A GIRL'S GOT TO BREATHE

HOLLYWOOD LEGENDS SERIES
CARL ROLLYSON, GENERAL EDITOR

A GIRL'S GOT TO BREATHE

THE LIFE OF

Teresa Wright

DONALD SPOTO

UNIVERSITY PRESS OF MISSISSIPPI • JACKSON

www.upress.state.ms.us

Designed by Peter D. Halverson

The University Press of Mississippi is a member of the Association of
American University Presses.

Unless otherwise indicated, all photos appear by courtesy of
the family of Teresa Wright.

First printing 2016

∞

Library of Congress Cataloging-in-Publication Data

Spoto, Donald, 1941–
A girl's got to breathe : the life of Teresa Wright / Donald Spoto.
pages cm. — (Hollywood legends series)
Includes bibliographical references and index.
ISBN 978-1-62846-045-2 (cloth : alk. paper) — ISBN 978-1-62846-046-9
(ebook)
1. Wright, Teresa, 1918–2005. 2. Actors—United States—Biography. I. Title.
PN2287.W75S55 2016
791.4302'8092—dc23
[B]
                                        2015031971

British Library Cataloging-in-Publication Data available

for Irene Mahoney, OSU
5 May 1921–9 May 2015

CONTENTS

INTRODUCTION &
ACKNOWLEDGMENTS

TERESA WRIGHT WAS ONE OF MY CLOSEST FRIENDS. FROM THE FIRST day we met (June 26, 1974) until her death (March 6, 2005), we were never out of touch for more than a week or two.

The occasion of our introduction was simply a professional expedient: I interviewed her as an expert for my first book. For the three decades following, our relationship was one of unalloyed and uninterrupted friendship, enriched by visits and phone calls, and travels near and far. We shared a deep confidence and mutual devotion not only when we met but also in our correspondence. We had countless happy times together and some challenging days, too.

I was grateful to be among those invited by her family to speak at her memorial service. And I was greatly honored when her daughter and son—Mary-Kelly Busch and Niven Terence (Terry) Busch—invited me to be Teresa's authorized biographer. They have granted me unrestricted access to her letters and papers, and to those of Teresa's second husband, Robert Anderson, whose Estate they also represent.

This book could never have been undertaken, much less completed, without their help. Mary-Kelly and Terry neither demanded nor requested editorial control. They replied—sometimes daily—to my requests for information, advice, opinions, clarifications and facts regarding their mother's ancestry, her life, times and relationships. I cannot imagine any biographer being more fortunate than I to have such confidence and trust as they have given me. Like their mother, they, too, have become my friends. I regret only that I never knew their father—Teresa's first husband, the writer Niven Busch.

Christine Miller, the cousin of Mary-Kelly and Terry, was also an important source of family memories and of valuable anecdotes.

Teresa's was a rich, complex, magnificent life, during which she made signal contributions to the golden age of film, theatre and television.

There was no indication, from her shockingly difficult childhood, of the successes that followed. In this regard, I have tried to demonstrate that Teresa Wright was not merely a winsome ingénue or an attractive supporting player: she was also—if we consider the depth, consistency, volume and range of her achievements—one of the great actresses to emerge in mid-century America and to go from strength to strength for over fifty years.

∽

My research took me to places where I was welcomed and assisted by dedicated librarians and archivists.

The vast collection of the papers of Teresa Wright and of Robert Anderson are maintained at the Harvard Theatre Collection. My work there was greatly facilitated by Dale Stinchcomb, curatorial assistant, for whose kindness and alacrity I am very grateful.

The Main Branch of the New York Public Library, the Stephen A. Schwarzman Building, contains the Neil McFee Skinner Papers and the Edith Warman Skinner Papers, which cover the history of the Wharf Theatre in Provincetown, Massachusetts, during the years when Teresa was both student and performer. I am grateful to Tal Nadan, reference archivist at the library, for his kind assistance.

Teresa Wright was under exclusive contract to the great producer Samuel Goldwyn from 1941 through 1948. Not long before his death, my friend Samuel Goldwyn Jr. graciously granted me permission to examine and to cite the papers of Samuel Goldwyn Productions held at the Margaret Herrick Library of the Academy of Motion Picture Arts and Sciences, Beverly Hills. I am grateful to Barbara Hall for her help in sorting through the materials in a timely manner. Barbara also indicated the relevant files in the Fred Zinnemann Papers and the Hedda Hopper Papers, all of them of considerable value in the preparation of this book.

Also at the Herrick Library, Stacey Behlmer, who is extraordinarily knowledgeable about film history, helped me as always through the thickets of obscure sources and documents.

In 1959, Teresa sat for a long recorded interview about her career for the Columbia University Center for Oral History. Breanne Loren LaCamera, editorial assistant at the Butler Library, very kindly helped me to obtain a transcript of that interview, which is oddly misidentified in the collection as the Reminiscences of Theresa [sic!] Wright for the Popular Arts Project.

Teresa appeared in more than one hundred movies and television dramas. I have seen and studied all of her twenty-seven feature films, and each is considered in this book. I am grateful to Tony Greco for enabling me to see two of Teresa's films that are extremely difficult to locate.

As for her seventy-eight television appearances, I have seen more than half of them—some, alas, have vanished. Those to which readers may have easy access (on YouTube, for example, or at The Paley Center for Media in New York and Beverly Hills) are treated here as well. Teresa's fans know that she has two stars on the Hollywood Walk of Fame—one for her films (located at 1658 Vine Street) and one for her television appearances (at 6405 Hollywood Boulevard). Flowers are often left there in her memory.

Teresa also had more than forty roles onstage, many of which I attended. Her theatre tours in America and abroad, her dramatic readings, radio performances and interviews, appearances at schools and universities and her long list of tributes to others are literally innumerable. I was privileged to be present at a number of them and also to have sponsored a few.

∽

I am grateful to the people who knew and worked with Teresa and generously granted interviews: Arvin Brown; Mila Malden Doerner; A.R. Gurney; Margaret Hunt; Michael Kahn; the late Karl Malden; Mona Malden; Vivian Matalon; Christine Miller; and Maryann Plunkett. For additional contributions and assistance, I offer my thanks to Brooks Baldwin, Bernard F. Dick and David Lloyd Olson.

Once again, my brother-in-law John Møller worked his technical wizardry, repairing, refinishing and preparing for publication the photographs in this book.

Leila Salisbury, director of the University Press of Mississippi, is the ideal publisher, always ready with wise and encouraging words. Leila's gracious and efficient editorial associate Valerie Jones and the gifted and keen-eyed copy editor Peter Tonguette made this book a memorable chapter in my life's work. I am grateful to both of them and to the entire art and production department at the University Press of Mississippi.

As always, I owe more than I can say to my husband, Ole Flemming Larsen. He helped with challenging research travels, read portions of the manuscript and provided encouragement every day during the process.

∽

As you will see, I have considered it inadvisable to disregard myself as I treat those events in Teresa's life to which I was a direct witness and sometimes a participant. She and Bob Anderson were uncommonly generous not only in extending the long arm of their friendship to me: they also introduced me to others close to them, among whom were Broadway and Hollywood luminaries who soon became my friends, too. Many of them appear in these pages.

In my previous books, I rigorously excised myself from the narrative, in the firm belief that an author should disappear. But in this case that seemed to me both injudicious and a prime example of false humility; it would also have weakened important accounts for reasons that will at once become clear.

D.S.
Sjælland, Denmark: Easter 2015

A GIRL'S GOT TO BREATHE

CHAPTER ONE

March 4, 1943

ON THIS DATE, MORE THAN A THOUSAND GUESTS WERE SEATED AT dinner tables in the Ambassador Hotel, located at 3400 Wilshire Boulevard in downtown Los Angeles. Rechristened the Cocoanut Grove soon after the hotel opened in 1921, the former Grand Ballroom had become, hands down, the hottest nightclub in town—which it certainly was that evening.

Everything about the Grove, as frequent patrons called it, was immense; not a millimeter of space was unadorned or unpainted or left unembellished. It might have been a microcosm of Hearst's San Simeon as Orson Welles reimagined that grand folly in *Citizen Kane*. Or it might have been a prototype of Disneyland, an explosion of fantasy that required another dozen years before it became, in 1955, a variant on reality right there in the Southern California desert.

The Grove's floors were expensively tiled. In great hearths made of Italian marble, fires roared even on warm Los Angeles evenings. The elevated ceiling was awash with twinkling bulbs. The scent of night-blooming jasmine, hyacinths, lilac and orange blossoms drifted in from a tropical courtyard. A waterfall splashed down one wall. Mechanical monkeys with glowing eyes glared down from artificial palm trees saved from the set of Rudolph Valentino's 1921 movie *The Sheik*. The Ambassador was an extravagant testimony to Jazz Age excess, a Mediterranean-Revival palace whose private rooms, public spaces and clients defined Hollywood hedonism.

During the hotel's first decade, Joan Crawford regularly showed up for the Charleston contests and, it was said, took home the winner's cup almost every time. Charles Chaplin was a frequent customer, escorting this or that compliant starlet. Howard Hughes ambled in alone but strutted out with a female companion, usually a hopeful aspirant to stardom. Clara Bow made her way among the tables, winking, crooking a finger and daring some man she fancied to follow her outside or upstairs or only the bellman knew where. Sometimes on the arm of her producer and lover Joseph P. Kennedy, Gloria Swanson nodded regally to her admirers. The list of regulars was long, the names glistened from the page of the maître d's engagement book and the gossip columns of the newspapers.

These notables were among the countless Hollywood folks who just had to be seen at the Grove. In the 1930s, regular patrons included Errol Flynn, Jean Harlow, Clark Gable, Katharine Hepburn, Cary Grant, James Stewart, Marlene Dietrich, Lana Turner, John Wayne, Henry Fonda, Ginger Rogers and Gary Cooper. Miss Harlow lived for a time at the Ambassador, as did John Barrymore and a score of other celebrities. On at least one occasion, Barrymore brought some live monkeys to the Grove, but they were annoying and messy—especially when they scampered up the palm trees toward their mechanical cousins and dislodged plaster cocoanuts onto the heads of such as Lucille Ball, Loretta Young, Spencer Tracy and Norma Shearer. Unlike Barrymore, these guests were not amused.

At precisely six o'clock on that evening of March 4, 1943, a platoon of waiters emerged from the hotel's vast kitchens, balancing trays of chicken croquettes, French fried potatoes and peas. The meal was consumed with unusual haste while dozens of newspaper reporters and photographers snaked along the walls of the Grove, their pads and pencils at the ready and flashbulbs in prodigious supply.

But there was more important activity than the usual dining, dancing, flirting and business schmoozing. Patrons were not there for the food, or to hear the crooners or the dance band. By formal invitation from the Hollywood producer Walter Wanger, president of the majestically named Academy of Motion Picture Arts and Sciences, the crowd had gathered for the sixth time at the Cocoanut Grove, for the fifteenth annual presentation of the Oscar statuettes, honoring exceptional achievements in acting and the various technical and artistic departments of film production in 1942.[1] (For news of Oscar night, the public had to depend on

---

1. The annual presentations of the Academy Award began in 1929, honoring films for 1927 and 1928. The origin of the name "Oscar" is much debated and remains unclear, although a popular story maintains that on seeing it for the first time, the Academy's librarian, Margaret Herrick (later executive director) remarked that it resembled her Uncle Oscar. Hollywood columnist Sidney Skolsky used the nickname in 1934, but the Academy did not officially adopt it until 1939.

newspaper reports until 1944, when the evening was first broadcast on radio; television transmission of the event began in 1953.)

Among the most lucrative movies released in 1942 were *Bambi, Casablanca, The Pride of the Yankees, Mrs. Miniver, The Road to Morocco* and *Yankee Doodle Dandy.* The most profitable male stars were Bing Crosby, Gary Cooper, Humphrey Bogart, Mickey Rooney and Bob Hope; for the fourth time, Hope was also the host of the evening's festivities, a role he eventually undertook or shared a total of nineteen times. Betty Grable and Greer Garson headed the shorter list of bankable female stars.

The most famously photographed "pinups" were Miss Grable, Rita Hayworth and Lana Turner. Gene Tierney was the Hollywood fashion icon, thanks to her dark, elusive beauty and the talents of her husband, costume designer Oleg Cassini.

ぷ

During 1942, over 500 feature films were released in the United States— the greatest number ever; seventy years later, that number had dropped to fewer than 200. When the average price of a ticket to the movies at the height of World War II was 25 cents and the nation's population was 136 million, more than 75 million Americans went to see Walt Disney's animated feature, *Bambi.* Impressive though that was, Disney had hoped to match the runaway success of *Gone With the Wind,* which 227 million people had seen in its first release. Moviegoers were lining up two and three times to hear Vivien Leigh's opening salvo as Scarlett O'Hara, bored with the talk of "War, war, war . . ." and Rhett Butler, walking into the mist as he declares his indifference to Scarlett's future, "Frankly, my dear, I don't give a damn"—surely one of the most famous lines in book and film history.

Movies were the primary form of mass entertainment until the arrival of television sets in postwar American households. In 1943, the Office of War Information, on the alert for treasonous, subversive or even a vague critique of the government, began to censor every American movie retroactively to 1942—a massive task, since about 1,500 titles (including imports) were released in a two-year period. This remarkable if misguided scrutiny was perhaps unnecessary, as Hollywood was producing a staggering number of patriotic movies, created to inspire and support. Among these were the documentaries *Memphis Belle* and *Why We Fight;* and the features *Yankee Doodle Dandy, Wake Island, Bombs Over Burma, Mrs. Miniver, Winged Victory, A Yank in the R.A.F.* and Disney's animated Technicolor feature, *Victory Through Air Power.* This pattern of sometimes jingoistic photoplays in fact paralleled the completion and dedication of two great national buildings in 1943, the Pentagon and the Jefferson Memorial—achievements resoundingly celebrated in movie house newsreels.

At the peak of the war effort, the average cost of a new home in America was $3,600 (the equivalent of $50,000 in 2015); the average national wage was $1,880 ($28,000 in 2015). A gallon of gas cost 15 cents, a bottle of Coca-Cola 5 cents, a new car $920 ($12,000), a first-class stamp 3 cents. For the first time, the government levied withholding taxes on wages and salaries from paychecks: the enormous cost of World War II made this Revenue Act necessary.

The war brought food rationing to America in March: there were already limits on gasoline, and now there were strict controls (by means of allocated coupons) on the amount of beef, pork, lamb, butter, cheese and canned fish that a family could purchase; the sale of poultry was not affected. This moderation imposed on the American household did not seem to affect the denizens of the Cocoanut Grove or of nightclubs like Ciro's and the Mocambo—these and such places as the Brown Derby Restaurant were full each night.

There were more democratic forms of amusement than California nightspots. On December 31, 1942, a vast mob of hysterical teenagers jammed New York's Times Square and blocked city traffic for hours—not for New Year's Eve revelry, but because a twenty-seven-year-old singer named Frank Sinatra, America's first teen idol, held forth at the Paramount Theatre. Fourteen blocks north, at the venerable Carnegie Hall, Duke Ellington and his orchestra performed in January for a sold-out audience, raising money for war relief.

In the same venue, a few months later, the sudden illness of the New York Philharmonic's conductor required a last-minute substitution. To the rescue came a relatively unknown twenty-five-year-old musician named Leonard Bernstein, who at once became the darling of New York's classical music scene. The *Times* noted that the audience was "wildly demonstrative" by the end of the evening, and that Bernstein gave "a thrillingly good performance" that made for "a good American success story . . . a triumph that filled Carnegie Hall and spread far over the air waves."

Across the country, Americans in record numbers were reading hardcover books: best-selling novels of 1943 included Graham Greene's *The Ministry of Fear*, Betty Smith's *A Tree Grows in Brooklyn*, William Saroyan's *The Human Comedy* and Vera Caspary's *Laura*—all of which were quickly turned into polished and popular motion pictures. Poets and philosophers found wide readerships, too—among them, Reinhold Niebuhr and Jean-Paul Sartre, Carl Sandburg, Langston Hughes, Stephen Vincent Benét, Archibald MacLeish and Edna St. Vincent Millay. On Broadway, theatregoers had a choice of seventy-three shows running in 1943—among them *Life With Father*, a popular holdover since 1939 that endured until 1947; Thornton Wilder's Pulitzer Prize-winning *The Skin of Our Teeth*, starring Tallulah Bankhead, Fredric March and Montgomery Clift; and Rodgers and Hammerstein's innovative musical drama *Oklahoma!*

∽

In 1943, Franklin Delano Roosevelt, in his eleventh year in the White House, became the first president to travel by airplane: in January, he went to Morocco to discuss the progress of World War II with England's prime minister, Winston Churchill.

On America's home front, there were pitched battles of another sort. In Mobile, Alabama, twelve African-American workers were given promotions in their jobs at a shipyard—an action that triggered a violent protest by Southern white laborers. Race riots also occurred in California, New York, Michigan, Texas—wherever a number of non-Caucasian manual workers were promoted or sometimes merely hired.

The *Jackson (Mississippi) Daily News* blamed the national riots on First Lady Eleanor Roosevelt's efforts toward racial equality: "In Detroit, a city noted for the growing impudence and insolence of its Negro population, an attempt was made to put your preachments [about racial integration] into practice, Mrs. Roosevelt!"

Similarly, Representative Martin Dies of Texas, chairman of the House Un-American Activities Committee, absurdly assigned blame for the Michigan riots on Japanese-Americans. It was these citizens, said Dies, "who had infiltrated Detroit's Negro population to spread hatred of the white man and disrupt the war effort." His committee had already gone on record stating unequivocally that they had information on an English writer named Christopher Marlowe, who was now apparently at work in America as a member of the Communist Party. Never mind that Marlowe, the Elizabethan playwright, had died in 1593.

Furthermore, according to the committee, a nefarious Greek writer named Mr. Euripides was preaching class warfare right here in America. The committee briefly considered opening investigations into the Ku Klux Klan but decided against doing so: as that proud racist Senator John E. Rankin of Mississippi said, "After all, the KKK is an old American institution!" Such was the startling moral intelligence of a powerful government organization, seeking whom it might devour for decades to come.

Things fared better in the nation's medical laboratories. Penicillin had first been given to an American patient in 1942, when the drug was imported from England. (Alexander Fleming had developed it there in 1928.) Clinical trials of penicillin began in the United States in 1943, when it was proven to be an effective antibacterial agent. By the end of the year, production was greatly increased and made available for Allied troops fighting in Europe; infections had to be treated with multiple injections of the drug, and two million doses were rushed to soldiers wounded during the invasion of Normandy in June 1944. The general population in the United States had access to penicillin from March 1945.

∽

Daily, the atrocities of World War II continued. As the movie business was celebrating itself that evening in March 1943, more than 1,000 French Jews were being deported to Maidanek, where only three people survived, and 34,000 Dutch Jews were shipped to Mauthausen and to Auschwitz (where Dr. Josef Mengele performed atrocious tortures, his "medical experiments" on doomed victims). Very few lived to see the end of the war. In the Ukraine, 23,000 Jews who had been expelled from Hungary were executed by machine-gunfire or by being buried alive. Virtually the entire Jewish population of Greece was arrested and subsequently eradicated at Auschwitz.

There was dissent. Hitler ordered the deportation and execution of Jews in Occupied Denmark, but his orders were ineffective: many Danish Christians risked their lives by secretly transporting endangered Jews at night by rowboat to neutral Sweden. Within Germany, members of the student anti-Nazi resistance movement in Munich floated banners urging "Down With Hitler!" and "Long Live Freedom!" For their acts of moral outrage, all the young people were apprehended and beheaded within days. In Berlin, Hitler gleefully watched the lynching of captured Allied pilots.

Catholic bishops in Belgium excommunicated Nazis and Nazi sympathizers. But perhaps the most effective and influential protest against the ideology was lodged—from the earliest days of the tyranny right through to the end of World War II—by the German nobleman, Count Clemens August von Galen. A highly respected prelate, he used his position as a Roman Catholic cardinal and a member of one of Germany's oldest aristocratic families to oppose openly every program of the Nazi party and the SS right up to open confrontation with the highest German leaders.

Von Galen's thunderous weekly anti-Nazi sermons in Münster Cathedral were printed and circulated throughout the country, where they inspired countless protest movements. But Hitler could not touch the cardinal: von Galen was a revered member of the historic German nobility, born in the Grand Duchy of Oldenburg and linked to a heroic and distinguished family. He was also the living and beloved symbol of the old province of Westphalia, which the Führer could not risk alienating.

The air forces of the British and American armies escalated their attacks, bombing noncombatant locations as well as military targets in Germany. In two hours, Britain's Royal Air Force killed 45,000 civilians living in Hamburg, while among the targeted cities, Kassel, Pforzheim and Mainz were almost obliterated.

༄

The United States was never a war zone, but at its best the nation's popular culture knew how to condemn the evil and praise the valiant. Occasionally, the movies did that—none of them more successfully, nor with more authentic emotion, than a Metro-Goldwyn-Mayer picture called *Mrs. Miniver*, loosely based on a series of English stories. Without a single combat scene in wartime, it was an exemplary treatment of the triumph of the human spirit amid the dreadful circumstances of World War II.

The movie had already been nominated for twelve Oscars, and at the Academy gala on March 4, it won six: for best black-and-white cinematography (presented to Joseph Ruttenberg); for best screenplay (to George Froeschel, James Hilton, Claudine West and Arthur Wimperis); for best direction (to William Wyler); for the best performance by an actress (to Greer Garson); for best picture (to Sidney Franklin, the film's producer at Metro).

Additionally, as it happened, two players in *Mrs. Miniver* had been nominated for the sixth award, in the category of best supporting actress. The venerable doyenne of the English stage and screen, Dame May Whitty, was seventy-seven years old and nearing the end of a long career that had begun onstage in 1881 and continued in motion pictures in 1914. This was the second time May Whitty was nominated as a best supporting actress.

The other nominee in that category was present that evening at the Cocoanut Grove not only for her performance in *Mrs. Miniver*. She had also been nominated in the best actress category, for her leading role in *The Pride of the Yankees*. She was twenty-four years old and had appeared in four major movies in just twenty months, from the spring of 1941 to the fall of 1942: Wyler's *The Little Foxes* and *Mrs. Miniver*; Sam Wood's *The Pride of the Yankees*; and Alfred Hitchcock's *Shadow of a Doubt*. The moviegoing public loved her, and Academy members obviously approved of her, for she was nominated for an Oscar for her first three films. She justified the cliché about a meteoric rise to stardom.

Bob Hope called out her name as the recipient of the best supporting actress of the year 1942. It took a moment for the announcement to register with her, but at last she stood, received a kiss from her husband and hurried to the makeshift stage.

The evening's exhilaration and the Hollywood accolade were perhaps not so unexpected after her theatrical training, her previous achievement on Broadway and a nomination the previous year. But in light of a dreadful situation that repeatedly blighted her childhood, no one—least of all herself—could have imagined her ultimate success. Of the past she spoke but rarely, and only to a very few people. Along with her earnest work ethic, her straightforward character, her direct manner and the complete absence of a star complex, she was also a deeply vulnerable but tough young lady. Her name was Teresa Wright.

⌀

CHAPTER TWO

1918–1935

SHE WAS BORN IN THE AUTUMN OF 1918, DURING A DOUBLE WORLD-wide disaster. The Great War claimed 16 million lives between 1914 and 1919, while a horrific epidemic—the deadliest illness since the medieval plagues—killed almost 100 million in one year. Between March and October 1918, more people succumbed to the so-called Spanish Influenza than to any disease in recorded history. In Spain alone, 21 million people—40 percent of the country's population—died in May 1918. No area of the world was unaffected by the illness.

The population of the United States in 1918 was 104 million: 29 million people were severely sick, and 875,000 died. There were no vaccines or antiviral drugs, and no antibiotics to prevent the flu from its typical course—bacterial pneumonia, which often killed healthy people within hours. Newborns, the young and the elderly were particularly vulnerable, but the epidemic spared no age group and no section of the country, from the crowded Eastern cities to the remote wilds of the Alaskan territory. President Woodrow Wilson fell ill with the flu while negotiating the Treaty of Versailles to end the war; he recovered, only to suffer a massive stroke that left him incapacitated and the White House largely under the control of his wife.

In the town of Trenton, New Jersey, for one example, more than 15,000 cases were listed in the city's population of 110,000. In more populous Chicago, 500 cases and over 300 deaths were reported daily during October.

But the disease was especially rampant in New York City in the autumn of 1918, when the population was 5.5 million. In just one month—from September 18 to October 17—the Health Department recorded that "only [!] 48,024 deaths have been reported . . . and that during one 24-hour period ending on the morning of October 5, there were no fewer than 2,070 deaths."

In the borough of Manhattan alone, corpses were hurriedly removed from homes and hospitals, while ferries and yachts were pressed into service as makeshift morgues. Suddenly, often overnight, thousands of children were orphaned—from the Lower East Side slums to the posh apartments farther north; helpless girls and boys stood mute as no doctor or nurse could prevent their parents suffocating from pneumonia. Dr. Royal S. Copeland, the city's health commissioner, somehow managed to prevent the additional epidemic of mass panic, even as he informed Governor Charles S. Whitman that it was necessary to order restricted hours for public gatherings in theatres, churches, courtrooms and all places where more than ten people gathered. Mayor John Francis Hylan of New York City directed that signs be posted, requiring the public to use handkerchiefs for sneezing, coughing and spitting—a precaution that, alas, had little effect on the spread of disease. Public funerals were prohibited, and burials had to be completed within twenty-four hours of death.

ço

The child later known as Teresa Wright was born in a hospital in the Harlem section of Manhattan on Sunday, October 27, 1918. That week, the Public Health Service of the United States recorded the peak of the influenza epidemic that month: 12,357 deaths in New York City. Many of the citywide casualties were newborns and infants, and the survival of the one simply identified as "Wright baby" was, like all births, not guaranteed.

The single pervasive danger in neonatal wards was widespread impaired breathing, with contagious pulmonary infection and then deadly pneumonia acquired right there in the hospital. The mothers and available attending staff were urged to constant vigilance: "The children have to breathe!" as signposts admonished. But precisely what was to be done was not specified. The survival rate among newborns was the lowest in eighty years.

The precise location of the hospital where the baby was born is unknown, as the epidemic made it impossible to register many births; in this case, too, there was no official birth certificate. Years later, the child's father signed a sworn affidavit:

My wife, at the time I embarked for overseas duty with the American Expeditionary Forces in June 1918, was five months pregnant. Four months later, I received a cablegram from my mother advising me that my child had been born in New York City on October 27, 1918. When I returned to the U.S.A. I applied to the Hall of Records for her birth certificate and was advised that her birth had not been recorded. This was apparently due to neglect on [the] part of the hospital, as it was at a time [that] a severe flu epidemic was raging in that area.[1]

Not long after the child's birth, she was christened Muriel Teresa Wright: the first name was popular at the time; the second was her paternal grandmother's middle name.

Arthur Hendricksen Wright, the baby's father, was born on September 3, 1891, in the home of his parents, at 142 West Sixty-second Street, Manhattan; he was the fourth son and last child of John Wright and Mary Teresa Wright, who was often called by her maiden name, Mary Kelly. Forms of the surname Wright can be traced in Britain for 1,500 years. The designation refers to a craftsman or maker of something, and the word survives linguistically in, for example, the words playwright, shipwright and wheelwright.

John Wright had six children by two wives who had died before his marriage to the much younger Irish immigrant Mary Kelly. He lived and worked in New Jersey as a hatter and maker of small fur pieces until his death in 1897. This left Mary a widow with four boys to support; the youngest was six-year-old Arthur. She then worked for various families as a housekeeper and later remarried at least once.

Of Arthur's early years very little is known. He completed high school, held a variety of jobs and by the age of twenty-six was living and working in Philadelphia. In April 1917, President Wilson asked Congress for a declaration of war against Germany, and the following month the Selective Service Act authorized a military draft. In October, Arthur was inducted into the U.S. Army and began training in New Jersey. Finally, in late June 1918, he was shipped to France for active duty in the Great War. The huge number of recruits wracked by disease in trench warfare required an influx of medical personnel, and Arthur was quickly assigned to the Ambulance Service.

---

1. See the Note on this affidavit.

But not for long. After less than two months of service, Arthur was sent to England to recuperate—either from a battlefield injury or, more likely, because he contracted the virulent Spanish influenza or dysentery or typhoid fever. In the town of Winchester, an hour southwest of London, the Allies had established a major transit point for troops destined for the Western Front. There, where several large infirmaries cared for wounded Allied soldiers, Arthur remained from August 14 to October 18. He was then sent back to France, where he received from his mother in New York the announcement of his daughter's birth.

The Armistice marking the end of hostilities was declared in France in November 1918—in a railway carriage in the forest of Compiègne. But the formal peace treaty between Germany and the Allies was not signed until June 1919, at Versailles, after protracted meetings involving the so-called Big Three—Prime Minister David Lloyd George of England; Prime Minister Georges Clemenceau of France; and U.S. President Woodrow Wilson. From the fall of 1918 to the summer of 1919, American troops remained in France, returning home in designated consignments. In early March 1919, after almost nine months abroad, Arthur arrived for demobilization at Camp Dix (later Fort Dix), New Jersey; on the twenty-first, he was honorably discharged as Sergeant Arthur H. Wright.

∽

The twenty-seven-year-old veteran came home to find his five-month-old daughter named Muriel Teresa, whose baptism Grandmother Kelly had evidently arranged, and with whom she shared her own middle name. Arthur also returned to the baby's mother, his wife.

Martha Espy claimed that she had been born in New York City (or a town in Delaware, or Maryland, or somewhere elsewhere, depending on her fancy at the moment) in 1895 or 1896; hence she would have been twenty-two or twenty-three at the time of Muriel's birth. But Martha was an unreliable guide to the facts of her life. She altered her past to suit her mood, she disdained both custom and the law and she left few traces of her unpredictable itinerant life.

No archives or public records attest Martha Espy's marriage to Arthur Wright—there is neither a wedding certificate nor a divorce decree before his subsequent, post-Martha marriages. That Martha and Arthur were indeed husband and wife must be accepted solely on Arthur's word. That they were the parents of the child he also swore; that Martha was the biological mother was never questioned. Of Arthur's paternity Muriel had occasional vague doubts, but finally the physical resemblances between them, his lifelong pride in her accomplishments and his constant manifest devotion convinced her that he was her biological father.

The absence of a marriage certificate is no proof that Arthur and Martha were not married. A ceremony may have been formalized somewhere not scrupulous in keeping records—there were many such locations a century ago. But Miss Espy's previous marriage is clearly documented and notarized—certificate number 3822 in the Marriage Records Division of the Department of Health of the City of New York. On November 18, 1916—less than two years before Muriel's birth—Martha W. Espy and a Canadian named Joseph Charles Peachy were married by a city clerk at the Municipal Building, 4 Columbia Street, Manhattan. She said she was twenty-one and unemployed; that she had been born in New York City; that John B.W. Espy was her father and Charlotte Edwards Espy her mother; and she swore that this was her first marriage. Peachy, age twenty-two, claimed that he worked as a clerk; that his parents (in Ottawa) were Joseph and Angelina Peachy; and that his address was the same as Martha's: 532 West 138th Street, Manhattan.

But there is no record of Martha's divorce from Peachy. Did they simply go their separate ways? If so, this further raises the question of the legality of the Wright-Espy marriage. Did they not marry because she was still wed to Peachy? Or was the Wright-Espy wedding, if it occurred, a polyandrous marriage—with Martha simply ignoring her legal standing as Mrs. Peachy and adding one husband to another? Even in her maturity, Teresa Wright was (as her daughter recalled) "never sure that her mother [Martha Espy] ever divorced that man [Joseph Peachy]."

Divorce or no, Martha was soon living apart from her husband Joseph, or at least pursuing passion elsewhere: fifteen months after she had been wed to Joseph Peachy, Martha was pregnant with Mr. Wright's child.

∽

Whatever term is used to describe their relationship, Arthur and Martha presented themselves to the world as Mr. and Mrs. Wright (which suggests that Peachy was nowhere in sight). By the time Muriel was two, in 1920, they were living in Manhattan's 10th District, Central Harlem. Arthur was twenty-nine, and he told census takers that he worked as a "theatrical treasurer" at a repertory theatre. There are no details of this job, which may have been temporary; his daughter had no memory of it, or of her father taking her to a show. In any case, he was soon working as a traveling insurance salesman.

The strongest presence in Muriel's early years was her paternal grand-mother, the widowed Mary Teresa Kelly Wright, the only grandparent the child ever knew. She doted on Muriel, visited her often, and dressed, fed and cared for her during Arthur's business travels and Martha's mysterious absences. "My mother was a troubled person," Teresa said, "and she was not around." She never said anything more on the record, but years later she was more forthcoming with a few people close to her.[2]

Granny was loving, dependable, generous, eccentric. "My grandmother wore the three dresses she owned—all of them at the same time, layer on layer, rotating them one on top of the other," Teresa recalled years later. "And she always carried a shopping bag or a valise, full of every card and note her sons had ever sent her. I never saw her angry unless someone tried to help her. Then she would say, 'Take your hand off my bag!' in her thick Irish brogue. She could be very funny—sometimes without knowing it."

Before the child was old enough for school, her grandmother's visits became less frequent. Eventually, Mary Kelly Wright met a house painter named Thomas Reese. As it happened, he lived in a basement flat on Charles Street in Greenwich Village, ten miles from the Wright apartment in Harlem. Here, the newlyweds made their home—much to Mary Kelly's relief, for she was always fearful of being caught in a fire on an upper floor.

Arthur's job continued to require out-of-town travel, and his wife and daughter were alone in the small apartment. In a letter she drafted in 1975 but never sent, Teresa Wright wrote, "I've never talked about my mother publicly and I don't expect I ever will." There were several reasons for her silence.

More and more often Martha was, as her daughter said, "not around." Before she departed for her many outings, the mother issued the odd command that Muriel had to keep the door and windows of the apartment shut at all times, regardless of the outdoor temperature. But this was not the worst imposition on the child.

Martha Espy, known as Mrs. Wright, was (in the words of the Jazz Era) a woman of easy virtue: in fact, she was a prostitute who invited her clients right into the apartment and into the bed she shared with the child. Understandably, Teresa shared this information with very few people, primarily her daughter, Mary-Kelly Busch: "When Martha brought men home, she took them into bed while Muriel was there." The sounds

---

2. The incidents that Muriel never forgot are discussed below.

of sex terrified the child, who thought that her mother was being killed, and that maybe she would die, too. Without a means of escape, she lay there frightened and traumatized, feigning sleep and scarcely breathing. Years later, her second husband wrote to a friend that her early life "was so miserable, I know she doesn't want to go into it."

✐

Eventually, the peripatetic Arthur deposited Muriel with various friends or relatives in New Jersey, and before Muriel reached adolescence, Martha Espy vanished forever from her daughter's life. "I didn't have much of a home life before this, and then I lived with a lot of people, friends and relatives of my father. I was in and out of houses and apartments. Very early, I got to know a lot of different lifestyles. I just had to adjust." She was no longer subjected to the anguish caused by her mother, but life was insecure, confused and lonely. "I was boarded out. They all treated me very well, but my problems were never their problems. I had to decide all kinds of things for myself."

Finally, Muriel was sent to board at the Rose Haven School for Girls in Bergen County, New Jersey, about eighteen miles from New York City. Founded in 1920 in a picturesque eighteenth-century Dutch Colonial manor house, the school was set on twenty acres of rolling lawns, stately trees, verdant orchards and broad fields for sports. By 1926, Rose Haven was a prestigious academy where the students had spacious bedrooms in the manor house and sat at desks in a bright and airy classroom building. In addition to the standard curriculum, the girls were offered ballet and music lessons, dramatics and art. Muriel was almost two years older than her classmates, but she was petite and demure, and (as she later recalled) she passed for their contemporary.

"I didn't know anybody, and I didn't know what they were talking about, so very often I just looked out the window, daydreaming. But then I discovered acting—or at least a child's version of acting. From the first grade on, I was in every school play that came along." She made her debut, somehow, as a rippling brook and then appeared in the role of Little Eva—complete with a wig of golden curls—in an abridgement of *Uncle Tom's Cabin.*

Within a few years at Rose Haven, Muriel was known as the star performer. One afternoon on the playing field, she was struck on the face by an errant croquet mallet. Two teachers rushed her, bleeding and weeping, to a doctor. "This girl cannot be scarred or have anything happen to her face!" they cried. "She is an actress!"

At the age of ten, she appeared (on June 3, 1929) in a colorful Rose Haven pageant; she sang a lyric poem called "Blue Birds" and acted in the school play, a fantasy called *Butterfly Wings*. The following year, she took piano lessons at Rose Haven and joined classmate Betty Powell for a simplified Diabelli duet at a school assembly; she also performed in three tableaux.

Students were permitted to return to their families on weekends, and the girls did—except Muriel, whose guardians said she would be better off remaining at school. When she did visit this or that temporary home, "she was really like a kind of Cinderella," according to her daughter. "She soon learned to make clothes from castoff garments, and she sewed the top of one old dress onto the bottom of another." Muriel had few possessions—very little apart from what the school provided—but when referring to this time, she neither complained nor presented herself as a tragic waif mistreated by wicked keepers. It was simply the way things were. By all accounts she was not a melancholy child when staying with these surrogate families, but she was always happy to return to the teachers at Rose Haven and to peers like Dixie Alexander, with whom she formed a lifelong friendship.

Even before she was a teenager, Muriel was known for her pointed impersonations of teachers, classmates, movie stars, relatives—anyone was fair game for her good-natured humor, and she had no trouble attracting an audience.

Whereas she excelled in performing, Muriel was only an average student in regular courses. "I liked to dance as well as act, and the grownups always said that I was going to be an actress. I thought they said that because I was too dumb to be anything else."

In 1930, two wise and kind ladies, Mary Brichard and Ruth Van Strum, began their tenure as directors of the school. Brichard died in 1938, but for almost forty years Van Strum continued to own and run Rose Haven. A serious educator and gifted administrator, she was also noteworthy for a gentle, unpossessive mothering quality.

During Muriel's school years, Arthur continued to travel, courting new insurance business along the East Coast. After divorcing Martha (perhaps for abandonment, as there is no divorce record), he married a young woman with whom he temporarily set up house on Hicks Avenue in Brooklyn. After a divorce from her, Arthur married a divorcée named Edna, whose maiden name and first married name are unknown; he adopted the children from her first marriage.

∾

When she was fourteen, Muriel transferred into grade seven at the Columbia High School, on Parker Avenue in Maplewood. Twenty miles west of lower Manhattan, the municipality had a small-town atmosphere but a wide-ranging culture in about four square miles of Essex County. Here, Muriel lodged with other relatives and friends of Arthur.

The first sight of Columbia is impressive to this day, and it must have seemed especially grand in the fall of 1932, at the height of the Great Depression. There had been a school in Maplewood since 1700, but after various tents, cabins and buildings had been constructed, demolished or rebuilt in new locations around town, a vast new structure was completed in 1927 to accommodate more than a thousand students.

Designed by the architectural firm of Guilbert & Betelle in the Collegiate Gothic style, it was widely praised by artists and professional journals and celebrated in the 1930 edition of the Encyclopedia Britannica. The building featured carved limestone, numerous chimneys, pitched slate roofs and a seven-story clock tower. Inside, there were an observatory with a refractory telescope, a large swimming pool, hallways with faience tiles and mosaic inlaid terrazzo floors—and capacious classrooms, some with fireplaces. In the huge auditorium was a three-manual Skinner Organ, majestically played at every major school function.[3] When Muriel arrived, an industrial arts center was nearing completion—an addition that helped to meet the need for special skills during the economic crisis.

Muriel gained friends quickly. Known to her pals as Moochie or Tess, she was popular at Rose Haven for her accurate, hilarious but never unkind impersonations of faculty and students. For the next six years her interests were mainly focused on acting in plays, and gradually it became clear that this was much more than a schoolgirl's diversion or a leisure pursuit: Muriel was serious to the point of eventually stating her aspirations as an actress. She joined the school's drama group—the Parnassian Society, which had staged plays without interruption since 1905 and had developed into a major school activity under the tutelage of Mildred Memory.

Muriel certainly enjoyed performing, but as she said, "there's also the important little matter of getting some encouragement from someone besides yourself—someone whose opinion means something to you. One of the most important people in my life was Miss Mildred Memory.

3. Alfred C. Kinsey graduated from Columbia High in 1912 and Drew Middleton in 1931. Among many celebrated later alumni: Roy Scheider, Richard Meier, Frank Langella and Paul Auster.

When I was at Columbia High School, she encouraged me in her gentle, brilliant way and made me know I was really going to be an actress. She knew that I had never been to the theatre, and so she invited me to go with her to see Cornelia Otis Skinner."[4]

Skinner was a noted actress, humorist, author and exponent of high comedy. She appeared on Broadway in plays by Congreve, Wilde, Shaw and Maugham and was justly famous for her one-woman shows. From November 22 to December 10, 1932, Skinner was appearing at the Lyceum Theatre on West Forty-fifth Street, in a presentation of what she called her "character sketches." Muriel and Miss Memory went to a performance over the Thanksgiving weekend—"the first live thing I ever saw."

The sketches were unforgettable: "A Southern Girl in the Sistine Chapel," "A Lady Explorer," "In a Gondola" and "A Picnic in Kentucky," along with a dozen more—brief, mostly hilarious vignettes, and sometimes touching or trenchant monologues, too. "For months afterward," Muriel recalled, "I was exhilarated by that experience." Her humorous sendups at school continued after that, for Cornelia Otis Skinner had validated the art of impersonation.

During her years at Columbia, Arthur came to as many of his daughter's staged performances as his schedule permitted: "My father always encouraged me and seemed to be pleased [with my efforts]." And for six years, Mildred Memory remained Muriel's mentor, protector and guide. Appreciative of her nascent talent and perhaps sensing a sad family history, Miss Memory gave her an elegant teacup on her birthday one year ("Every lady must have a nice teacup," she said) and continued to send one to Muriel for many years thereafter. The collection of teacups was carefully kept for the nurturing love they represented and which she had never received from her mother.

∂

---

4. Cornelia Otis Skinner was not related to Ernest M. Skinner, the noted designer and builder of pipe organs, or to Edith Warman Skinner, the celebrated speech teacher soon to be so important in Muriel's training.

CHAPTER THREE

1935–1939

"WHEN I COULD GET FIVE CENTS TO GO TO A MOVIE, I WENT TO SEE Helen Hayes, and I listened to her whenever she was on the radio."

The First Lady of the American Theatre, as she was known, marked her thirty-fifth birthday in 1935. She acted frequently on Broadway since childhood, was in films since 1917 and received a best actress Oscar in 1931. "I just adored Helen Hayes when I was a kid. She was my idol when I was in school."

Just five feet tall, Hayes was equally adept at tragedy, romance and comedy: she portrayed passionate, grief-stricken and angry women without inflated emotion and roles of high humor without mannerisms. By 1935, she was a famous American exponent of James M. Barrie (*Dear Brutus* and *What Every Woman Knows*), Oliver Goldsmith (*She Stoops to Conquer*) and George Bernard Shaw (*Caesar and Cleopatra*). Offstage, Hayes was admired for her unpretentious warmth and unaffected benevolence. In art and in life, Helen Hayes was precisely the kind of actress Muriel Wright aspired to become; at school, she kept Hayes's photograph in her room.

At seventeen, Muriel had reached her full adult height of five-feet-two. She weighed 106 pounds, had beryl blue-green eyes, luxuriant brown hair and alabaster skin. To no one's surprise, boys took notice, and one of them was dragooned as an escort for an outing that certainly left him surprised.

The day after Christmas, Helen Hayes began a six-month run on Broadway as the title character in *Victoria Regina*. Muriel was resolved to see the play at the Broadhurst Theatre as soon as possible. Early the following spring, she hatched a plan.

"I think it was the only time in my life I've ever used a young man. He wanted to take me to [the amusement park] Coney Island, but before he knew what was happening, we were going to *Victoria Regina* instead. So there we were—in the first row of the balcony, and I was in seventh heaven. He was looking at this play and probably thinking, 'God, it must be great at the beach today.'" During their return journey to Maplewood, as she later repeatedly recalled, Muriel's hopes became a firm purpose and her future took shape: "Seeing that play fed additional vitamins to my ambition." For later theatre outings in 1936, Muriel joined a group of classmates who traveled by train to New York, where they saw Katharine Cornell in *Wingless Victory*.

In Hayes's performance, what was it that so fervently transported Muriel and reinforced her aspirations?

First, as she recalled, there was an early scene in *Victoria Regina* in which the teenager is told that she has become queen of England. With her long hair cascading down her nightdress, the actress stood silently, but by some subtle alchemy of expression and gesture conveyed bafflement, apprehension and youthful optimism.

In subsequent scenes, Hayes communicated a Teutonic stubbornness when that was appropriate—and, when it was natural but perhaps unexpected, she showed passionate abandon in the arms of Prince Albert (played by twenty-four-year-old Vincent Price, in his Broadway debut). Still later in the play, at Albert's death, Victoria seemed to wear a mask of grief and dread. In the final scenes, with her makeup of inflated cheeks, lowered eyelids and grim composure, Hayes made herself unrecognizable as the wizened, puffy, aged monarch.

∽

At Columbia, her speech and oratory teacher, Stanley Wood, offered Muriel further encouragement—and more. During the summers, Wood worked with the playwrights and actors at the nonprofit Wharf Theatre in Provincetown, Massachusetts. In the spring of 1937, he was sufficiently impressed by Muriel's stage presence and her evident earnestness that he wrote to colleagues at the Wharf, recommending her for an internship that summer. On the alert for new talent and confident in Wood's reference, the small company accepted Muriel along with a dozen other theatre aspirants. Like everyone else in the company, she would receive no salary; her father paid the $125 tuition for eight weeks and subsidized her living expenses on Cape Cod during July and August.

When she arrived in Provincetown at the end of June, Muriel found a situation for which austere is too modest a word: the theatre company consisted of a small rented room in which classes were held, and—in a derelict space on a rickety pier—a performing space and room for an audience of 160.[1]

The site had formerly been the home of the historic Provincetown Players. From 1915 to 1924, they were a ragtag, radical, groundbreaking band of actors, writers and directors that had included Susan Glaspell, Edna St. Vincent Millay and Eugene O'Neill, who supervised the premieres of his plays there. Bette Davis was an apprentice with the Provincetown Players before her 1929 Broadway debut with them in two O'Neill plays; by then, the group had relocated to New York, and the Cape Cod pier became the home of a new company—the Wharf Theatre.[2]

Memorable productions were somehow staged on that ramshackle pier, including an acclaimed revival of Eugene O'Neill's 1933 comedy *Ah, Wilderness!* Muriel cheerfully pitched in to help paint makeshift backdrops, to concoct improvised props, to sell tickets, to sweep the theatre and to sew battered costumes. "I had an opportunity to learn, learn, learn, and the chance to take on a few bit roles. I was the youngest, smallest and shyest in the group. After the high school plays, this was the nearest I ever came to real study for the theatre."

Since 1928, the Wharf had been owned and managed by Margaret Hewes, who recruited some major stars to work for almost nothing for summer performances. In 1935, Hewes decamped to work at a London movie studio, and her brother-in-law, the actor Neil McFee, assumed the job of managing director. His wife, Margaret's sister Edith Warman Skinner, was appointed director of the Summer Theatre Workshop School. She also lectured on Voice Development and Stage Speaking, and on Stage Movement.

The visiting faculty at the Wharf that summer was impressive: Douglas McLean of the Carnegie Institute of Technology (later Carnegie Mellon University) and E. Stanley Pratt, a director, taught Technique of Acting; Paul Wing, a radio director for NBC, and Jean King, an MGM newsreel

---

1. In February 1940, a winter storm washed away the pier supporting the Wharf Theatre, and everything collapsed into Provincetown Harbor.

2. The New York home of the Provincetown Players was for many years located on MacDougal Street in Greenwich Village. Remarkable performances were offered from its tiny stage before an audience of just over a hundred. As a high school student, I saw an extraordinary, chilling production of *Macbeth* at the Provincetown Playhouse in 1958.

commentator, taught Radio Training; and there were guest lecturers speaking about stage design and lighting.

But most of all, the Wharf School meant Edith Skinner. She was a widely respected and influential speech teacher at Carnegie Tech. Thirty-five years old, an attractive brunette fluent in five languages, she taught Muriel and the other neophytes what she considered proper speech for each different role.

"I use many recordings of [President] Roosevelt's addresses to teach boys and girls how to talk," she said that year. "Besides being a purist without affectation, the president has a most intimate way of speaking that inspires confidence." As examples of clear diction, she also imported some recordings of the voices of England's Queen Mary, Leslie Howard, Beatrice Lillie and others whose speech she admired; her teaching methods affected generations of American actors.[3]

That summer, Edith also provided her class with pages of the typescript that soon became her published manifesto in a book still in print almost eighty years later:

> The speech of the character [in a play] must bring to life the character itself. If the role calls for refined utterance, the audience must receive that impression . . . If the character speaks a dialect, then the actor must create the illusion by changes in sound and melody . . . Distinct utterance is the prime requisite of an actor. In fact, the audience should be able to take for granted that they can hear and understand everything the actor says, without straining to do so.

"She seemed like a visitor from another era or another century," recalled one of her later students, the dialect coach Brooks Baldwin. "She was always dressed to the nines—sometimes eccentrically—and she wore lots of gold jewelry. Among her maxims was: 'Darlings, there are two things in this world that you can't have enough of—little plastic bottles and gold.'"

---

3. Later, Edith Skinner was a consultant in speech at the American Conservatory Theatre, at the McCarter Theatre, at Lincoln Center, at the Guthrie Theatre and at the Brooklyn Academy of Music. From 1968 to her death in 1981, she taught at the Juilliard School while maintaining a full schedule at Carnegie Mellon. She was also in demand by celebrated working actors: at various times, she coached Laurence Olivier, Elizabeth Taylor, Meryl Streep, Rosemary Harris, Christopher Reeve and Robin Williams. Directors like Ellis Rabb and William Ball often called on her expertise.

Edith Skinner was a lively and surprising teacher completely devoted to the art of correct speech. One day, she announced to a startled class, "Today, we're banishing the jews." After a dramatic pause, she continued: "No more *couldjews, wouldjews, didjews,* and *hadjews*!" Her students spent the remaining hour practicing "d" followed by "y" in the next syllable—"could you, would you"—without muddying the glide.

Except during her summer months in Provincetown, Edith was a weekly visitor to the venerable Elizabeth Arden salon on Fifth Avenue, Manhattan, where she had her hair dyed a custom tint; perhaps in her honor, that color was discontinued after her death in 1981, at the age of 79.

Plays by Ibsen, Millay and O'Neill were among those studied in July 1937, as students performed semi-staged excerpts. Among the newcomers was Sally Rand, the notorious burlesque queen and fan dancer, eager to become a Serious Artiste. She appeared in a play called *White Cargo*, and Muriel never forgot the unintended hilarity of Rand's performance as the seductive native woman intoning the line, "I am Tondelayo." (The words were later immortalized by Hedy Lamarr in the 1942 movie version.) For her curtain call, Sally Rand appeared in a long blue gown and broad-brimmed hat: the ecdysiast with an arrest record and a tarnished public reputation transformed herself into a cool aristocrat.

In August, Edith Skinner assigned Muriel the role of Andrée in *By Your Leave*, a comedy by Gladys Hurlburt and Emma Wells. One of Muriel's co-stars was Doro Merande—an actress whose whiny, nasal, sometimes warbling tone and impeccable timing made her the perfect comic spinster, pathetic widow or gossipy neighbor in scores of plays and movies. Then in her forties and destined for a long and busy career, Doro had already appeared on stage and screen, and she recognized young talent when she saw it: that season, she became a kindly advisor to Muriel. *By Your Leave* was warmly received by the audiences when it was staged for six performances at the end of August.

"It was an education of sorts," Muriel recalled about her work and her roles that summer. "There was no room for self-indulgence or self-importance, and that lesson alone was a good antidote to anyone's notion that the theatre is a glamorous life."

∽

Back in Maplewood for her final academic year, Muriel won the leading role in Alberto Casella's *Death Takes a Holiday*. As the ingénue forced to confront death personified in a strange visitor, she was remembered for her portrayal of the character's charm, her confusion, her terror and the mystical sensibility the part required. Columbia High School's yearbook named her "the actress most likely to succeed." Commencement exercises were held on June 23.

That summer, Stanley Wood secured a scholarship for Muriel's return to the Wharf. Her expenses were therefore paid by a small fund in Provincetown, and soon she was back with the players for a ten-week season. There she met Vivian Vance, who had appeared four times on Broadway and became a new friend. (Vance was later most famous as Ethel Mertz, Lucille Ball's sidekick on the long-running television show *I Love Lucy*.)

Early that summer, Muriel was assigned a good role with several affecting scenes, as the teenage daughter, Blossom, in Rachel Crothers's literate comedy *Susan and God*, which had just completed a successful Broadway engagement. Arthur Wright sent his daughter a telegram before opening night:

HAVE BEEN THINKING OF YOU ALL WEEK HOPING THAT YOU LIKE YOUR PART AND WILL DO WELL WITH IT. TOMORROW BEGINS YOUR FINE OPPORTUNITY. WILL BE THINKING OF YOU AND WISHING SO HARD FOR YOUR SUCCESS AND WAITING TO HEAR FROM YOU. EDY [Edna, his fiancée, later his wife] JOINS ME IN SENDING YOU LOVE AND BEST WISHES—DAD

Two weeks later, for her role in the comedy *All's Fair*, Muriel was mentioned in the press for the first time: "Muriel Wright, a youngster, drew applause for her spontaneous performance as [the] younger sister." Another local critic added, "Muriel Wright is outstandingly good."

Good she may have been, but she was also very shrewd about the inadequacies and hazards of summer theatre and stock work in general, and she balked at being rushed from one part to another, with rehearsals overlapping performances. As she said years later, "You can't do a really good job when you rehearse for a short time as they did in stock companies.

Repertory is something else. In rep, actors who have really worked and studied roles learn from doing them continually. You might work on three or four different roles in one week, but you have time, a lot of time, to work on those roles before performing them. That's a lot different from the stock or summer theatre thing, when you rehearse one week and go onstage the next—and while you're doing that, you learn a role for the following week.

I'm glad I had the experience as a kid in summer stock, but I think if I had continued to do only that, it wouldn't have been very good. Actors who worked only in summer stock were perhaps not as good or as deep in their performances, or skilled or finished at all. There were a lot of excuses made for them, as one knows from all those old jokes: "We know the line [of dialogue], but who says it?" and "What play are we doing tonight?" and "How am I doing and what am I doing?" It made for a hit-or-miss kind of performance.

∾

Before the Wharf troupe disbanded at summer's end, Muriel had a letter from Doro Merande, who was appearing on Broadway as the town gossip Mrs. Soames in Thornton Wilder's Pulitzer Prize-winning play, *Our Town*. Doro invited Muriel to come to the play as her guest that autumn, and then to visit backstage.

And then things happened quickly.

Muriel hurried to Maplewood, visited Arthur and Edna at their home in nearby East Orange, and announced that she wanted to move to Manhattan to pursue her theatrical career. Her father was once again on her side and provided some cash to get her started. In early August, Muriel found a modest two-room apartment at 314 West Ninety-fourth Street, which she shared with another young working woman.

She then saw *Our Town*; visited Doro backstage afterward; was introduced to a number of cast members; and met the leading lady, Martha Scott, who was having great success as Emily Webb. As it happened, Doro had already mentioned Muriel to Martha, who was planning to leave the play in early September—to go to Hollywood for a screen test (for the role of Melanie in *Gone With the Wind*). The leading role was to be taken by Scott's twenty-four-year-old understudy, Dorothy McGuire, in her professional debut. Hence Jed Harris, the producer-director of the play, and Thornton Wilder, who had the right of cast approval, were earnestly seeking an understudy for Dorothy.

Muriel was encouraged to audition for Wilder and Harris—at the convenience of Harris, as usual. But a meeting with this notoriously difficult man, known for his bad temper, rudeness and mercurial personality, was virtually impossible to schedule: he made and broke appointments without warning and according to his momentary whimsy.

First, Muriel's audition was set for late in the evening of September 10: Harris preferred to have business meetings at the Morosco Theater, after the final curtain of *Our Town*. Muriel arrived on time and waited . . . and waited . . . and waited. Harris never appeared, and she went home at about one o'clock in the morning. His secretary then rescheduled the audition for September 15, same time, same place—but with the same result. Another appointment was made for September 21.

That was the date of what became known as the Great Hurricane of 1938. Winds howled through Central Park at sixty miles per hour; the waters of New York Harbor overflowed by seven feet; disaster affected tens of thousands from Long Island to Maine and destroyed hundreds of homes; and there were power failures, injuries and deaths over the course of three days. Announcements were constantly heard on the radio, warning people to remain in their homes.

But a telephone call to Muriel at home advised her that Harris would definitely see her at 11:30 that stormy evening. Unwell with a sore throat and cold, she wrapped herself in layers and boarded the nearly deserted subway train for the theatre. Shivering with anxiety and not in her best voice, she waited while two other actresses read for the director. "I was terrified of him—he was quite an unpredictable man—and I was frightened of the process of reading for him."

Muriel stepped onstage to read three brief scenes for the aloof, cranky and dispassionate Jed Harris. When she finished, he said nothing, his assistant thanked her, "and I remember going out into the hallway and bursting into tears—of relief, as much as anything." Home she went, certain that she had failed. But next morning, she was awakened early with the news that Harris (who had highly praised her to Wilder) had decided that Muriel would be Dorothy's understudy, beginning immediately. McGuire had been onstage as Emily since September 5 without a contracted standby. Marilyn Erskine, who was also in the cast, knew the role and was available in an emergency, but a permanent understudy was both desirable and required.

Muriel quickly memorized the major role of Emily, and for the next two weeks she attended every performance of the play, although she never had the opportunity to assume the role on Broadway. But backstage and on Sundays, she spent a great deal of free time with Dorothy: the two became firm and devoted friends and confidantes, and so they remained forever.[4] Thornton Wilder also extended to Muriel the long arm of his

4. Contrary to many published statements, Dorothy McGuire's understudy never stepped

friendship and became an influential advocate and champion—and he was especially active on her behalf four years later, in Hollywood.

Also in the cast were two men with whom Muriel formed lifetime friendships—Thomas Coley and William Roerick, who were twenty-five years old that year. These two met during rehearsals, fell in love and lived as a devoted couple for fifty-one years. Like Dorothy McGuire and Doro Merande, Tom and Bill had long and distinguished careers on Broadway, in films and on television.

Muriel's new job required her to join the actors' union, and so she applied for membership in the Actors' Equity Association. On October 18, she paid a $26 initiation fee, valid until her twenty-first birthday a year later, when the dues would increase. The receipt from Actors' Equity was written to Muriel Wright.

But at once there was a problem. In May 1934, an Equity member named Muriel Wright had appeared on Broadway at the Mansfield Theatre in the small role of "Woman Guest" for all seven performances of a flop called *I, Myself*, by Adelyn Bushell. This Muriel Wright had not worked since that time, but she was still registered with Equity—and so the twenty-year-old immigrant from Maplewood and the Wharf Theatre had to alter her identity. She took an obvious and easy route, excising her first name and henceforth using only her second. Her Equity card, mailed to her apartment on November 1, was issued to Miss Teresa Wright; thus she was listed as Dorothy's understudy in the playbill for *Our Town*, and so she was known from that time.[5]

Our Town closed on November 19, 1938, after 336 performances, but in a way it has never closed, and there can be no doubt that it must be ranked among a handful of great American plays, along with *The Glass Menagerie*, *Death of a Salesman* and *Long Day's Journey into Night*, to name but three other American masterworks that have become classics. As of 2015, there have been four Broadway revivals of *Our Town*, three film versions, a handful of television adaptations (one a musical) and an

---

into the role: Dorothy appeared in every performance from September 5 to the play's closing on November 19.

5. A few people (e.g., some of the players in *Our Town*) called her Tess, and one or two preferred the pronunciation Ter-ESS-a. But so far as I can ascertain, almost everyone called her Teresa, with the second *e* traditionally pronounced as a long vowel; she never corrected this usage. Her first husband and members of his family sometimes called her Muriel; to her second husband, she was always Teresa.

opera based on it; an Off-Broadway revival ran for 648 performances in 2009 and 2010; and repertory and school productions are literally past counting.

In the first twenty months after Wilder's agents authorized the release of amateur and stock rights, in April 1939, the play was performed more than 700 times throughout the United States and Canada; by 1943, it had been seen in Switzerland, Italy, Norway, Sweden, Finland, Spain, Rumania and Japan (these were mostly illegal productions); and experts claim that the play has been translated into more than fifty languages. It seems that some group is performing *Our Town*, somewhere, every day or evening.

∽

Teresa was engaged for the national tour of the play, which began in early 1939. At first, she did not play Emily but was assigned the role of eleven-year-old Rebecca because in some American cities, children under sixteen were not permitted to participate in professional stage productions. Rebecca is a minor part, and Teresa could easily be credible in it. Though the role was brief, Rebecca has a crucial speech that expresses one of Wilder's major themes. At the close of the first act, speaking of a letter sent by a minister to a sick friend, Rebecca says:

> He wrote Jane a letter and on the envelope the address was like this: It said: Jane Crofut; The Crofut Farm; Grover's Corners; Sutton County; New Hampshire; United States of America; Continent of North America; Western Hemisphere; the Earth; the Solar System; the Universe; the Mind of God—that's what it said on the envelope.

From January 1939, Teresa played Emily at theatres in Philadelphia, Cleveland, Toledo, Pittsburgh, Lexington (Kentucky), Boston, Providence, New Haven, Los Angeles, Chicago—and in Maplewood, where her father joined the townspeople in a Welcome Home celebration after the performance. At the conclusion of the Boston engagement, on April 24, Eddie Dowling (who produced the tour and played the Stage Manager) stepped forward at the curtain call and, according to the critic E.C. Sherburne, "took occasion to compliment Miss Teresa Wright on her performance, in which he was roundly seconded by the audience. She has a glow that sets her apart. She brings to Emily, both as child and woman, a completeness of assimilation," by which Sherburne probably meant that she seamlessly conveyed Emily's character development.

∽

Each generation has discovered the mysteries and timeless meanings within the simple manners of *Our Town*, and its universal themes are presented with disarming simplicity. Wilder insisted that there be no sets for the play—only a few chairs, perhaps a lectern, a ladder, a few pieces of wood laid down to suggest the perimeters of a house. "No curtain. No scenery. The audience, arriving, sees an empty stage in half-light." Wilder also stipulated that the actors must mime their actions with invisible "props." So begins the text of the play.

Often misunderstood and dismissed as a sentimental romanticizing of life in a small New England town in the early twentieth century, *Our Town* is nothing of the sort. Like all great works, it cannot be reduced to a classroom summary, but it is perhaps fair to say that the play radiates a belief in the eternal value of ordinary lives. Emily, after her death, revisits Grover's Corners and her home. As she leaves, she says,

> I didn't realize. So all that was going on, and we never noticed. Good-by, Good-by, world. Good-by, Grover's Corners . . . and Mama and Papa. Good-by to clocks ticking . . . and Mama's sunflowers. And food and coffee. And new-ironed dresses and hot baths, and sleeping and waking up. Oh, Earth, you're too wonderful for anybody to realize you.

And then she turns to the Stage Manager: "We don't have time to look at one another," Emily says ("through her tears," Wilder writes in the stage directions). "Do any human beings ever realize life while they live it—every, every minute?" The Narrator/Stage Manager replies, "The saints and poets, maybe."

The play's profoundest, most poignant moment occurs when George Gibbs comes to the grave of his wife, Emily, who has died in childbirth. The "dead," detached and serene, are seated in chairs as a graveyard. Sobbing, George falls at the feet of Emily. With the wisdom of eternity, she turns to her mother-in-law:

--"Mother Gibbs?"
--"Yes, Emily?"
--"They don't understand, do they?"
--"No, dear. They don't understand."

∽

CHAPTER FOUR

1939–1941

THE NATIONAL TOUR OF *OUR TOWN* CONTINUED UNTIL JUNE 1939. When Teresa returned to New York, Francis G. Cleveland, a cast member in *Our Town* (and the son of Grover Cleveland, former United States president), invited her to join the Barnstormers, a renowned professional company that Cleveland had co-founded in 1931. During the summers, this group of actors, based in Tamworth, New Hampshire, traveled throughout the New England countryside in caravans and old trucks, "barnstorming" from town to town, offering eight plays in eight weeks. They performed in school auditoriums, halls and theatres, and attracted enthusiastic audiences in large cities and small hamlets. After minor parts in two plays, Teresa won the major role of Leone in *The Vinegar Tree*, by Paul Osborn.

A Broadway success in 1930 and 1931, the comedy dealt with suppressed sex and marital tedium: Nineteen-year-old Leone ("a very pretty, attractive young lady," according to Osborn's notes) is rejected by her boyfriend because of her lack of "experience." Lamenting her innocence, she flirts outrageously with a forty-year-old artist and tries to make him a tutor: "I am a virgin," she complains. "It's an unintelligent state to be in. I think about sex all the time. But I shouldn't. I want to put it in its proper place so that I'll have time to think of more important things. My mind is fairly sophisticated for a girl my age, but my body is so naïve that it disgusts my mind." Teresa played the role with a deft and amusing blend of innocence and seductiveness: she did not often have a part that was both droll and racy, and she savored every moment.

In early August, the Barnstormers performed at the Lakewood Theatre in Skowhegan, Maine, and Cleveland and his troupe prepared to
depart for their next venue just as another production was moving in
with its cast and sets. This new play, having a pre-Broadway tryout, was
a comedy called *Life With Father*; it was under the uncertain control of a
fledgling producer named Oscar Serlin, and Teresa (who had completed
the run of *The Vinegar Tree*) remained in Skowhegan to see the show.

Life With Father was based on Clarence Day's popular stories, first published in *The New Yorker*, about the comic adventures of a large New York
City family in the 1880s. Oscar Serlin and the director, Bretaigne Windust, were making minor adjustments to the play and found that a few
cast members had turned out to be unsuitable in their roles. Especially
worrisome was a young actress in the role of "a pretty, wide-eyed girl of
seventeen," as the playwrights Howard Lindsay and Russel Crouse described the character—not a cameo role but an important one.

Gossip, news and rumors invariably spread among theatre and movie
people, and never more so than when employment is or might be available. Teresa learned of the possible replacement, and she was eager to
read for the part. But there were two problems: she did not have a theatrical agent, whom she would have to engage before proceeding with
any efforts to audition for a role; and the producer and director had not
formally announced that they were seeking a new young actress.

She hurried back to her Manhattan apartment, and after a few calls to
friends, she made an appointment to meet Louis Shurr—an agent who at
various times over many years represented Bob Hope, Robert Mitchum
and Kim Novak, among others. With no Broadway acting credits thus
far, Teresa feared that Shurr would not accept her as a client. But he
was also a talent scout for film studios, and he often smoothed the path
to Hollywood of many New York actors unknown to movie executives:
with additional income from movie studios for his finder's fee, this was a
welcome adjunct to Louis Shurr's primary function as a Broadway theatrical agent.

In September, Shurr arranged for Teresa to meet with Serlin and Windust. They told her that they wanted a blonde with an opulent figure
for the ingénue role, the romantic interest—and there she was, a petite,
slim brunette. But please, she said, would they allow her to read? Oh,
well: like Serlin's mother's chicken soup, it couldn't hurt. She read, they
listened, they asked her to wait a moment in the outer office and then
invited her back in for the verdict. She had the role of Mary Skinner. At

once she was rushed into the New York rehearsals of *Life With Father*, which moved to Baltimore for the last tryout, a week's engagement at the Maryland Theatre beginning on October 30—three days after her twenty-first birthday.

Mary Skinner is a winsome and impressionable visitor to New York, impressed with anyone or anything even vaguely cosmopolitan: "I never met a Yale man before!" she says almost breathlessly, just as she is stricken with a bad case of awe about a glamorous restaurant ("Delmonico's!") or an elegant New York lodging ("The Fifth Avenue Hotel!"). Mary is the welcome guest and the reminder of outside reality, as she becomes the romantic but clear-eyed love interest, stealing into the heart of the oldest son in this large and agreeably daffy family.

Playwrights Lindsay and Crouse had hoped for a decent run of the play—perhaps six to eight months. But their estimate was wildly inaccurate: *Life With Father* opened at the Empire Theatre, New York, on November 8, 1939. Later, the production transferred, without omitting a single show, to two other Broadway houses; after a total of 3,224 performances, the play closed on July 12, 1947. As of 2015, *Life With Father* remains the longest-running straight (that is, nonmusical) play in the history of the American theatre.

Teresa's dressing room at the Empire was near that of John Drew Devereaux, the actor who played young Clarence. She remembered that John had a fine singing voice and that he loved music, especially opera. "I learned a lot about good music during the run of that play." On her dressing table, as usual, she kept a signed photo of Helen Hayes, sent in response to a fan letter Teresa had mailed after seeing *Victoria Regina*.

The New York critics were rhapsodic about *Life With Father*. "Sooner or later, everyone will have to see 'Life With Father,'" wrote Brooks Atkinson, the longtime drama critic of the *New York Times*. "Last night, everyone in the audience was falling jubilantly in love with a minor classic in the library of American humor [that is, the stories on which the play was based] . . . Written and acted with infinite dexterity, it is no cartoon out of the funny papers . . . The dialogue is sparkling, the story is shrewdly told, and the acting is a treasure. The play is overpoweringly funny . . . and also enchanting . . . Teresa Wright plays with uncommon charm as a person and willowy skill as an actress." Audiences responded heartily to Teresa's pert, spirited manner, which was never overstated or played to the gallery. She remained in the cast for a year and a half and performed her role for 624 performances.

I ask myself how I could keep doing the same thing night after night, but it never bothered me. The only difficulty was that I didn't want to take a vacation. Everybody else did, but I was sure that if I took a vacation and stopped saying the words, I'd never be able to go on saying them again.

What kind of latent fear prompted this sort of hesitation? Teresa did not lack the professional self-confidence she needed for a role, but throughout her life she had no strong sense of self-esteem, which is something else altogether. Perhaps it would be too easy to trace her recurring qualms to the disturbing events of her childhood and the subsequent abandonment by her mother. But it would also be impossible to believe that her early experience of fear and loss did not affect her deeply and forever.

On the other hand, there was compensation for "doing the same thing night after night." Mary was a bright, loving girl, and if occasionally Teresa went to the theatre feeling ill or depressed about something, by the final curtain her spirits had much improved: "I felt much better, having had to play a part that was light and gay."

In addition, there was an extraordinary spirit unifying the cast of *Life With Father*.

What a way for a youngster to begin! Every person connected with that production grew up knowing theatre manners. I'm talking about backstage behavior; I'm talking about caring about the play, the other actors and the audience. To want to do your best, to be on time—at the theatre *and* with your cues. Always to do the best as if it's for the first time.

For the rest of her life, Teresa gratefully recalled the friendly mentorship of Howard Lindsay, the star and co-author, and of director Bretaigne Windust ("Windy" to his friends). And most of all—as she did with Dorothy McGuire during *Our Town*—Teresa formed another lifelong friendship from *Life With Father*. Katherine Bard was an actress just two years her senior: she had the role of Annie, the new maid in the household, and was also Teresa's understudy.

Just before the play opened, Katie Bard married Martin Manulis, a man of exceptional talent, destined to contribute greatly to the development of significant drama on live American television and the production of several memorable movies. At that time, he reviewed scripts for a theatrical business manager and was about to assume the directorship of the Bass Rocks Theatre in Gloucester, Massachusetts. Katie and Martin had an apartment on East Ninth Street, to which Teresa was a frequent visitor. In the decades to come, the Bards intersected Teresa's life with increasing professional and personal importance; their friendship was uninterrupted.

At twenty-one, Teresa Wright was suddenly a Broadway star, pressured to grant interviews and asked to speak about the show on the radio—which she did, while expertly deflecting any questions about her personal life. She was besieged for autographs at the stage door and received more than one invitation to step out with this or that smitten gentleman who had seen a performance. Within weeks of the premiere, she and Louis Shurr were fielding offers from Hollywood.

But Teresa was adamant in rejecting the idea of relocating to California for a movie contract: she did not want to be among a crowd in a big movie scene, or to be a bathing beauty for studio publicity, or to be photographed marketing a product, or (for the gossip columns) to be set up on a blind date with a young man also under contract—such was the usual fate of a legion of young actors transported to Hollywood. "I'd seen too many promising actresses go there for a career in pictures and end up with a career in picture magazines," she said. "I could see myself sitting around for months waiting for a bit part and meantime being photographed in bathing suits in every conceivable pose. I'm no glamour girl to begin with—so I made up my mind that I would give Hollywood a pass until I had the offer of a definite part."

Soon after the opening, Katharine Hepburn came backstage to congratulate Teresa. She also had a firm offer from her friend Howard Hughes, formerly (it was said) her lover and still a good friend. "Howard is preparing a movie called *The Outlaw*," Hepburn announced, "and you would be perfect for the part of the leading lady. Why not come out to Hollywood for a test? He will pay all your expenses and treat you very, very well."

"Oh, I couldn't," said Teresa before she could take back her own words. "I don't want to make movies. I want to be a *legitimate* actress"—this to an established star who already had won her first Academy Award. Teresa did not report Hepburn's reaction to this gaffe. But the notion of casting her in a role eventually assumed by Jane Russell—a production in which Hughes was transfixed by tricky ways of presenting Russell's opulent bust—was both ludicrous and hilarious. In any case, it is impossible to determine whether the invitation that evening originated with Hughes or Hepburn.

∽

Within a month of the premiere, Teresa received a strange letter from the comic actor Charley Chase, once successful in the silent-movie era. "I saw you Saturday night in the play and really thought you were terrific. The last time I saw you was in Pasadena where you were with the King Players, and that was so long ago. It doesn't seem possible that an old dame like you could play a young girl like Mary Skinner and get away with it. You were swell. Call me up and come to dinner with me."

Chase was obviously confused, and it is impossible to know of whom he was thinking when he wrote to Teresa. She had never acted in Pasadena; she did not know the King Players; and she was of course nothing like an old dame. Prudently, she ignored the letter. Six months later, in a fit of dementia caused by years of alcoholism and clinical depression, Charley Chase died at the age of forty-six.

She had to disappoint someone closer to home, too. Earlier—perhaps at Columbia High School, perhaps during the Maplewood performance of *Our Town*—her grandmother had cried out: "There's my baby! There she is!" to the acute embarrassment of her granddaughter onstage, and to the consternation of the audience. Teresa could not risk that again, and so, very gently, she asked Granny to postpone her visit. The matter never arose again: the beloved Mary Teresa Kelly Wright Reese—who always preferred to use all her names, to wear her three dresses simultaneously and to haul her family correspondence everywhere in a large reticule—died during the run of *Life With Father*.

∽

When she first joined the cast, Teresa met a genial, handsome man exactly her own age. Jean Barrere was the understudy to John Drew Devereaux. After graduating from the American Academy of Dramatic Arts in 1936, Jean had a brief career as an actor before becoming an occasional understudy and a skilled stage manager. He was Teresa's date around town on Sundays; he invited her to dinner at bistros patronized by theatre folk; and he escorted her to the movies.

Before the end of 1939, Jean was regarded (at least by some cast members and the New York press) as Teresa's boyfriend. That seemed to be confirmed when a magazine published a photograph of them, standing just outside her new apartment at 25 Minetta Lane, near Washington Square Park in Greenwich Village. (Now that she was paid $80 weekly as a working actress, she could afford the rent of $32 per month for her own rooms.)

On one of those "dark" Sundays (January 28, 1940), when no performance was offered at the Empire, *Life With Father* moved to the National Theatre in Washington, D.C., for a command performance honoring President Franklin D. Roosevelt's fifty-eighth birthday. Afterward, the cast, crew and understudies were invited to dinner at the White House. "I'll never forget it," Teresa recalled. "Mrs. Roosevelt managed to sit for a while at every single table, and we were a big company. She somehow accomplished the feat of making everyone feel like a special guest."

∽

Six days later, on February 3, Lillian Hellman's third Broadway play, *The Little Foxes*, closed after 410 performances. There was a bidding war for the film rights, and negotiations with Hollywood moguls continued throughout the spring and summer of 1940 while Hellman temporized, raised her price and demanded script, director and cast approval.

But from the start, there was really no doubt about who would bring *The Little Foxes* to the screen. Hellman had already worked on four screenplays for producer Samuel Goldwyn—*The Dark Angel*, *These Three* (based on her play *The Children's Hour*), *Dead End* and *The Westerner*. Goldwyn, who had produced Hollywood's first feature picture (*The Squaw Man*, directed by Cecil B. DeMille in 1913), was arguably the greatest independent producer in the history of Hollywood. At sixty-one, he had earned a reputation for making not the greatest number of movies annually, but for making what he considered the best—one at a time—with the finest stars, the best writers and the most talented directors. Goldwyn handily won the movie rights to *Foxes*.

As the director of the film, Hellman and Goldwyn at once chose William Wyler, who had been working in Hollywood for more than fifteen years and had already directed many hugely successful pictures—most recently, *Dodsworth*, *Jezebel*, *Wuthering Heights* and *The Letter*.[1] At that time, he had a multi-picture deal with Goldwyn. Despite the daily dust-ups that normally occur before, during and after every production, Hellman, Goldwyn and Wyler were a mutually respectful troika.

The Little Foxes is an intense drama of larceny, greed and unchecked, callous ambition in a Southern family at the turn of the twentieth

---

1. In the course of his long career, Wyler directed more than seventy movies and won three Academy Awards as best director—for *Mrs. Miniver*, *The Best Years of Our Lives* and *Ben-Hur*. His later successes included *The Heiress*, *Roman Holiday* and *Funny Girl*.

century. The triumphant Broadway production owed as much to its gifted players as to the astringent dialogue, solid structure and sharp characters.

Casting for the Goldwyn-Wyler-Hellman movie began with a clear decision. The leading lady in the play had been Tallulah Bankhead, but for a movie version, Bankhead was not bankable as the viperish Regina Giddens: her eccentric qualities and often wild mannerisms onstage were frequently impressive, but there was perhaps too much of her muchness. Movie audiences of the time were not keen on Bankhead, and her few films were box-office failures. Instead, Goldwyn borrowed Bette Davis from Warner Bros., and from the Broadway cast, five actors were signed to repeat their roles for the movie.

But there was a problem. A principal character in the play is Alexandra Giddens—Regina's seventeen-year-old daughter, the moral center of the story, and the untainted one among the ruthless vultures. It is she who tries to protect her dying father from her unprincipled mother and rapacious uncles. Hellman and Goldwyn had already expanded the role of Alexandra, and for the movie, the playwright created a love interest for her. At the same time, the producer set out to find a new actress for the part—one who could pass for seventeen, could communicate glowing innocence, a clear conscience and an inchoate maturity tempered by keen intelligence. Alexandra was no cliché and required the most delicate shadings of an actress's craft.[2]

Unable to find a satisfactory Hollywood actress for the role, Goldwyn asked Hellman to scout New York talent. She saw *Life With Father*, was keen on Teresa, and sent a cable to Goldwyn, who hurried to New York to see for himself. Teresa had read the play, knew of the impending movie and thought that here at last might be a reason to consider going to Hollywood. But she also thought the odds in her favor were slim indeed.

Everything changed when Goldwyn made his way backstage. "I knew she was a great actress before the end of the first act," he told *Time* magazine. "Miss Wright was seated at her dressing table when I was introduced, and she looked for all the world like a little girl experimenting with her mother's cosmetics. I had discovered in her—from the first sight, you might say—an unaffected genuineness and appeal."

---

2. At various times, Goldwyn had a roster of men under exclusive contract: Will Rogers, Ronald Colman, David Niven, Farley Granger, Danny Kaye and others. Director William Wyler and cinematographer Gregg Toland were also committed to Goldwyn—and at one time, the actress Miriam Hopkins. But when Teresa signed with the producer, he had no other woman under contract.

On the spot, he offered Teresa the role of Alexandra in a one-picture deal. The following day, before the producer left town, he had spoken to Louis Shurr, who turned Teresa over to his Hollywood colleague, Abe Lastfogel, head of the William Morris Agency. Teletypes clacked across the country, and an agreement was quickly sealed. There would have to be the *pro forma* screen test to examine her hair and skin tones before the camera, and to hear how her voice registered for microphones. But Goldwyn was convinced he had his new star.

As for Teresa, she was predictably delighted at the prospect of joining such a prestigious production, but she was equally pleased that her time in Hollywood would be limited to one picture, and that soon she would be back among her friends onstage at the Empire Theatre. She was given the opportunity to submit to the test in New York, but sensibly she wanted every possible assistance from studio professionals; hence she preferred to travel to Hollywood for the test.

Teresa's contract with Oscar Serlin to perform in *Life With Father* had begun in the autumn of 1939 and continued until June 1, 1940. They maintained a friendly trust, and as the term date approached, Serlin did not ask her to sign a run of the play contract (which would bind her until forever, as she said). "This means," as Shurr wrote to Lastfogel, "that she can be available for a test or for production on two weeks notice. But Teresa's relationship with [Serlin] is much too pleasant, and she has no intention of taking advantage of the two-week privilege. Also, she is taking no vacation, which has been offered to her—so Oscar will certainly grant her a leave to make the screen test."

Lastfogel took up the cause with Goldwyn, who for some reason did not reply with a firm date for the test. "Do you want Teresa or not?" Lastfogel cabled edgily across town to Goldwyn on July 17, 1940; that evoked an immediate response—the test would be set for four weeks hence. But in the ways of Hollywood, one month stretched to eight. Finally, Teresa arrived in Los Angeles for her screen test, which was completed on March 6, 1941; it thoroughly impressed Wyler and confirmed Goldwyn's initial zeal. Perhaps planning for Teresa's eventual withdrawal from *Life With Father*, Goldwyn sent a note of gratitude to Oscar Serlin on March 24, thanking him for permitting Teresa to fly to California for the test.

She then hurried back to New York. Declining the limousine Goldwyn had ordered to meet her at the New York Municipal Airport (later La-Guardia Field), she hopped into Jean Barrere's waiting jalopy and went straight to the Empire Theatre. And that, it seems, was the last time Jean and Teresa met, a separation due to their respective professional plans.

Whether this friendship was ever romantic cannot be determined; the couple may have been just amiable colleagues and companions during this brief period of time. Then and later, Teresa never mentioned him, but her silence implies nothing. In any case, when she left the production, Jean Barrere faded into her history. He married, had three children, continued his busy career as a stage manager and died in 1977 at the age of fifty-nine.

∽

On March 17, 1941, the *New York Times* reported that in Hollywood, Teresa Wright "was signed to a five-year contract by Samuel Goldwyn." That was a proleptic announcement that skewed the facts: there was as yet no countersigned contract, and she had only verbally agreed to work for Goldwyn on just one picture, *The Little Foxes*, after which she expected to return to *Life With Father*. She did not leave the cast of the play until after the Saturday evening performance on April 5 and did not depart from New York until the following Thursday, April 10. Her friend Katie Bard assumed the role of Mary Skinner on Monday, April 7.

The Goldwyn contract was finally ready for everyone's signature in May, when the filming of *The Little Foxes* was well along; for those he liked and trusted, Goldwyn was satisfied with a handshake until his agents and attorneys settled details. After several emendations demanded both by Abe Lastfogel and by Goldwyn's legal department, the agreement was concluded.

Teresa was guaranteed $500 weekly for the first forty weeks of employment, with raises to $750 weekly for a second year if Goldwyn chose to renew. Over the next six years, her income would eventually rise to $3,000 weekly. She was permitted to work only for Goldwyn, whose privilege it was to loan her out to another studio for any fee; as usual in Hollywood, he pocketed any difference between her contracted salary with him and the income from a loan-out.[3] This was often the means by which studio bosses realized exorbitant wealth. On her side, Teresa

---

3. After withholdings for the 45 percent federal tax then in effect at her bracket; and after deductions for California taxes, for Social Security, for dues in the Screen Actors Guild and for commissions to her agent, Teresa took home approximately $220 a week of the contracted $500. But her annual net income of about $8,800 was very handsome in 1941, when the average American earned $1,490 a year.

was allowed to work in the theatre for six months of every year—at the sacrifice of her Goldwyn salary, of course.

∽

When she returned to Los Angeles, she did not have the remotest idea of what clothing she needed or where she would live. A Goldwyn fashion consultant and a woman in his costume department quickly resolved the first issue; they took her shopping, issued sound professional counsel and charged to Goldwyn's account those clothes suitable for every occasion. The ladies were perhaps surprised when Teresa insisted on the simplest outfits for her personal use.

With the help of another Goldwyn assistant, Teresa found a two-room furnished apartment south of Wilshire Boulevard and north of Olympic Boulevard. The place was down a partly hidden driveway, the former guest room over a homeowner's garage, in what was considered the déclassé sector of Beverly Hills. The rent was $45 a month, which (unlike the clothes) she would have to pay.

This area was regarded as the wrong side (or in this case, the south side) of the rail-car tracks that ran along the median on Santa Monica Boulevard. Teresa could have afforded a more upscale residence, but as always she selected a simple, unpretentious place to live. As her son said years later, "She always disapproved of ostentation, of crass materialism, or a belief that wealth is somehow proof of worth."

Of Beverly Hills south of Wilshire, wrote the novelist and screenwriter Viña Delmar,

> No place in the country has a more candid, less flexible division between the right side and the wrong side of town. The swimming pools are scarce, if indeed any at all exist . . . and [there are] fewer servants, fewer cars of exotic makes, fewer unlisted telephone numbers—for wealth and importance are rare south of Wilshire.

By contrast, Delmar continued, in Beverly Hills north of Wilshire, "screen stars commit suicide with little red sleeping pills . . . Bugsy Siegel was shot to death . . . and Howard Hughes crashed and burned a plane. These things happen north of Wilshire."

Modest though it was, the apartment quickly bore the stamp of Teresa's personality. She sewed and installed new curtains and purchased a few bibelots; her entire expenditure came to $34.52.

During her first months in town, and often when she had free days during production, Goldwyn subjected Teresa to the usual studio buildup and the rigors of the publicity machine. At an early session, a photographer told her to run her hands through her hair, to look up at a key light, to lick and part her lips alluringly, to recline in a nearly diaphanous silk gown on a chaise—and to look bored . . . or seductive . . . or disenchanted. Then an attending "hack," a publicist, fired questions he might use to entice magazines:

"What do you want most of all in Hollywood?"

"Above everything, I want to be a good actress."

This was not the sort of scintillating reply the man wanted.

"Tell us something original about your work at the studio."

"If you want something entirely original, just say that I hate the hours. I don't see how anyone has time to go to Ciro's [a nightclub] as they all claim."

This was not going well.

While other newcomers were appearing in newspapers and magazines, it was hard to place Teresa. "She is not the glamour type," Goldwyn's minions told their boss—to which Teresa replied that she agreed, that she felt she had none of the attributes for artificial poses. "I said I would have to make good on my acting ability, which was the only attribute I could offer."

Goldwyn was not anxious: *The Little Foxes* would vindicate his faith in her talent and her looks. At the same time, she was relieved not to be considered glamorous. Her lack of typical movie-star allure certainly did not mean she lacked real beauty, however—although, typically, she never thought of herself as particularly attractive when it came to assessing her looks.

Teresa depended on her understanding, her intuition and her expressive eyes. She saw herself as Plain Jane; in reality, she radiated a rare kind of direct, unstudied warmth and an appealing freshness that was never cloying or childish, always recognizably honest and candid. Directors and audiences immediately understood her spontaneous, natural charm, which contrasted mightily with the studio-generated images of, for example, Rita Hayworth, Lana Turner, Betty Grable, Jane Russell and, earlier, Greta Garbo and Marlene Dietrich—none of them without talent, all of them perhaps too much the invention of powerful men.

After regarding what Goldwyn considered her overly casual hairstyle, he bought her an expensive new hairbrush and told her, "Go home and

brush your hair 100 strokes in the morning and 150 strokes at night."
He then added a typical Goldwyn *non sequitur*: "I want you to be natural
in every department."[4] How that kind of regime was natural he did not
explain.

∽

At that time, film crews worked six days a week, and normal working
hours could extend from six in the morning to late evening; later, the
Screen Actors Guild, the Directors Guild and the technical unions obtained major reductions in these schedules.

From the time of the first rehearsals and then filming (which began
on April 28), Teresa routinely rose from her folding bed at four o'clock
in the morning. She drove her secondhand car about three miles east to
the Goldwyn Studios, at 7200 Santa Monica Boulevard, where *The Little
Foxes* was in production.

Many stage actors need time to adjust to the different demands of
movie technique: the necessity to moderate the voice, to modify gestures, to allow the director and his camera to find on the face the intima-
tions of feeling that require something larger or louder or more obvious
onstage, where the patrons in the upper balconies must see and hear
things clearly.

"I didn't find it difficult to adapt to the camera," Teresa said years later,
"and I think that was because I didn't have a lot of experience on the
stage, and I was young enough to be able to adapt. I hadn't set any kind
of pattern. I feel that my 'style,' whatever it may be, is rather a small one
anyway—so that it adapted itself well to the camera."

At first, the difference primarily had to do with the director—in this
case, William Wyler, who was notorious for demanding take after take of
a scene or even an individual shot, until he finally saw what he wanted.
According to Bette Davis, whom Wyler had already directed in *Jezebel*
and *The Letter*, "He was inarticulate about what he wanted." Laurence
Olivier, who had acted in Wyler's *Wuthering Heights* in 1939, spoke for
many when he said that Wyler asked for so many takes of one or another scene that an exasperated Olivier finally asked, "Willy, how in God's
name do you *want* this scene?" To which the director replied, "Better."
Soon, Olivier understood that Wyler did not want to see him acting—or

---

4. Goldwyn had these precise instructions about hair brushing inserted into the script for *The
Little Foxes*, in an exhortation by the housemaid Addie (Jessie Grayson) to Alexandra Giddens
(Teresa).

overacting: "Where the hell do you think you are, at the Opera House in Manchester?" Wyler cried.

"Willy required a certain something from you that he seemed unable to put into words," Teresa recalled.

> But when I think about it years later, I'm not sure if he was actually unable to articulate what he wanted—or if he simply did not want to impose himself or a certain idea on the actor. I think that sometimes there was some special quality Willy was waiting for. And he actually hated to see "acting"—he wanted to see something real. To tell the truth, Willy wasn't interested much in actors: he was interested in creating an effect on film, and that's what he did so beautifully. Like Goldwyn, Willy knew what he *didn't* want, and he was so right about it that it turned out well.

Teresa's relationships during production were uniformly agreeable. Bette Davis did not suffer fools or lazy amateurs gladly; she excoriated unprepared colleagues or undisciplined members of a cast or crew; and she frequently intimidated actors on movie sets. But she could also be helpful and kind to neophytes—and so she was to Teresa, who was making her debut in a difficult and demanding role with a company of seasoned professionals. "Bette was very generous," Teresa recalled. "I had come through the theatre, as she had, and she welcomed stage actors. She was too much of a pro to steal scenes. She just played her part. She was marvelous to all of us, and as helpful as she could be."

There was no friction between Teresa and Bette (who already had two Oscars, one of them thanks to Wyler's direction), but sparks were ignited between Davis and the director. When he saw her makeup test, the director was livid: what was all this rice-powder on her face? She looked like a refugee from the Kabuki theatre! She looks old, harsh and shabby! She should look wittier, sexier!

Well, replied the star, this is how Lillian Hellman wrote the part of Regina—a woman in her forties, not soft but furiously ruthless. Davis was only thirty-three, she reminded Wyler, and she had to look at least old enough to be the wife of the actor Herbert Marshall (then sixty-one) and the mother of seventeen-year-old Alexandra. Their disagreements on the set were certainly aggravated by the 100-degree heat wave that smothered Los Angeles that spring and summer, and by the heavy, neck-to-toe period costumes the women players had to wear. Eventually, the discord between Davis and her director became louder and more bitter, until she stormed off the set and out of town for three weeks; Wyler had to shoot around her. But when Davis heard rumors that either Katharine Hepburn or Miriam Hopkins would replace her (which Goldwyn and Wyler circulated as a rumor to frighten Davis), she made her peace with the director and finished the picture.

This episode was duly chronicled in the *New York Times*, but a notable, contrary element concluded the essay: "One newcomer to the cast is exciting great enthusiasm in the company. She is Teresa Wright. Wyler says she is the most promising young actress he has ever directed." A reporter from *Variety* visited the production, too; he later saw a preview screening and reported: "Miss Wright is a newcomer to the screen and is magnificent in a very difficult part. A less talented actress in her place could have ruined the picture." Goldwyn almost crowed with pride.

The number of Teresa's friends was increasing. Patricia Collinge, then forty-eight, had played the tragic figure of alcoholic Aunt Birdie in the Broadway production of *Foxes* and was now repeating her role in the movie. She became a motherly friend to Teresa, and both of them some-times giggled helplessly at some of Hollywood's technical jargon: "Put the baby on her and let it dribble on Ben," cried one of the lighting techni-cians—moviespeak for "Put a tiny spotlight on a stand and let it shine softly on the character of Ben Hubbard," and "Shut the barn doors!" a reference to a set of attachments that focus a certain kind of floodlight or lantern.

∽

It would have been easy for Teresa to portray Alexandra as a cardboard character—a one-note rendering of vulnerable and naïve innocence. But she understood that the girl grew and matured, becoming gradually aware of the horrifying, murderous family greed that was concentrated in her rapacious mother. Hence her performance removed Alexandra from the borderline of cliché and made her a figure who experiences a moral education. The girl's decency and integrity, in other words, are tested and become credible through her strength of character. It is not axiomatic that any young actress could just recite the dialogue to make Alexandra a fully realized young woman.

For the final moments of the picture, a confrontation between Alex-andra and Regina, Wyler placed the two actresses on a winding staircase, an arrangement he often favored in his films. As Bette Davis ascends the stairs, Teresa remains below:

Regina: You'll feel better when we get to Chicago. I'm going to get you the world I always wanted.

Alexandra: I don't want the world, Mama. I'm not going to Chicago with you.

Regina: You're upset, Alexandra. Let's talk about it tomorrow.

Alexandra: There's nothing to talk about. I'm going away from you—because I want to. Because I know Papa would want me to.

Regina: You know your Papa would want you to go away from me?

Alexandra: Yes.

Regina: And if I say no?

Alexandra: Say it, Mama—say it and see what happens.

Regina: You're serious about this, aren't you? Well, you'll change your mind in a couple of days. [pause] Alexandra, I've come to the end of my rope! Somewhere there's got to be what I want, too. Life goes too fast. You can go where you want, do what you want, be what you want. I'd like to keep you with me, but I won't make you stay. No, I won't make you stay.

Alexandra: You couldn't, Mama, because I don't want to stay with you—because I'm beginning to understand about things. Addie said there were people who ate the Earth and people who stood around and watched them do it. And just now Uncle Ben said the same thing, really the same thing. Well, tell him for me, Mama, that I'm not going to watch you do it. Tell him I'll be fighting as hard as he is—someplace where people don't just stand around and watch.

Regina: Why, Alexandra—you have spirit, after all. I used to think you were all sugar-water. [pause] We don't have to be bad friends, Zan—I don't want us to be bad friends. [She continues her slow ascent, glancing toward the door behind which lies the body of her husband, who has just died from her deliberate failure to provide medicine. Then, slowly, sadly:] Would you like to talk with me, Alexandra? Would you like to sleep in my room tonight?

Alexandra: Why, Mama? Are you afraid?

These are the last words of *The Little Foxes*, which Teresa spoke quietly, as if uttering a kind of painful threnody—calmly, sadly and almost with compassion for the devil. Few films have dared to fade out with a moral triumph so pacific.

❦

The praise for Teresa was rapturous when the picture was released, just five weeks after the final scene was shot. Edwin Schallert, senior film critic for the *Los Angeles Times*, spoke for many when he described her debut as "one of the most remarkably brilliant for a young player in Hollywood."

When the Academy Award nominations for 1941 were announced, ten people were cited in eight categories for *The Little Foxes*: best picture, best actress (Bette Davis), best director (William Wyler), best scoring of a dramatic picture (Meredith Willson, who later wrote the book, music and lyrics for *The Music Man*), best screenplay (Lillian Hellman), best black-and-white art direction (Stephen Goosson and Howard Bristol), best film editing (Daniel Mandell)—and best supporting actress, the category in which both Patricia Collinge and Teresa Wright received nominations.

The Little Foxes was a great success for Goldwyn that year, although it failed to win a single Oscar. For Teresa, however, an Academy nomination for her first motion-picture performance was very gratifying, but it was not enough to keep her in Hollywood. Samuel Goldwyn was disappointed when she announced that she would now return to the theatre, but there was the matter of her contract, which permitted just that.

Before *The Little Foxes* opened nationwide in August, Teresa was back in New York, summoned by Oscar Serlin. He chose to exercise his contractual right for her participation in a play after one movie, and he assigned Teresa a major role in *The King's Maid*, by Ferenc Molnár. And so she traveled first to New York and then on to Gloucester, on the picturesque north shore of Massachusetts, where the play would be tested prior to a Broadway premiere. As the ancient cartographers wrote in another context, "Here lie dragons"—but now they lurked not in the sea or in caves.

CHAPTER FIVE

❧

1941–1942

BORN IN BUDAPEST, WHERE HIS NOVELS WERE FIRST PUBLISHED AND his plays performed, Ferenc Molnár was recognized as a master of both modern drama and romantic comedy. In 1940, he fled to the United States to escape the massacre of the Hungarian Jews and, settling in New York, he continued to write—but without realizing the success of earlier works like *The Swan* (filmed several times) and *Liliom* (the basis for the musical *Carousel*). A curious product of his last years, his play called *The King's Maid* was an honorable but misguided attempt at an ecumenical drama: the action concerns an aging Jewish peddler who finds a copy of the New Testament and discovers Jesus for himself.

After reading the play and translating it from the Hungarian, Oscar Serlin regarded *The King's Maid* as a potential Broadway hit to follow the success of *Life With Father*. He and Molnár polished the text and turned it over to Martin Manulis, now the director of the Bass Rocks Theatre in Gloucester, Massachusetts. A summer staging of the play, the playwright and the producer reasoned, would provide the opportunity for revisions prior to an autumn premiere in New York.

By early August 1941, Serlin had engaged his leading players: Sam Jaffe, well known from more than a dozen Broadway plays; Karl Malden, already established as a major actor onstage (in *Golden Boy*, *Key Largo* and *Flight to the West*) and soon to commence a long career in Hollywood; and Teresa Wright in the leading female role.

During rehearsals, she received a letter from Sam Goldwyn following a press preview of *The Little Foxes* in Los Angeles: "The reviewers, while liking the picture, liked you as much. You made a very fine impression

49

which pleased me very much and which ought to make you very happy." Her reply from Bass Rocks, written after the premiere of *The King's Maid*, was a good example of her ability to whistle in the dark:

> Thank you for your kind note about the reviews [of *The Little Foxes*]. I haven't seen the picture yet, since we left New York for Gloucester a week before the picture opened. We have worked day and night here before we opened [on Monday, August 25] and the reviews were most favorable, which makes us all very happy, as it was a tremendous job to do in a week. Mr. Serlin and Mr. Molnár were able to discover from this tryout just what the play needs before being brought to Broadway. Our audiences have been deeply moved by it, and Mr. Serlin feels he has an important play in this new work. I am extremely grateful for the opportunity to play the role, as I feel it will mean a great deal to my career. Thank you again for your kind remembrance of me.

But *The King's Maid* was a failure. "The play was not good," recalled Karl Malden. "Some things looked okay on paper, but once we began rehearsing, it was clear this was not going to work. We tried and tried— Manulis worked very hard, and no one was more hopeful than Teresa. But the play was beyond repair."

"In addition to the problems with the play, Oscar Serlin was not a good producer," added Karl's wife, Mona Malden. "Karl was always complaining about him as being very inept, because Oscar really didn't understand the theatre. But Karl and I liked Teresa from the first day we met her, and we thought she was very talented. We had seen her in *Life With Father*, and she was always an integral part of the play. While watching her onstage, you didn't say, 'Oh, what a great performance!' It *was* a first-rate performance, but she seemed to belong there naturally— she wasn't at all self-centered, and she didn't push herself forward. She was what she should have been, a member of a particular cast." That summer, Teresa added the Maldens to her list of friends.

Contrary to Teresa's report to Goldwyn, *The King's Maid* meant nothing for her career, nor for the future of anyone involved. The critical response to the play was unfavorable, and audiences found it hopelessly sentimental; despite its noble subject, it was without any recognizable focus. As the *New York Times* reported, "Sam Jaffe and Teresa Wright were praised for their performances in the leading roles, but the script was said to need more substance before [a] Broadway presentation." Convinced that the play's wrongs could be righted before New York, Serlin stormed

ahead, imprudently booking the play for an additional tryout in Baltimore. But *The King's Maid* expired there, never to be seen again.

At the end of the Gloucester week, Serlin freed Teresa from any future
obligations with the play, and so ended her theatrical contract with him.
Kurt Frings, now her agent, immediately relayed this news to Goldwyn,
who was eagerly awaiting her return.[1]

◌∕∕◌

As soon as she returned to Los Angeles, Goldwyn confronted Teresa with
new demands. More insistently than before and in light of her Oscar
nomination that autumn, he wanted to publicize and glamorize her, to
place her photos nationwide, and to show the world that she was not
only an important new talent but also a fetching twenty-three-year-old.

But he did not foresee the extent of Teresa's strength. To the press
and to viewers who saw *The Little Foxes*, she might have seemed willowy
and demure (adjectives repeatedly hauled out during her career), but
like Alexandra Giddens, she was not made of sugar-water, nor was she
diffident to the point of self-abnegation. After hearing Goldwyn's plans
for her, Teresa put her graceful little foot down firmly and instructed
Abe Lastfogel to add a codicil to her renewed contract. Such a step was
unusual in Hollywood, but she wanted to clarify the manner of her presentation to the world by the Goldwyn machine, and so she composed a
list of demands:

> I will not pose for publicity photographs in a bathing suit—unless
> I'm doing a water scene in a picture. I will not be photographed on
> the beach with my hair flying in the wind, holding aloft a beach
> ball. I will not pose in shorts, playing with a cute cocker spaniel. I
> will not be shown happily whipping up a meal for a huge family. I
> will not be dressed in firecrackers for the Fourth of July. I will not
> look insinuatingly at a turkey on Thanksgiving. I will not wear a
> bunny cap with long ears for Easter. I will not twinkle for the cam-
> era on prop snow, in a skiing outfit, while a fan blows my scarf.
> And I will not assume an athletic stance while pretending to hit
> something or other with a bow and arrow.[2]

---

1. Actors typically had several agents during a long career. Teresa was at various times
represented by Fred Amsel, Fifi Oscard, Stark Hesseltine and Robert Lantz, among others.
2. Goldwyn's staff duly transformed Teresa's composition into legalese: "The aforementioned
Teresa Wright shall not be required to . . . Neither may she be photographed . . . Nor may she
pose . . ." etc.

As she later admitted, Teresa had great fun drafting these serious conditions; decades later, they remain a clear window onto the requirements often placed on contracted stars in the golden age of Hollywood. This must have been one of the rare occasions that Samuel Goldwyn had to swallow his pride. He very likely had a sore throat for days, but he did add Teresa's terms to the deal.

"I hoped that my acting was better than my figure," she said years later, "and I knew that another actress could do bathing-suit photos better." As her daughter said, "One of the benefits of her difficult childhood was that it made her strong."

೧⁄෨

Nineteen twenty-four had been a turning point in Hollywood history, the year when merely profitable entertainment first became huge corporate business. A film production company called Metro Pictures had fallen on hard times in 1918, when one of its executives had departed to form a company he named for himself—Louis B. Mayer Pictures. New York theatre-owner Marcus Loew, requiring more product for his vast nationwide chain, soon purchased both Metro and Mayer Pictures, and brought over Louis B. as chief officer. Together, they then forced Samuel Goldwyn out of his own Goldwyn Pictures and acquired his company, too. He immediately became an independent producer at his own Samuel Goldwyn Productions and had no role in what, from 1924, was known as Metro-Goldwyn-Mayer (called simply Metro by Hollywood insiders).

Goldwyn then leased space at the United Artists Studios, at the corner of Formosa Avenue and Santa Monica Boulevard, and over time he added sound stages and other facilities. He released his independent pictures through United Artists and often through RKO, and because he preferred to make one good film at a time rather than a wave of them simultaneously, he frequently raised cash by loaning out his contracted players.

That was precisely the case in the autumn of 1941, when Louis B. Mayer wanted to borrow William Wyler to direct a movie based on a best-selling novel by Jan Struther called *Mrs. Miniver*. The book celebrated the forbearance of ordinary British citizens under siege since the war began in 1939.

At the same time, the Office of War Information in Washington was in constant contact with Mayer, in order to guarantee that the film would be not merely a family melodrama but much more: it would support

Roosevelt's Lend-Lease Policy Act, which supplied Britain and other nations with food, oil and materiel for the war. This suited Mayer's patriotic instincts perfectly; he also envisioned an international box-office sensation—and so for his production, he paid Goldwyn a hefty fee to borrow William Wyler.

In October, MGM's top female star, Greer Garson, was assigned to play the title role. When Wyler read the screenplay (by a quartet of writers), he immediately called Goldwyn: Wyler could see no other actress but Teresa in the role of Carol Beldon, an aristocratic, spirited and deeply democratic young English lady who marries Mrs. Miniver's son and dies at the picture's conclusion. Negotiations to borrow her were concluded swiftly, and she was working at MGM in Culver City when production began in early November. Filming was interrupted for only one weekday, after the bombing of Pearl Harbor on December 7.

As with *The Little Foxes,* Wyler liked to rehearse before film rolled in the camera, "but he didn't talk a great deal about your character or give you a lot of instructions," according to Teresa. "He was painstaking about getting everything right." Regarding the actor's contributions: "If you handle Mr. Wyler properly, you can put your ideas across. I wish you could have seen how Greer Garson got her way with him. She was very sweet and charming and said, 'Willy, don't you think that we ought to do it this way?' That was the way to handle him, and once or twice I followed her lead."

Although this was an American picture, it was of course about English people in England. Prudently, Wyler did not impose British accents on the American actors, insisting that they would sound hopelessly artificial, that good diction would offset the need for precise local inflections, and that audiences would not be bothered. He was on the mark. Greer Garson did not have to alter her mild English accent, and Walter Pidgeon (in the role of her husband, Mr. Miniver) was Canadian and could pass.

Teresa was convincing as an English girl because she perfected the proper lilt and flow of British English and had impeccable speech, the result of her training with Edith Skinner. Unfortunately, the New York-born newcomer Richard Ney, playing the Miniver son and the young swain, attempted to be an authentic Englishman in accent and gesture—and he completely failed.

With the United States now at war, *Mrs. Miniver* hurried to a successful conclusion before the wartime financial and technical restrictions on moviemaking went into full effect. Wyler, born in Europe and Jewish, was eager to join the American fighting forces and did so soon after the final editing.

"*Mrs. Miniver* became a very popular and necessary kind of thing," Teresa recalled. "It brought the war into our homes and made us aware of what the British were going through. We all felt and sought to convey the profound determination that dramatized those days. It was a picture produced in the shadow of headlines, and those of us who appeared in it never forgot it."

Everyone involved knew that the aim of the picture was to influence American public opinion toward stronger support for Great Britain, and that goal was quickly achieved. When the picture was released in June 1942, Lord Halifax, Britain's ambassador to the United States, publicly stated that the picture could not fail to move all who saw it, and cabinet member Lord Beaverbrook praised it for supporting England in its darkest hour. Most notably, Prime Minister Winston Churchill told President Roosevelt and the American people that the film was worth an entire regiment.

By the time MGM's accountants did their sums for 1942, the film had grossed over $5 million in North America and more than $3 million abroad, making it by far the most financially successful film of 1942.

Critics ransacked their vocabularies. Trade and consumer publications placed it at the top of their lists. "Masterful" and "faultless" were words that often recurred, and the *New York Times*, no pushover for this sort of movie, quietly observed, "It is hard to believe that a picture could be made without a cry for vengeance and could crystallize the cruel effect of total war upon a civilized people. This has been magnificently done in *Mrs. Miniver*." Of 592 critics polled worldwide by the trade publication *Film Daily*, all but thirty-seven named *Mrs. Miniver* the best film of 1942.

Remarkably, *Mrs. Miniver* retains its emotional power and authentic sentiment many decades later. This is a war movie without a single battle, a story that presents the effects of war on ordinary people. The performances have the ring of truth, of recognizable reactions, suspicions and fears—of the small things that enliven and the gestures that can ennoble life under the most frightening circumstances. Youngsters and small animals were often included for easy sentiment in American movies, but this was never so in a William Wyler picture: in *Mrs. Miniver*, the children—and even the family cat—act with artless spontaneity.

This was Teresa's second Oscar nomination, for her second picture, and she was, in the language of the time, the toast of the town and the country. Contrary to the revered Hollywood custom, she readily admitted her true age to the press. But this the journalists found hard to accept: her talent and her swift rise to stardom surely indicated that she must be much older, and that she had to be a regular patron at the beauty salons of Marcel Machu or Ann Meredith or Saks Fifth Avenue, all in Beverly Hills. No, she replied, she was really twenty-three; and no, she relied only on soap and water and could not afford expensive beauty treatments (nor, indeed, did she need them).

Reviewers praised Teresa's humorous, tenacious and finally heroic portrait in *Mrs. Miniver*—and her notable ability to *listen* to another character. In a way, this was a *modern* performance, free of pretense, tics and tricks. Her Carol Beldon comes alive on the screen, defying verbal approximations; even the most articulate critics were left stammering. Once again, she was (thus *Variety*) "box-office gold for Goldwyn."

Seventy years later, film historians were still mightily impressed: "Much of the heart in *Mrs. Miniver* comes from one of William Wyler's favorite actresses of the time, Teresa Wright. She exudes integrity and sincerity . . . [and] the basic honesty of this propaganda picture over the majority being made in 1942 can be seen in her final scenes."

∽

Principal photography was completed in February 1942, when Goldwyn offered Teresa her first leading role—not a supporting part—in a movie that changed her life forever: *The Pride of the Yankees*, the story of a recently deceased baseball star and American hero.

From 1923 to 1939, Lou Gehrig was one of the country's most celebrated and admired baseball players. Among other singular achievements, he played in 2,130 consecutive games for the New York Yankees (a record unbroken until Cal Ripken Jr. of the Baltimore Orioles surpassed it in 1995). At the height of his professional life, Gehrig was stricken with amyotrophic lateral sclerosis, a rare, inevitably fatal neuromuscular disease that reduced him to complete paralysis, unable to speak or swallow but left his mind intact. Forced to retire in 1939 at the age of thirty-six, he was cared for by his wife, Eleanor, until his death two years later. From that time, this terminal illness has been widely known as Lou Gehrig's Disease.

Universally esteemed for his "absolute reliability," Gehrig was a modest, likable man. "He could be counted on," said one sportswriter. "He was there day after day and year after year. He never sulked or whined or went into a huff. He was the answer to a manager's dream."

Immediately after Gehrig's death in June 1941, one of Goldwyn's story editors approached his boss with the idea that Gehrig's life would be a superb motion picture. But Goldwyn was wary of films about athletes: usually, they failed at the box office, if for no other reason than women decided which movies they and their men attended. But the story editor persisted and asked Goldwyn to listen to a portion of Gehrig's farewell speech at Yankee Stadium, with the dying man's famously moving statement, "I consider myself the luckiest man in the world." Goldwyn's obduracy melted as tears filled his eyes. How quickly, he asked, could they make the movie?

As it happened, the story editor was a sports fan and had a wealth of material about Gehrig; in fact, he had published a major profile of the athlete in *The New Yorker* on August 10, 1929. His name was Niven Busch, and he had co-written Goldwyn's recent film *The Westerner*, directed by Wyler and starring Gary Cooper. The actor had never played baseball or even seen a game, but Goldwyn was not deterred: he had Cooper under contract, and a month earlier Cooper had won the best actor Oscar for *Sergeant York*. Hands down, he was one of the most popular actors in the business.

Teresa was unsure that the public would accept her as Gehrig's wife, a woman who was alive and still very much in the press; and like Cooper, Teresa was also completely ignorant of baseball. But she liked the story treatment, which located the core of Gehrig's heroism in his courage and humility. She accepted the part of Eleanor Twitchell Gehrig, and her participation was announced on January 21, 1942. Even before production began, Mrs. Gehrig herself became an important element in the success of *The Pride of the Yankees*. The entire film was completed between February and April—including the sequences filmed at Wrigley Field in Chicago and the second unit footage at Yankee Stadium, New York.

Eleanor Gehrig did not have official cast approval, but Goldwyn wisely and courteously wanted her endorsement. "When Sam first told me that Teresa would play me," Eleanor recalled, "I felt that she was much too young. I preferred someone like Barbara Stanwyck or Jean Arthur, or an actress with more experience. But I learned that no one could do better, or even as well, as Teresa. Of course she's prettier and younger than I, but then no woman could object to that, could she?"

∽

As filming began, so did romance.

Teresa had first met Niven Busch a year earlier, during production of *The Little Foxes*. He was story editor, writer, script doctor and unofficially an associate producer for Goldwyn, who had asked Niven to polish the final screenplay of *Foxes*. Goldwyn had "a gut feeling" about scripts and stories, Niven recalled. "He knew what the audience was going to buy. I got along very well with him—he had much more ability than, for example, David O. Selznick. Knowledgeable and disciplined, Goldwyn was a natural, intuitive intellectual, while Selznick was a pretender and a great entrepreneur who had no talent as a writer."

Niven's position gave him access to the set, and one day, he and Teresa chatted during a break in shooting. "Goldwyn," Niven recalled, "did not like that at all. He felt I'd have more influence on her than he did."

⁓

Briton Niven Busch was born at the home of his parents on West Fifty-fifth Street, New York, on April 26, 1903. Always called by his second name, he came from a prosperous family of sturdy Brooklyn bankers that had invested wisely during the late nineteenth and early twentieth centuries. Niven's mother was English, and his father ("a dandy and a big dress-up guy," as his son recalled) was a stockbroker, monitoring portfolios and investing on behalf of a group of Wall Street entrepreneurs. During Niven's childhood and adolescence, the Busch family fortunes grew impressively.

Papa was also the treasurer and investment supervisor for film distributor Lewis J. Selznick, and so it was natural for the Busch family to go often to the movies; in addition, Niven's mother sometime typed screenplays for Selznick. "Lewis J. was much more intelligent than his peers," Niven said years later, recalling his father's experience. "He was also crookeder than a dog's hind leg."

One day, in Selznick's New York office, young Niven met Lewis's son, David, who was one year older, little more than an errand boy and almost possessed by the idea of making movies. Even as a teen, David Selznick (who latter added the "O" to distinguish himself from an uncle) was making big plans. But the senior Busch's connection to the movies was severed when Lewis Selznick's company relocated to Hollywood, where it soon collapsed.

Niven's father could afford a fashionable prep school for his son, and in 1921, he enrolled the eighteen-year-old at Princeton University. "Even then, I was writing poetry, stories and skits," Niven recalled. From his room in town, situated directly over a movie theatre, he could hear the music accompanying silent films. And so he dispatched his school assignments as quickly as possible and then raced downstairs to buy a ticket.

Although a respectable achiever at Princeton, Niven was forced to leave before graduation and work for a living when his family lost a vast amount of money in the failure of certain foreign investments. After a series of odd jobs, he landed a position in 1927 as a junior editor for *Time* magazine, writing capsule movie reviews. Simultaneously, he went on staff at *The New Yorker*, where for over two years he published more than forty articles on contemporary topics illuminating various aspects of the Jazz Age: speakeasies during Prohibition; corruption in the New York City Police Department; the hell of city jails; the risky atmosphere of Chinatown; the comings and goings of crooks; and tales of glamorous Manhattan socialites.

At *The New Yorker*, Niven was a master at composing gripping short stories and literate biographical profiles of famous people, Lou Gehrig among them. He made a deal with Doubleday Doran to bring out a selection of these life-sketches, and that company published his first book, *21 Americans: Being Profiles of Some Famous People in Our Time*.[3] By the summer of 1929, Niven was earning $15,000 a year (over $200,000 in 2015 valuation).

A handsome, articulate, well-dressed and sophisticated man about town, with a perpetually ruddy face from his habit of daily jogging, Niven had only to stand still while a flock of adoring women gathered around. He rarely turned them away and was often seen escorting this or that young lady to dinner, or to the fights, or to the theatre. At times, he resembled a more rugged version of young Joel McCrea, but fuller of face and perhaps not as lithe. Niven Busch might have been the prototype of a Jazz Age character in the pages of F. Scott Fitzgerald—fiercely charming, forever self-confident and, when necessary, able to operate with a kind of heedless cunning.

But in the autumn of 1929, his carefully cultivated life was altered when his savings and investments—along with those of countless others—were lost in the October crash that effectively began the Great Depression. Thereafter, Niven often regaled friends with his account of lying in a hospital bed early in November, when he was recovering from

---

3. In addition to Gehrig, the book included profiles of Henry Ford, Fanny Brice, Adolph Zukor and seventeen others.

a tonsillectomy. Forbidden to speak above a whisper, he attempted in a hoarse murmur to command the family broker: "Sell! Sell!"

Thanks to his family's earlier association with the film business, the powerful agent Myron Selznick arranged for Niven to decamp for Hollywood. There, he obtained work at Warner Bros. and wrote the screenplay for a Howard Hawks picture—*The Crowd Roars*, starring James Cagney. A number of writing assignments followed throughout the 1930s, for Edward G. Robinson, Bette Davis and Mary Astor, among others. In 1937, the Academy nominated him for the best original story that was the basis of *In Old Chicago*, starring Tyrone Power and Alice Faye.

Niven was glad to work, but he resented the Hollywood screenwriting system. "You nearly always collaborated, because they thought that two minds were better than one. And even if you turned in a very good screenplay, they handed it to somebody else just to mess around with it." This brought him "a certain amount of stress and was something you wanted to get away from, but you had to put up with it," which he did until he turned from writing screenplays to novels. In 1940, Goldwyn brought Niven over to write *The Westerner* for Gary Cooper, and in short order, Niven was promoted to the job of story editor.

By that time, Niven had been married and divorced twice and had two sons—Peter Briton Busch (born in October 1932), by his first wife, Sonia Frey; and Briton Cooper Busch (born in September 1936), by his second wife, Phyllis Cooper.

Until Teresa came on the scene, the lives of these boys were less than completely happy. Peter's mother, Sonia, blithely gave up the boy when he was born. At first, Niven hired a nurse to look after him, and then Peter was sent to live with a foster family. Until he was an adult, he never knew his mother. Phyllis Cooper, the mother of Briton (always called Tony), refused to keep him when she entered into a new marriage with an actor.

When Niven began to court Teresa, in early 1942, he was a single father with two lonely sons age nine and five; evidently neither of their mothers had a molecule of the maternal instinct. Niven was thirty-nine, Teresa twenty-three, but the age difference did not matter to her: she liked not only his rugged charm and swagger, but also his obvious gifts of intellect and humor.

Throughout her life, Teresa was attracted most of all to creative people. Writers and the craft of writing intrigued her, and she was an ardent student, an eager learner—especially of those things that enriched her. Contrary to her protestations of ignorance and her lack of an advanced education, she was highly intelligent, a woman who read widely and had a broad knowledge of every aspect of theatre and film production. Her letters reveal a grasp of what Gerard Manley Hopkins termed "the dearest freshness deep down things"; they also show her profound awareness of the complexities of human nature.

These talents and insights invariably deepened her understanding of a wide variety of roles. She was intuitively able to cut quickly to the heart of plays and screenplays—just as she was able to condole with friends and to understand human foibles and faults. But there was nothing of Pollyanna in her: Teresa was strong to the core—and sometimes even stubborn—and in life she had nothing of that bogus sweetness that cheapens life.

∽

Then and later, friends and colleagues inquired about her experience of working with taciturn Gary Cooper, whose many romantic liaisons were widely attested in Hollywood and beyond. "Oh, we got along very well on the set, although there was almost no chitchat," she told me, "but I never really knew him. When he wasn't needed for a shot, he rode his bike outside or went into a corner, where he whittled a stick. He wasn't unfriendly at all—just a bit remote, which was okay with me, because we had a tough shooting schedule. In the movie I kissed him, but it was just a movie kiss.

"But once, he prolonged the kiss—his lips seemed glued to mine, until I was forced to break away and ad lib, 'A girl's got to breathe!'" Cooper, the director Sam Wood and the crew burst out laughing—and at Cooper's request, Teresa's *sotto voce* line went into the finished film. Goldwyn wanted to assign a magazine writer to ghost a story: "How It Felt to Kiss Gary Cooper for the First Time." No way, said Teresa, or words to that effect.

In the end, the collaboration with Cooper was pleasant except for one thing, as she said at the time: "They can't do anything to shorten Gary," who was six-feet-three-inches tall, "so they're doing everything they can to make me taller than five-feet-two. I am partial to low heels, so I am suffering for my art for the first time—wearing heels that are miniature stilts!"

His performance was a wonder. Cooper captured Gehrig's diffidence and awkwardness as well as his fearful inhibition—and he played for comedy the scenes of the mother's pathological possessiveness. "Gary studied every picture of Lou," said Eleanor Gehrig years later. "He had every one of his mannerisms down to a science, and he is so like my husband in the picture that there were times when I felt I couldn't bear it."

No less a great character actor than Charles Laughton regarded Gary Cooper as the ultimate film actor, as Laughton's biographer Simon Callow has written: Cooper's "voluptuously gentle masculinity and *nearly* wooden delivery [was] spellbinding [and] essential to filmmaking."

∾

Sam Wood was a very different director from William Wyler, as Teresa quickly discovered to her surprise and to her dismay. "He preferred to direct horses," she said, "which he did very well on *Gone with the Wind*, when he replaced his friend, director Victor Fleming, for several weeks. But he didn't seem to care much about people. Coop and I were really on our own. And Sam really needed that great production designer we had, William Cameron Menzies."

Menzies was one of the geniuses of the old Hollywood. He was responsible for the design of several important pictures—among them *Gone With the Wind*, for which he and artist J. McMillan Johnson drew more than 2,000 detailed watercolor sketches that effectively provided the look of every scene. Menzies also directed the memorable "burning of Atlanta" sequence in that movie, as well as the arresting ninety-foot crane shot of Vivien Leigh amid wounded and dying soldiers that ends with a high, panoramic shot and a torn Confederate flag floating on the breeze.

As with that epic, Menzies planned every camera angle, all the lighting, props and actors' positions for *Our Town*, *Kings Row* and *For Whom the Bell Tolls*. Alfred Hitchcock brought him onto the production of *Foreign Correspondent*, for which Menzies designed the exterior of the Amsterdam Town Hall sequence, the interior of the windmill, the plane crash into the sea and the final harrowing scenes. William Cameron Menzies accomplished what many others could neither imagine nor achieve.

"Bill Menzies drew a sketch for every scene of *Yankees* for Sam Wood," Teresa added. "Each one was well conceived, beautiful and specific. All Sam had to do was look at a sketch, position us, check the lights, and he would have a perfect shot—when he wanted one."

Portraying not a fictional character but a real person who was actually present before and during production, Teresa gave the role of Eleanor Gehrig the precise blend of humor, intense love and finally a tragic bravery that was never maudlin. She had moments of raucous slapstick and vaudevillian antics, and scenes of great passion and of deep, private grief. Among the many personal items that Eleanor brought to the set was a bracelet Lou had given her on their fourth anniversary, made of medallions commemorating his world championships and all-star games. It is seen in a tight close-up in the picture, and Teresa wore it in every subsequent scene.

She and Eleanor Gehrig became good friends. "I know she was happy with the film," Teresa recalled. "I think it meant a lot to her. With the sadness of Lou's early death, I think, in a way, it gave him back to her for a while. Having her on the set occasionally, where she was so warm, friendly and supportive, only helped."

The Pride of the Yankees was released in July 1942, just thirteen months after Lou Gehrig's death, and one month after the release of *Mrs. Miniver*. *Time* magazine, summarizing the critical consensus, considered that Teresa Wright's performance in *Yankees* "cemented her rise to stardom. If moviegoers like her, she may become [Hollywood's] foremost dramatic actress. If they don't, she can remain what she is: one of the best young actresses Hollywood has turned up in many a talent hunt."

౭౨౦

CHAPTER SIX

1942–1944

WHEN THE ACADEMY NOMINATIONS FOR 1942 WERE ANNOUNCED, sixteen people who worked on *Mrs. Miniver* were cited in eleven categories: best picture (producer Sidney Franklin), best director (William Wyler), best actor and actress (Walter Pidgeon and Greer Garson, as Clem and Kay Miniver) best supporting actor (Henry Travers, as the stationmaster who cultivates prize roses), best supporting actress (Teresa Wright, as the well-born, unaffected Carol Beldon, and Dame May Whitty, as her crusty but benevolent grandmother, Lady Beldon), best black-and-white-cinematography (Joseph Ruttenberg), best editing (Harold F. Kress), the quartet of screenwriters headed by James Hilton and best special effects (A. Arnold Gillespie, Warren Newcombe and Douglas Shearer).

At the same time, *The Pride of the Yankees* was cited in eleven categories that included fifteen people: best picture (producer Samuel Goldwyn), best actor (Gary Cooper), best actress (Teresa Wright), best original story (Paul Gallico), best screenplay (Herman J. Mankiewicz and Jo Swerling), best black-and-white cinematography (Rudolph Maté), best black-and-white art direction (Perry Ferguson and Howard Bristol), best sound recording (the Goldwyn Sound Department), best editing (Daniel Mandell), best special effects (Jack Cosgrove, Ray Binger and Thomas T. Moulton) and best score for a dramatic picture (Ray Harline).

In just one year—from April 1941 to April 1942—Teresa had appeared in three motion pictures (*The Little Foxes*, *Mrs. Miniver* and *The Pride of the Yankees*). She had been nominated by her peers for her performance in each of them—twice as best supporting actress (for *Foxes* and *Miniver*) and once as best actress (for *Yankees*); she was then nominated in the same year as both the best actress and the best supporting actress. At the age of twenty-three, she won the latter award, for *Mrs. Miniver*; for the same picture, Greer Garson was voted best actress.

With the completion of *Yankees*, Teresa and Niven were able to spend more time together than during production. In late April, they were engaged, and for courtesy's sake, Teresa first informed Samuel Goldwyn. "This means what it used to mean," she said in early May. "It means we're taking time to think it over very seriously, before we marry." Then they shared the news with Niven's sister, Beatrix Miller (always called Bea), and her husband, the screenwriter Winston Miller.

During their engagement, the couple socialized with a few Hollywood writers and their wives—for Sunday evening barbecues or swimming pool parties, activities Teresa much preferred to evenings at the glamorous hot spots and nightclubs frequented by Hollywood insiders. They also visited Winston's sister, Patsy Ruth Miller, formerly a silent-movie star and later a novelist and playwright, and Patsy's husband, screenwriter John Lee Mahin.

That year, Winston began training at the U.S. Marine Corps Base, in San Diego County; Niven was thirty-nine, one year too old for the wartime draft at that time. Bea took an apartment near the base, and the Millers invited Niven to move from his apartment on South Spalding Drive, Beverly Hills, to their home at 13603 Hart Street, Van Nuys (just over the Santa Monica Mountains, in the San Fernando Valley). "It was a modest, ranch-style house with a backyard patio and a flagstone pool," recalled Christine Miller, their daughter.

Teresa and Niven did not think too long about marriage: the engagement was a short one, and on Saturday, May 23, 1942, they were married at the Miller house by a Congregational pastor.[1] Goldwyn, who usually found excuses for a little publicity, agreed with Teresa and forbade photographers: "Glamour might jinx the wedding," she said.

Before the nuptials, Teresa's father and stepmother swept into Los Angeles for a brief visit. They met Niven; Teresa gave them a tour of the Goldwyn Studios; and they were greatly impressed by her successes and her Academy Award. They also wanted to benefit from it.

---

1. In light of the couple's celebrity status, it is odd that the *New York Times* did not report correctly any details of the marriage: the newspaper reported the wedding of *Irving* Busch to Teresa Wright, wildly misstated their ages and identified the Millers as their "friends."

Arthur Wright was working for the Accident and Casualty Insurance Company in Manhattan, while he and his wife, Edna, were living comfortably in a house in East Orange, New Jersey. Edy was a broad-shouldered woman who tended to plumpness; perhaps most memorably, she affected the manner of a waiflike but confident princess. The youngest of four sisters, Edy believed that she deserved constant pampering, and her husband was happy to oblige. If she could avoid it, she rarely rose from a chair to fetch something: "Arthur, while you're up, would you get me . . ."

Quick to laugh but often frivolous, Edy was a demanding woman who stirred in her husband a new and persistent habit: asking Teresa for money. She loved her father deeply, but she greatly resented that she virtually had to support her father because of his wife's materialistic demands.

Despite her annoyance, Teresa could not refuse her father: He loved her, and she him, while Edy put on such airs and made certain that Arthur was dependent on his daughter. Edy's attitude—that she was highly born—convinced the family that there was something lacking in grandpa's judgment. He was a sweet man, and he adored and worshipped his wife. But this meant nothing to her, and she always discounted his evaluation of her.

∽

The newlyweds departed for a honeymoon along the California coast, and on May 25, Teresa wrote to her boss from the La Playa Hotel in Carmel:

> Saturday, Niven and I were married in the garden of his sister's home in the Valley. It was a beautiful ceremony, and I want you to know I was grateful for your blessing and good wishes. I'm very happy, enjoying every minute of our trip and eagerly looking forward to seeing Pride of the Yankees when I return.

Back home from the honeymoon, Teresa and Niven moved all their belongings into the Miller home—and brought with them Niven's sons, Peter and Tony, who that year marked their tenth and sixth birthdays. Far from resenting the sudden inheritance of two active boys, Teresa gave them the attention and devotion their mothers did not, and she dedicated herself to providing a loving home for them. Peter and Tony never forgot her great kindness, her patience and generosity—maternal qualities that might not have been inevitably expected of a woman who had endured a lonely and frightening childhood and who was abandoned by an abusive mother.

Even before the wedding, Goldwyn had decided to loan out Teresa to Jack Skirball, a producer at Universal Studios who was in turn negotiating with David O. Selznick to borrow Alfred Hitchcock. Teresa did not like the Hollywood tradition of loan-outs—she considered it professional servitude, not to say a system that left actors with a considerable loss of income: on loan-outs, the actor's boss (in this case, Goldwyn) pocketed a handsome profit, receiving a small fortune on the loan-out yet paying his contracted player only the salary fixed by their contract.

But the prospect of working with Hitchcock was irresistible. On August 11, Teresa countersigned the contract, and two days later she joined the director and cast for two weeks of location filming in Santa Rosa, sixty-five miles north of San Francisco. As it turned out, Hitchcock later called the film his personal favorite in the catalogue of his works—just as Teresa invariably named it as her own favorite. There was good reason for their shared estimation: *Shadow of a Doubt* is a work of sheer genius, a profound and disturbing picture remarkable for superb performances and haunting black-and-white cinematography; in every sequence, it reveals the touch of a master filmmaker.[2]

In addition to the recent Oscar that made her an advantageous star, Teresa had been most enthusiastically recommended to Hitchcock by none other than Thornton Wilder, who was chosen to write the screenplay for *Shadow* because the story was in many ways the dark underside of *Our Town*. In June 1974, she recounted for me in detail her first meeting with Hitchcock:

> When he told me the story as we sat in his office, it was as if he had already finished the picture. He had it completely planned in his mind, along with every sound effect, and he told me the entire movie, scene by scene. He used anything on his desk as a prop—a drinking glass, a pencil or a book. He stepped around. If a character was strumming his fingers on a table, for example, it wasn't an idle gesture—Hitch put a beat to it, like a musical pattern or a refrain. If someone was walking or rustling a newspaper, tearing an envelope

---

2. For detailed studies of *Shadow of a Doubt*, whose structure consists of an almost infinite series of doubles, see my trilogy about the director: *The Art of Alfred Hitchcock*, pages 115–27; *The Dark Side of Genius: The Life of Alfred Hitchcock*, pages 256–65; and *Spellbound by Beauty: Alfred Hitchcock and His Leading Ladies*, pages 116–23.

or whistling, or if there was a flutter of birds or an outside sound, Hitch had everything carefully orchestrated.

As for the filming process:

Hitch made us all feel very relaxed, and his direction never came across as mere instruction. We felt we could trust him, and although he guided us carefully, he also gave us a sense of freedom. He was very calm, as if we were contributing to something that was already a foreseen success. No one plans a film as thoroughly as Hitch, and no one saw it as clearly as he did from the start. Other directors often let things happen during the shooting, but with Hitch's planning, everything was more serene during production, and therefore more enjoyable . . . What luck it was for me—this was a wonderful role, a girl who starts off one way and then changes and grows before your eyes as she's dealt this awful problem. At the conclusion, it was the end of innocence for young Charlie, because now she knows evil exists, and in the one person she and her mother love the most. She has grown up and learned that someone she has loved and been loved by can literally kill people.

There were some uncomfortable moments during filming, however. Often-just before he called "Action!" Hitchcock whispered to Teresa something obscene, "usually," she said, "having to do with a young bride on her honeymoon, which I had just returned from." Hitchcock also made some inappropriate comments about Niven relative to his age difference from Teresa. "I tried to cope with this by smiling, as if I didn't understand him, or as if he was uttering the most polite compliments."

This was neither the first nor the last time Hitchcock indulged in verbal mischief with one of his leading ladies. Perhaps he wanted a reaction, a sudden expression of dismay or shock before a certain difficult shot; after all, such tactics are not rare. In this regard, Hitchcock's professional wardrobe, invariably a suit, white shirt and tie; his tranquility during the workday; his refusal to shout or cause a fracas; his deliberate air of bourgeois respectability—all these habits contrasted with unexpected utterances of the crudest kind.

Shadow of a Doubt (for which Teresa received first billing in the opening credits) is the story of a serial widow-murderer, Uncle Charlie (played by Joseph Cotten), who attempts to escape the police on the East Coast by visiting his sister (played by Patricia Collinge, Teresa's friend from

The Little Foxes) and her family in Santa Rosa. Charlotte, age nineteen or twenty, is one of his nieces, named for him and also called Charlie. The film charts the girl's moral education as she progresses from innocence and untested idealism to a firsthand experience of the eruption of evil amid everyday reality—and the murderous tendency to depravity that is latent in human nature, indeed in everyone.[3]

Teresa filmed her role calmly, but inside she was, perhaps for the first time, tearing herself to pieces, enduring a nervous stomach and losing weight while, under Hitchcock's tutelage, she thought out every moment of her character's abrupt introduction to the darkness in human nature. "I had to understand how this woman felt—how she developed to include a mature, tough side, too. After all, cardboard characters are no fun. There's no place you can go with cardboard, no depth."

Despite her anxiety, Teresa offered a virtual textbook in the art of film acting. "The shots of Wright," wrote the novelist and critic Stephan Talty, "have the raw power of those early silent close-ups in which an entire drama was played out on the face of the actor, [and her performance] remains one of the most lucidly beautiful in the cinema."

The picture was of course shot out of sequence: everything set outdoors in Santa Rosa was filmed there, before the interiors were photographed at Universal Studios. This made special demands on Teresa, who appeared in all but a few scenes of the entire picture, but throughout she demonstrated a supple intuition, so that young Charlie's ordeal seems both shocking and inevitable. Her youthful credulity is never cloying, her threats of murder both horrifying and believable: "I don't want you here, Uncle Charlie. I don't want you to touch my mother. Go away, I'm warning you. Go away, or I'll kill you myself. See? That's the way I feel about you."

Teresa did not portray young Charlie as the killer's victim, but—after her initial romantic infatuation for her uncle is destroyed by knowledge of his crimes—she plays young Charlie as his challenger, his rival. And her character was conveyed mostly through her eyes. "You must be thinking the right thing," she said, "because it will show if you're not.

---

3. This is mainstream Hitchcock, central to many of his motion pictures—most notably the quartet of *Shadow of a Doubt, Strangers on a Train, Psycho* and *Frenzy*. Each of these films expresses the theme in an accumulated series of doubles and doubling which associate (but do not identify) good and evil. This use of the doppelgänger motif is also commonplace in literature: it informs, for example, Joseph Conrad's *The Secret Sharer*, Edgar Allan Poe's story "William Wilson," Robert Louis Stevenson's *Dr. Jekyll and Mr. Hyde*, Graham Greene's *Brighton Rock* and works of fiction past counting.

When there's a close-up of your eyes, you can't be thinking of making the 11:45 train or something."

In scenes with Henry Travers—he had played the stationmaster in *Mrs. Miniver*—and with Patricia Collinge as her mother (Aunt Birdie in *The Little Foxes*), Teresa was an acute listener—hence our identification with her character deepens as we listen *with* her. Opposite the pliant lure of perilously attractive Uncle Charlie (Joseph Cotten), another actress might have been diminished precisely because his character is so fiercely idiosyncratic and unpredictable. But Teresa allowed young Charlie's moral education to emerge without forcing the issue of a life lesson—and so she left a nuanced, exquisitely rendered performance that gave *Shadow of a Doubt* its coherence and complexity.

"She was lovely to work with," producer Jack Skirball wrote to Samuel Goldwyn after the picture was released. "And in my opinion, she has no superiors and few equals as an actress. I was very impressed."

Hitchcock only rarely had a good word to say about actors, and he usually kept a polite distance from them. But in this case, he was uncharacteristically lavish in his praise: "I got along very well with Teresa. If she can't act a line in a script, there's something wrong with the line. She was always prepared and completely professional, she knew what she was doing, she always got things right, and she gave a great deal to the picture."

As for Teresa, she was candid for the rest of her life: "At the time we made this picture, we all thought it was a great film. But I don't think any of us had an idea that it would have such an impact on generation after generation."

But two mysteries remain.

The first was the critical reaction. When *Shadow* was released in January 1943, the consensus was that the movie had succumbed to mediocrity. The intervention of years was necessary before the movie's reputation grew like Topsy; seventy years later, *Shadow* is rightly deemed a masterwork of the cinema.

But even at the height of World War II, the critics applauded Teresa. Howard Barnes of the *New York Herald-Tribune* commended her "quietly authoritative performance that elevated the film into a screen classic." William Wyler, continuing his advocacy of her, said that Teresa was "an actress who can do no wrong," and critic Alton Cook claimed that Teresa was "one of the great new actresses of our time." *Time* summarized the matter by calling her "Hollywood's best young dramatic actress."

The second mystery emerged when the Oscar nominations for 1943 were announced: *Shadow of a Doubt* was listed only for best original story (a six-page summary by Gordon McDonell); it lost to *The Human Comedy*, by William Saroyan. This was neither the first nor last time that a Hitchcock masterwork was overlooked for an industry award.[4] In addition, many moviegoers, then and later, could not comprehend the absence of Teresa Wright's name from the list of nominations for best actress of the year 1942.

∞

In January 1943, the weather in Southern California was uncommonly chilly, and Teresa, along with Niven's two boys, were not exempt from the chronic chest colds that swept Southern California. While she was recovering at home, she learned that Samuel Goldwyn was pressing his case for her to play the leading role in his production of Lillian Hellman's *The North Star*, a film about heroic Ukrainian villagers during the Nazi invasion of Russia.

Audaciously, Goldwyn had already announced—just when Teresa was on her way to Santa Rosa to begin work on *Shadow of a Doubt*—that she was definitely cast in *The North Star*. This was not only a proleptic announcement but also a remarkably discourteous one: she had not even read the script, much less given her *pro forma* assent to it. This episode was the first time Samuel Goldwyn lost major points with Teresa Wright.

As he pressured her further, she was adamant. "I didn't like the script too much," she said later, "but I had to turn him down because of illness, and I didn't want to go into another production without any preparation, just two weeks later [which *The North Star* in fact did]. Goldwyn always suspected that I withdrew because I didn't like *The North Star*, but that wasn't the case. True, I didn't like it. But the reason for turning him down was sickness."[5] (The part went to nineteen-year-old Anne Baxter.)

---

4. Hitchcock was nominated five times as best director—for *Rebecca, Lifeboat, Spellbound, Rear Window* and *Psycho*. He never won. Years later, the Academy granted him an honorary accolade for lifetime excellence as a producer—the Irving G. Thalberg Memorial Award, which was not an Oscar statuette but a bust of Thalberg. Hitchcock's entire acceptance speech consisted of five words: "Thank you very much indeed."

5. Most sources state that Teresa withdrew from *The North Star* because of pregnancy, but this is inaccurate. The film was produced in February and March 1943, and Teresa was not pregnant with her first child until March 1944. Nor did she suffer a miscarriage, as other sources theorized.

But it was also true that Teresa wanted more time with Niven, Peter and Tony. "My family has always been more important to me than anything," and she did not relish the role of absentee wife and mother. As her daughter said years later, "Having the boys around kept her busy, and she loved it," and Teresa's son agreed: "Peter and Tony were important to her. She was a wonderful stepmother to them both, and they loved her. She gave them something their own mothers couldn't or wouldn't."

From that time, Teresa rejected several Goldwyn projects that were either inferior or unsuitable for her; her judgment was vindicated when several were never produced (something called *Bid for Happiness*, for example, never went further than an outline, while *Up In Arms* was produced solely for the antics of Danny Kaye).

The consequences of Teresa's apparent recalcitrance were immediate: beginning on February 20, Goldwyn placed her on suspension for as long as she failed to work for him. This was an extraordinary measure—indeed, it was an act of retaliation for what he considered downright insubordination. Suspension meant that she received no salary, and that she was enjoined from accepting offers of work elsewhere. For all of 1943, the lines were drawn and no quarter given.[6]

The "illness" of which she had spoken was neither an invention nor an exaggeration. Teresa's physician had strongly advised six months of rest at home after they both wrongly thought she was pregnant. "I was feeling very low," she wrote years later, "having just been told that I was not going to have a baby, but a tumor, and I had to rest and get built up for the operation." Her treatment suggests that Teresa had suffered from nonmalignant fibroid tumors, and after the surgery, she was fit and ready both for work and pregnancy.

On March 4, Teresa and Niven attended the Academy Awards ceremony at the Cocoanut Grove—with muted expectations, given the competition. The press, however, noted that at the age of twenty-four, she had already appeared in four major films in eighteen months. Her fellow nominees in the category of best supporting actress were Dame May Whitty (also for *Mrs. Miniver*), Gladys Cooper (for *Now, Voyager*), Agnes Moorehead (for *The Magnificent Ambersons*) and Susan Peters (for *Random Harvest*). When Teresa's name was called, she paused for a moment as if

---

6. During the suspension period, RKO offered Teresa the leading role in *The Enchanted Cottage*. She loved the project and later played the part on television, but at the time she was forbidden to work elsewhere than for Goldwyn. Instead, she recommended that her good friend Dorothy McGuire play the role, which she did magnificently.

she had imagined the announcement—and then she hurried to receive her award.

"It was an evening of mixed emotions for all of us who worked on *Mrs. Miniver*," she said later. "Willie Wyler, in service overseas, could not be with us to share the thrill that the picture received six awards. It was also an unbelievably exciting night for me." It was also the last time Teresa Wright was nominated for an Academy Award.

That evening, she received not the traditional Art Deco-style Oscar statuette, the stylized bald knight, standing on a reel of film and discreetly holding a sword. Until 1943, limitations imposed on the use of metals except for wartime materiel prohibited the Academy from manufacturing the award for any winners except the best actor and actress, and the producer and the director of the best picture. All the others, Teresa included, received small wooden plaques. (Beginning the following year, however, supporting actors also received statuettes.) At the end of the war, those who had received plaques were invited to exchange them for the real thing. This Teresa did with great pleasure.

According to custom, Oscar-winning actors return the following year to present awards. Thus, on March 2, 1944, it was Teresa's turn to hand a statuette to the best supporting actress of 1943—Katina Paxinou (in *For Whom the Bell Tolls*). Backstage at the new venue, the 2,258-seat Grauman's Chinese Theatre, she waited for her call to go on—"as nervous as if I had to perform. Suddenly I realized that I was sharing the darkness with a beautiful man with white curly hair, a sad-comic face and a huge harp—my favorite Marx brother. I was so delighted to see him that I couldn't keep my eyes off him—a fact which he noticed, because he broke his famous silence to say, 'Young lady, are you flirting with me?'"

⚬⁓⚬

Meanwhile, Niven was busy writing—but no longer for Goldwyn. In 1941, his novel *The Carrington Incident* was published, a melodrama set in Nazi Germany. He then went to Twentieth Century-Fox, where he wrote the story basis for *Belle Star*, a Civil War romance. By 1943, he had completed the novel *They Dream of Home*—about a group of returning American Indian and African-American veterans that was unrecognizable when it became the movie *Till the End of Time*. That same year, he was writing a novel called *Duel in the Sun*, published in 1944, a far better work than the movie David O. Selznick later made of it.

"I always wanted to write a novel," Niven recalled. "I started two or three, then dropped them when a film job came along"—because screenplays were more lucrative than novels. Nevertheless, he wrote as many novels as screenplays; among the latter, the most famous is certainly *The Postman Always Rings Twice* (1946), based on James M. Cain's novel. Niven's prolific output led to princely compensation in 1943—mostly from the sale of movie rights to his novels—and this was particularly welcome income in light of Teresa's suspension from work.

The day after Christmas, Goldwyn lifted the penalty when Teresa returned to work, and on New Year's Eve, he announced that she was soon to co-star once again with Gary Cooper, this time in a comedy eventually titled *Casanova Brown*—a loan-out to International Pictures for their first production, which began in February and was completed in late March. The Nunnally Johnson production paid Goldwyn $100,000 for Teresa; her salary, determined by her Goldwyn contract, earned her about $15,000.

"I thought that was one of the most amusing and sweetest scripts I ever read," said Teresa,

> but the picture turned out to be miserable—mostly because of Sam Wood [who had directed her and Cooper in *Yankees*]. Wyler and Hitchcock knew how to film a scene with several characters—they showed the whole group reacting simultaneously to something, and that method worked especially in a comic sequence. But Sam directed the entire scene in a close-up on one person—and then he shot the scene all over again with a close-up on another character, and another and another. Well, after you've done this with six or seven actors in twenty-five takes, you've lost the spontaneity—and the humor, because all you've seen is close-up after close-up after close-up. I remember thinking that *Casanova Brown* might have been saved if Sam had William Cameron Menzies working with him again. But he didn't, and all the comedy and all the logic vanished when the picture went from the page to the screen.

She was on the mark, for the movie is a hopeless and hapless muddle that began nicely and with satiric humor mostly supplied by actor Frank Morgan. But after about a half-hour, the movie collapses. Cooper was forced to play the title role as a farcical dope, and Teresa—who appears in no more than a quarter of the movie's running time—was reduced to scenes of mawkish emotion and improbable passion; her character, bright and optimistic, was virtually lost in the final cut.

Her co-star once again impressed her. "You could watch Coop on the set and think that nothing was happening, and then you saw it on the screen and it was perfect. It was what acting really is—making people believe that you're thinking what you're saying. He acted with such simplicity, presence and power that the audience accepted anything he said, any way he said it."

Teresa's happiest memory of *Casanova Brown* was yet another reunion with her good friend Patricia Collinge. As in *Shadow of a Doubt*, Pat played Teresa's mother—this time, a daffy astrologist who consults the stars on every possible occasion. Pat stole the show with calibrated hilarity.

This unfortunate picture was Teresa's fifth film, released almost two years after *Shadow*, and it is perplexing that her talent was so badly employed. ("You can just forget about *Casanova Brown*," she said years later.) The movie did her career no good; Cooper, on the other hand, was such a masculine idol that he was never hurt by appearing in an inferior production.

∽

Immediately after concluding her work on the picture, Teresa learned that she was pregnant. By the time Goldwyn had another assignment for her, it was too late—"and I had to stop working, which irritated Mr. Goldwyn no end. I thought he would fire me on the spot." Not yet.

While they awaited the birth, Niven told his wife to read his work in progress—*Duel in the Sun*, in which, he insisted, the leading character of the torrid seductress Pearl Chavez could be a striking change of image for Teresa in a film version. At the same time, Niven hoped to write the screenplay for it, and his agent sold the movie rights to David O. Selznick. But Niven went further: believing that he could strike a deal with Selznick by acting as his wife's *de facto* agent and arranging for her to assume the role of Pearl, he asked Goldwyn to release her for that purpose: "This will make it possible for us to consummate a deal which we hope will prove of the greatest advantage and will lead to placing Teresa in a top-flight motion picture made by a major company, with a large participation in the profits." This was not the right way to approach Goldwyn, and Niven should have known that.

His hopes were dashed when Selznick, for financial reasons, cast the stars entirely from his own lineup of contract actors. But not even Jennifer Jones, Gregory Peck and Joseph Cotten could redeem what might be called an epic dud—its failure due in large part to Selznick's undying attempt to be a screenwriter, for which he took sole credit on *Duel in the Sun*.

For all her ability, it is not easy to imagine Teresa in the part of Pearl, which ill-suited her, Niven's idea to the contrary notwithstanding. She agreed that the role would dramatically alter her image, but she also felt it was violent and repellent—traits that always alienated her from a project.

And so her pregnancy was the occasion for another Goldwyn suspension.

"She has been and is now physically incapacitated," wrote Samuel Goldwyn to his legal department, interpreting pregnancy as illness. "She cannot perform her services under her contract of employment, and that incapacity will continue for some time. Miss Wright is therefore suspended again, both as to services and compensation, commencing April 27, 1944 and for so long a period thereafter as physical incapacity continues."

That meant until December, which saved Goldwyn about $60,000, the sum Teresa would otherwise have received according to her contract. This was a welcome economy for Goldwyn, but it also caused a serious gap in his roster and his schedule. There was nothing serious on Goldwyn's docket—only three facile comedies, two with Danny Kaye and one with Bob Hope.

Despite Teresa's Academy Award and highly praised performances in four major pictures, Hollywood as usual had a remarkably short memory.

CHAPTER SEVEN

1944–1948

EARLY IN 1944—WHEN THE MILLERS RETURNED HOME TO VAN NUYS—
Teresa, Niven, Peter and Tony moved to a short-term rental at 1014
Manning Avenue, in the area known as Westwood, between Beverly
Hills and West Los Angeles. While there, they began to look for a larger
house. During their time at Manning Avenue, on December 2, 1944,
Teresa gave birth to a boy they named Niven Terence Busch, the names
honoring both father and mother. When Teresa saw the baby's dark hair,
blue eyes and long lashes, she said with a laugh, "He looks like Elizabeth
Taylor!" Avoiding the confusion caused by the child's first name ("which
led to all sorts of misunderstandings," as he recalled), the boy was afterward known to family and friends as Terry.

Soon, mother and father found the right property to buy, at 4601
Balboa Avenue, in the San Fernando Valley neighborhood known as
Encino. Wooded lawns and citrus orchards surrounded the two-story
house, and there was room for a pool, which they later added.

There were also two garages. With the help of the architectural firm
Ayres and Fiegl, the Busches expanded one, adding a second floor in
1948 and upgrading it into a snug private suite for Peter and Tony and
their store of equipment for hobbies, sports and hunting. The second garage, closer to the house, was a ramshackle storehouse of castoff items,
mostly odds and ends and sheer junk. (Teresa found it hard to part with
anything, ever; she did so only when relocation made it necessary for her
to dispose of things.) The main buying point for Niven may have been
the space for his paddocks and horses; from the back of the house, one
could horseback ride over to the bluffs above Malibu.[1]

1. The house, grounds and pool were expanded and enlarged several times by subsequent
owners; in 2015, it was offered for sale at almost $3 million. In 1945, the Busches did not
pay much more than $5,000 for it.

Although born and raised an Easterner, Niven much preferred the West and its culture, which featured largely in his novels and screenplays. He routinely wore cowboy gear and often appeared more like the lead in a Western than its author as he rode up the trails into the uninhabited, rough hills. Teresa was not a rider, but Peter and Tony took to their horses easily, riding and hunting with their father. Young Terry was given a pony—"a vicious little Shetland named Dusty," as he recalled.

During Terry's childhood, household help was engaged when Mom and Dad were busy at work. Terry further remembered that, in the way of older siblings, Peter and Tony (who turned thirteen and nine in 1945) regarded him as

a pest or a pet, ranking somewhere between the high-status dogs and the lowly undifferentiated cats. I was hugely spoiled by nearly all the adults, and my brothers sort of balanced the scale, ensuring that I would not think I was the real ruler of the place.

The Encino location was ideal—not only for Niven's outdoor life but also for his friendships with those nearby who were also marinated in Western lore: Clark Gable, John Wayne, Joel McCrea, Gilbert Roland, Gene Autry and Roy Rogers. There were frequent weekend barbecue parties at the Busch home, but Teresa did not encourage games because, as she said, "games interfere with conversation. What's the use of getting interesting people together if you don't have conversation?"

There was no predominant style in the home furnishings, which were mostly pieces Niven and Teresa had collected over time. "It's just plain hodge-podge," she said, adding:

I seem to live in perpetual confusion. I get my accounts all mixed up, I can never remember whether or not I received change at a store, I am always promising myself to make lists of things, under the foolish impression that if I ever get around to it, life will magically become much simpler than it is now. I write notes to myself— and then I leave them all over the house in odd corners and usually can't decipher them when I finally find them!

That was a precise summary of habits Teresa never broke: throughout her life, she was disorganized in small things (shopping lists, for example) and sometimes even in larger matters (such as the paperwork necessary for the preparation of her annual taxes). Her genial but scatterbrained behavior was greatly annoying to some people, mostly her husbands. But she never forgot the essential things—the needs of family and friends—and those who worked with her always knew that she arrived with the most thorough preliminary research and preparation for her roles in plays or pictures. She read widely in every genre of literature, as her letters attest, and she never ignored matters affecting the poor and disenfranchised, on whose behalf she frequently wrote checks to charities.

With their house pets, three (and eventually four) children and professional lives that were often conducted on the moment, the Busches often lived amid a kind of household anarchy. But the atmosphere was cozy, cheerful and free of the pressures sometimes imposed on active boys taught to revere silence, discipline and good order. Living in Encino was also convenient for Teresa: it was just an easy ride through the canyons to the studios, the Millers and the shops in Santa Monica.

She preferred a set of friends different from those Niven cultivated: always there was Bea Miller, more of a sister than a sister-in-law; and Dorothy McGuire, who lived in Beverly Hills with her husband, the eminent photographer John Swope. Soon, Mona and Karl Malden, Jean and Richard Widmark, and Katie and Martin Manulis came to live in Los Angeles; each and all were very close to Teresa.

"I'm just another housewife with a part-time job," she told a reporter cheerfully. Indeed, since *Casanova Brown*, she had not worked apart from a few radio versions of her movie appearances. Radio adaptations were a popular format at the time, and Teresa was heard on the Lux Radio Theatre presentation of *Shadow of a Doubt*, with William Powell in Joseph Cotten's role.

✍

Niven was working on novels for which he received payment only on acceptance of the final draft. He was also beginning to work on the screenplay for *The Postman Always Rings Twice*, based on the novel by James M. Cain. Most of his fee would not be paid until the first day of filming in the summer of 1945.[2] The family, therefore, required income, and when Goldwyn finally lifted Teresa's suspension for another loan-out, she agreed to it without hesitation. Goldwyn, too, needed cash—and pocketed a profit of $125,000.

---

2. *The Postman Always Rings Twice* carries a credit for Harry Ruskin as co-writer. Ruskin was the producer's cousin, a radio gag-writer who added only a few lines of dialogue for the sake of a fee.

And so that spring, she was shipped over to Paramount Studios for two pictures: *The Trouble With Women*, produced from May to July; and *The Imperfect Lady*, made between September and November. In both, her co-star was Ray Milland, who had completed *The Lost Weekend*, destined to be a great success for Paramount and for him—he won the Academy Award as best actor of 1945.

In *The Trouble With Women*, Teresa had the role of a journalist confronting a pompous psychology professor who maintains that women have a suppressed desire to be controlled and manipulated by men. The picture, which was in many ways ahead of its time in puncturing the presumptions of sexism, gave Teresa a splendid opportunity for her capacious comic talents: no moment was overplayed, no gesture magnified. In a role that recalls Rosalind Russell in *His Girl Friday*, Teresa—who appears in almost every sequence—brought to life a lively, sassy, independent young woman. Seventy years later, *The Trouble With Women* remains sparkling entertainment.

The Imperfect Lady followed immediately. Teresa played a Victorian music-hall performer who marries an aristocratic politician (Milland) and is subsequently and wrongly suspected of immorality. The story moves smoothly from the world of the music hall and the East End to the plush salons of Mayfair and then to the exigencies of a courtroom drama. For reasons known only to Paramount executives at the time, *The Trouble With Women* and *The Imperfect Lady* were withheld from distribution for two years and are all but forgotten decades later. This is difficult to explain and impossible to defend, as the two movies are very enjoyable and nothing like the frivolous productions discounted by critics at the time.

∽

Meanwhile, Goldwyn and Wyler were preparing what became an historic motion picture—*The Best Years of Our Lives*, a classic on its release and a popular movie ever since. Produced from April to August 1946, it was arguably the most important production in the careers of the producer and director.

The story of three American servicemen returning from World War II, *Best Years* punctured every cliché: the men find not the fulfillment of their dream, but a nightmare of confusion, loss, rejection and the triumph of the class system in America. As critic Glenn Erickson has written,

A lot of the content of *Best Years* was daring stuff: alcoholism . . . a real amputee . . . an adulterous relationship . . . [and] the movie's frank views about callous business practices and a hostile work environment. The town [to which the men return] is no idealized Andy Hardy-land but a place of tight jobs and small minds . . . and the romantic conclusion has a bitter undertaste [that] shows a realistic awareness of the unfairness of the world.

One character, an Army sergeant (Fredric March) is alienated from his children and his career; another, a captain (Dana Andrews), finds temporary, underpaid work only as a soda jerk, and learns that the wife to whom he returns is now unfaithful and greedy; the third (Harold Russell) has endured a dreadful accident in which he lost his hands, now replaced by hooks.

The picture was loosely based on a blank-verse novel by MacKinlay Kantor, but the outstanding screenplay came from Robert E. Sherwood, formerly the senior speechwriter for President Franklin D. Roosevelt. Nothing in the Sherwood-Wyler *Best Years* is played for easy sentiment or jingoistic patriotism: the emotions are true and raw, the terrible circumstances readily recognizable to men returning from the war and to the families with whom they try to reunite and reconcile. Billy Wilder was a cynic in life and art—he directed, among other fine pictures, *Double Indemnity, The Lost Weekend, Sunset Boulevard, The Apartment* and *Fedora*. Wilder said that he began to weep copious tears five minutes into watching *Best Years*: "I cried through the whole picture, and I am not a pushover—I laugh at *Hamlet*."

As the love interest for the Dana Andrews character, and as the daughter of Fredric March and Myrna Loy, Teresa was at the emotional center of the picture. Her scenes with Andrews were finely tuned under Wyler's allusive direction, and the result was more poignant than merely provocative. As always, she watched and listened acutely to all the actors, and her performance was an amalgamation of delicacy, passion and bemusement.

It was not always easy for the cast to work with Dana Andrews, who went off several times on alcoholic binges that threw the production into disarray as he disappeared for a day or two before returning, weary and ill. "They had to go find him," Teresa recalled, "and we had to wait. They discovered him at some motel and brought him to the set and fed him a lot of coffee. He could work, but he was having a hard time. This happened more than once—but he gave a really wonderful, sensitive performance that amazed everyone."

Teresa, for one, always treated Dana Andrews with kindness and with respect for his considerable talent; Andrews remembered Teresa as "very quiet, intelligent, deep."

Those qualities remain evident in Teresa's every scene, as Stephan Talty has written:

> Wright brought the undercurrents to the surface as cleanly as any actress then working—as in the closing wedding sequence, where we feel her submerged love for Fred [Andrews] rise, heavy and sharp, into her eyes. She worked best with dialogue that was plain-spoken, but in which important things—new love, old deadly worries—lay hidden. When given that, she could make us feel a vibrato of silent emotion that remains undiminished and without distortion over time.

And no less a critic than novelist and poet James Agee wrote most perceptively in his review for *The Nation*:

> This new performance of [Teresa Wright's], entirely lacking in big scenes, tricks, or obstreperousness—one can hardly think of it as acting—seems to me one of the wisest and most beautiful pieces of work I have seen in years. If the picture had none of the hundreds of other things it has to recommend it, I could watch it a dozen times over for that personality and its mastery alone.

Apart from the occasional problems with Andrews, the only element of tension occurred between the producer and director, when Goldwyn came down to the set and began giving Wyler advice: "Then Willy just stalled and stalled. The lighting man stalled, the soundman stalled. Goldwyn got the message that nothing was going to be shot while he was there. So he would leave." But as he withdrew, Goldwyn shouted to Wyler: "You're too many pages behind schedule!"—to which Wyler quietly replied, "Okay, Sam—how many pages? Let's just tear them up and we'll be right back on schedule!"

As usual, Teresa won more new friends—in this case, Fredric March (and his wife, Florence Eldridge), Myrna Loy and Harold Russell. Their companionship did not end with the wrap of the film. "What a great actor!" Teresa said of March in 1980. "Freddie had a tremendous love of life and a tremendous honesty and authority. We all loved and enjoyed him so much that it just embellished our scenes with him."

The last of her trio of films under Wyler's direction was memorable for Teresa. "The movie captured the truth of what many people experienced," she said. "And Willie spoiled me for working with other directors. For one thing, he never let the technical people interfere with you. In *Best Years*, I had to scramble eggs, and the soundman objected to the noise of the fork in the pan. I said, 'Well, that's what happens when you scramble eggs.' Willie agreed: 'She'll scramble eggs, and you'll pick it up,' he said to the soundman. If you had a scene where you were supposed to be quiet, he'd tell sound, 'She's going to be quiet and you'll just have to catch it.'"

The picture was released in time for Christmas, and on March 13, 1947, the Academy distributed its awards for 1946. Seven statuettes were handed out for *The Best Years of Our Lives*: for the best picture (to producer Samuel Goldwyn); best director (Wyler); best actor (Fredric March); best supporting actor (Harold Russell); best screenplay (Robert E. Sherwood); best editing (Daniel Mandell); best musical scoring of a dramatic picture (Hugo Friedhofer); and a second, special Oscar to Harold Russell ("for bringing hope and courage to his fellow veterans"). Goldwyn also took home the Irving G. Thalberg Memorial Award.

On reflection, one aspect of *The Best Years of Our Lives* remains unclear, and that is the title. Early during production, the project was titled *Home Again* and then *Glory For Me*, but these were discarded. Sherwood and Wyler then settled on *The Best Years of Our Lives*. But precisely what do those words mean?

"The best years" cannot refer to the time of the war, nor to what preceded it—that would be too cynical and would reduce the significance of the heroic exploits of these men. Nor can the title refer to what is in the future—that would be hypothetical and, from a narrative standpoint, a cheat. Nor can the best years indicate what we see in the present, which is obviously a time of disillusionment and disappointment.

The title makes sense only if we understand it not literally but ironically. That is certainly the impact of the only moment in the picture when the phrase is spoken: when the character played by Virginia Mayo complains loudly to her husband (Dana Andrews), "I've given you the best years of my life!" In fact, she has given him nothing of the kind: she married him less than three weeks before he went off to war, and he has returned to find her frivolous, avaricious and adulterous.

In the final analysis, analysis may fail. *The Best Years of Our Lives* may have been invented as an allusion, a kind of wise trick to entice American audiences, who were disinclined to see yet another picture about the war. If this is so, it worked. Millions of moviegoers lined up to find out just what were the best years of their lives; what they got was something far richer to consider. In any case, the ambiguities of the title remain, and they are not to be blithely explained or easily resolved. The picture grossed $10 million in its first year, making it the most financially successful American movie since *Gone With the Wind*.

Best Years runs for almost three hours, but not a moment is repetitive, unnecessary or needlessly prolonged. In its register of superb performances, not one is off the mark; and in the economy of its authentic sentiment, the picture is as close to perfection as a movie can be. Many years later, it remains one of the greatest achievements ever to come from Hollywood.

∽

After filming was completed that summer, Goldwyn's publicists arranged for some cast members to be photographed for national magazines. Teresa's picture popped out from the pages of *American Home, Woman's Home Companion, Pageant, Movieland, Silver Screen* and *The Californian*, among many others. Most notably, a haunting portrait of her by Alfred Eisenstaedt appeared on the cover of *Life* magazine on December 16.

By then, Teresa had completed another picture. Immediately after the conclusion of *Best Years* in August, she traveled to New Mexico for four weeks of location shooting in a movie written especially for her by her husband and directed by Raoul Walsh. For months, Niven had continually badgered Goldwyn to set Teresa free for an image-changing role, and here it was: not Pearl Chavez in *Duel in the Sun*, but a character not entirely dissimilar, in a murky psychological Western called *Pursued*. Her co-stars were Robert Mitchum and Judith Anderson, and the picture was planned and marketed as a prestigious enterprise.

Decades later, *Pursued* is regarded as a kind of cult movie, and according to fans, it was the first *film noir* Western, suffused with allusions to classical myths and to Freudian psychology. That may be so, but it is also a nearly impenetrable account of a man (Mitchum) haunted by vague memories of uncertain parentage and a violent childhood in the Old New Mexico Territory. His adoptive sister (Teresa) falls in love with him and moves from love to hatred to vengeance and then back again to love when everything (for reasons not entirely clear) turns out all right.

"All I ever wanted to do was get hold of my material and control it," Niven said. "I had absolute control over that [movie], and [because] I needed a star, I got Teresa on loan-out. I was very happy with the result. I had a marvelous cast, a terrific crew, and the best cameraman in the world [James Wong Howe]. I was very proud of the story—it has kind of Greek overtones, incest and all that." It also has an egregious lack of logic and clarity.

Pursued was completed by October 1946 and released in March 1947. Teresa was surprised at the glorification of the movie years later; she was unhappy during the filming and as confused by the result as were many viewers. But she did confirm Niven's expectation, especially in a long and angry monologue, when she revealed an ability for the first time—the capacity to shift violently in one scene from emotion to emotion. Teresa as vengeful seductress was not anticipated onscreen in 1947, and she was so successful at the portrayal that many audiences rejected the picture for that reason alone. They would not accept that the wonderful girl from *Best Years* was a gun-slinging, man-hating woman of doubtful sanity.

"Niven Busch is a Pygmalion," wrote one perceptive journalist. "He has started a one-man campaign to take his wife out of the ingénue class and make her a femme fatale. How Teresa is going to take all this is still a mystery. It's the strange case of Teresa Wright, whose spouse wants her to inspire wolf calls and is making very sure that she does."

∽

In 1945, Goldwyn planned a film based on Robert Nathan's novel *The Bishop's Wife*, about a helpful angel who becomes involved in the lives of a troubled clergyman and his attractive spouse. On June 1 that year, Goldwyn announced that Teresa would star in the movie after her return from the Ray Milland films at Paramount. But the screenplay went through several difficult and disappointing drafts, and the production was delayed, even after Cary Grant and David Niven had been added to the cast.

The long postponement and the replacement of the director proved disastrous for Goldwyn's plans, for in early 1947, before the premiere of *Pursued*, Teresa was pregnant again and thus unable to perform in *The Bishop's Wife*. She at once informed Goldwyn, and this effected another, more serious contretemps with her boss, who had to look for a replacement to star in a production already far over budget.

At a party a few days later, Goldwyn angrily approached the Busches. "You think you know who you've been fucking!" he growled, his face turning red with rage as he poked Niven's chest. "Well, I'll tell you who you've been fucking—you've been fucking *me*!" For the rest of her life, Teresa from time to time hilariously recounted the incident, rendering Goldwyn complete with Polish-American accent and intonation. Loretta Young replaced Teresa in *The Bishop's Wife*.

For the remainder of 1947, Teresa lived quietly without the rigors of moviemaking. In a letter, she wrote eloquently of the emotions she felt during her pregnancies:

> Women are lucky when they are having a baby. They have that wonderful, fulfilled, "I'm creating" feeling, without any effort on their part. Usually at the beginning of pregnancy she's so filled with a sense of [the] wonder and beauty of it that she withdraws from the problems of the world and is content to spend hours by herself reading and thinking, or just lying still and listening to sounds, doubly aware of everything around her because of the life she knows to be inside her. Later, when she stops thinking of it as something wonderful and mysterious slowly happening, and begins to think of it as *the child*, the added responsibility who will soon be here, she often spoils it for herself, worrying about clothes and equipment for the baby, a nursery to be furnished, painted, curtained, etc.—all the things that poor little baby couldn't care less about. I know I made unnecessary worry for myself and Niven, worrying about such things. I envy the young woman who has the sense to do away with all that—who can just give birth to a child, wrap it in any old blanket and nurse it and just give it love and not all the accessories.

Teresa gave birth to a girl on September 12, 1947, and named her Mary Kelly, honoring a beloved grandmother. Premature and underweight, the baby was kept in the hospital for some weeks until she gained strength; called by both names that were soon hyphenated, she became known as Mary-Kelly Busch.

༄

The autumn was briefly eclipsed by the newborn's precarious health and then, for a longer time, by Teresa's nagging chest cold, aggravated by the demands of a large family and by daily travel to and from the hospital to see her baby in an incubator. By December, she was so weary that her agent wrote to Goldwyn, "Teresa said she would not be able to return [to work] until approximately another six months go by, which would be towards the latter part of May 1948. She is tired, does not feel well and just couldn't return to work any sooner."

This time, there was no suspension. As he cheerfully told Abe Last-fogel (who was representing her once again), Goldwyn was preparing a sublime motion picture for her and several other contracted play-ers—David Niven, Farley Granger and Evelyn Keyes. And so he waited and meantime supervised his fifth motion picture starring Danny Kaye, whose antics were pouring large sums into the Goldwyn treasuries.

At last, by the spring of 1948, Teresa was well enough and eager for work, perhaps especially because Niven was busy working on novels and had no movie deals after *Pursued*. Goldwyn finally sent her the script by John Patrick for a picture called *Enchantment*, along with the novel that inspired it—*Take Three Tenses*, by the British author Rumer Godden. Teresa was immediately drawn to this unique, almost mystical parable about several generations of a family, with love stories told simultane-ously as scenes move backward and forward in time. In fact, John Pat-rick's screenplay seemed to her more coherent than the book, and so it was.[3]

Enchantment is a period picture: Teresa's scenes were set in Edwardian England. Goldwyn ordered sumptuous costumes, expertly reproduced jewelry and wigs carefully reflecting the styles of the time. And when director Irving Reis began rehearsals in early May, Teresa arrived to find her old dressing room handsomely redecorated and banked with flow-ers. Goldwyn, in high spirits, was present to welcome her when principal photography began on May 12, and he frequently visited the set until the picture was completed in July.

George Jenkins had designed more than fifty Broadway produc-tions when Goldwyn brought him to Hollywood as art director for *The Best Years of Our Lives* and for *Enchantment*. George and his wife, Phyllis, quickly became Teresa's new friends that season; over many years, she visited their home in Santa Monica Canyon.

"Many producers reach a point where their productions are only about business—a job to make money, and they don't care how good the products are," Teresa said later.

---

3. A number of Godden's novels were brought to the screen, among them *Black Narcissus*, *The River* and *The Greengage Summer*. Her experiment with time in *Take Three Tenses* was surpassed in her later and more satisfying novel, *China Court*.

But Mr. Goldwyn was different—he always cared, more than anybody I ever met in Hollywood. I can't name anyone who was as artistic—he really wanted to create things that were good. Of course
he was a businessman, and that side of things was important, too.
But he was so dedicated to each production, and his record was
marvelous. I admired his involvement in every picture.

Neither critics nor audiences were much impressed by *Enchantment*,
and for many years it was all but forgotten; even after it became available on video formats, the movie failed to generate enthusiasm, much
less admiration. Perhaps this is due to the uncompromising, bittersweet
story of loves thwarted; perhaps it is due to the subtle performances,
the frequently poetic dialogue, the subtle methods of character development—and the technical brilliance through which a meditation on time
is expressed.

Whatever the stated reasons for the film's continual dismissal since
1948, this negative response seems to me entirely unjust. *Enchantment*,
shifting effortlessly and often from the early years of the century to the
bombing of London during World War II, is completely successful. The
performances—especially by Teresa and by David Niven—are unfailingly
right. As a young woman loved by her two adoptive brothers but hated
by their sister, Teresa counterpoises ardor with indignation in one of her
most complex and demanding roles. As one of those brothers, David
Niven is seen in flashback as a dashing rogue in Edwardian society; and
a half-century later in the story, during the bombing of London, he por-
trays a lonely old man, all but unrecognizable thanks to superb studio
makeup. Like Teresa's, David Niven's performance is uncontrived and
haunting: these two actors represent the art of screen acting at its highest level. There is more to admire in *Enchantment* than in almost any so-
called romantic film released in postwar America.

Perhaps more than any other production in his career, Goldwyn loved
this motion picture with passionate intensity—indeed, it elicited his celebrated comment, "I don't care if it doesn't make any money, as long as
every man, woman and child in America sees it."

⌒∕∂

When he released the movie at Christmas that year, Goldwyn ordered his
publicity department to organize a nationwide advertising and marketing campaign that obliged several supporting players to travel, to sit for
interviews and to perform the usual promotional tasks. Their schedules

were drawn up on the moment, and suddenly they received phone calls and were commanded to leave everything and everyone for the sake of Duty.

At first (contrary to every report published since 1948), Teresa tried to comply. She raced to complete Christmas shopping for the children, but her chores were impeded by her usual lack of organization. Perhaps because of anxiety, she had a relapse of her autumn illness, which was confirmed by her physician, Dr. Robert L. Sands. But Goldwyn insisted that his studio doctor examine her, and at this Teresa balked. "I've often been cast as mild and sweet," she said later, "but I'm not so soft. Determined is the nice word for it, but stubbornness is more accurate." She said she could not and would not leave home for the publicity tour, "and I refused to have my home invaded or my person examined by a physician hired by the studio to rule on my fitness to travel. My own doctor, a man of wide repute, was quite competent to inform the studio as to my condition."

The premiere of *Enchantment* occurred on December 11, and three days later, furious at what he considered Teresa's lack of cooperation, Goldwyn sent a telegram to her home: "You are hereby instructed to report to us immediately . . . to leave Los Angeles [and] to report to our office in New York for publicity interviews and to render such of your other required services as may be directed by us."

When Teresa refused again, Goldwyn terminated her contract on the spot, firing her once and for all, without suspension, without negotiation, without contacting her agent. Immediately, the details of this unhappy incident were publicized far more widely than the picture itself.

Goldwyn began with a forceful (if syntactically awkward) statement to the press on December 15:

> I think the time has arrived when studios must assert their rights more than they have in the past. No one has a greater appreciation of artists and no one wants to treat them more fairly than I have in my career. But I am sick and tired of seeing what is going on in this town—where people have no respect for their contracts and no respect for the money they receive and refuse to perform and cooperate.
>
> Making a picture is no longer sufficient. The picture has to be sold to the public, and particularly at this time, when it seems that everything is being done to unsell the public on Hollywood.

And then he drew out his big guns:

> My reason for cancelling the contract with Miss Wright is that she
> has been uncooperative and has refused to follow reasonable in-
> structions. As far as I am concerned, that is that—and irrespective
> of what anyone else does, I am through tolerating that sort of con-
> duct. Instead of showing gratitude, Miss Wright has done just the
> opposite. Hollywood had better get wise to itself. The day is over
> when stars can get away with this sort of behavior.

Teresa at once replied publicly and at length, revealing at last the depths
of her resentment:

> A discussion of my differences with Mr. Goldwyn would be of ben-
> efit to no one and of interest to few. However, for the record, I
> would like to say that I never refused to perform the services re-
> quired of me: I was unable to perform them because of ill health.

Then came the surprise: Teresa refused to renege on deeper principles,
and she refused to commence legal action:

> I accept Mr. Goldwyn's termination of my contract without pro-
> test—in fact, with relief. The types of contracts standardized in the
> motion picture industry between players and producers are archaic
> in form and absurd in concept. I am determined never to set my
> name to another one.
>   We in the acting branch of the profession are to blame for ac-
> cepting, in our eagerness to work, agreements under which we
> waive the natural equities prevailing in every other industry. We
> say, in effect, "We have no privacy which you as producers cannot
> invade. Treat us like cattle. Speak to us like children. Make us work
> eleven hours a day. Loan us out for ten or twenty times the sums
> paid to us at your discretion" . . . The time has come for actors to
> say, "Pay me less, only treat me with respect."
>   I have worked for Mr. Goldwyn for seven years because I con-
> sider him a great producer, and he has paid me well. But in the
> future I shall gladly work for less if by doing so I can retain my hold
> on the common decencies without which the most glorified job
> becomes intolerable.

I think the time has come for professional people to reject contracts like the one of which Mr. Goldwyn has so kindly relieved me.[4]

But another issue was at stake—one about which Goldwyn knew much more at the time, and which hung like a shadow over every day and every deal. The year 1948 marked the beginning of the studio system's inexorable decline. Anti-monopoly laws required filmmaking companies to divest themselves of movie theatres that guaranteed presentation of their own productions (the Loews chain for MGM pictures, for example). In addition, Americans were buying television sets in ever-greater profusion, and this brought a major threat to the motion picture industry.

As of Christmas 1948, Teresa's salary—then almost $5,000 a week—was terminated instantly, and she became one of the many unemployed actors in Hollywood. "I guess I wanted to be a kind of Joan of Arc," she said years later, "but all I proved was that I was an actress who would work for less money—$25,000 instead of $250,000. I wanted to be fired because I didn't like being owned, but the way I did it . . . I made a big mistake. Maybe I was wrong."

Years later, she regretted the entire episode. "Goldwyn was a fair man, and I should have gone straight to him, not just to my agent and the press. I didn't, and that was not very bright of me."

On the other hand, it is curious that Goldwyn did not make the overture and at least put through a call to Teresa at home. These were two people of good will, after all, with mutual respect. But in this case, the unhappy outcome was the result of mutual obstinacy.

---

4. In fact, Teresa did make a public appearance to promote *Enchantment*, at the San Francisco premiere, on March 8, 1949.

CHAPTER EIGHT

1949–1952

AS THE NEW YEAR BEGAN, AN OSCAR-WINNING MOVIE STAR WAS suddenly free to entertain offers from producers other than Goldwyn, to whom she had been exclusively attached for eight years. She was out of work and nearly out of funds, and in the unfathomable wisdom of Hollywood, not one independent mogul or studio stepped into the breach. One idea came through her agent in January—but it was, she said, "a dumb murder mystery they were to pay me $125,000 to do, but I rejected it." As Mary-Kelly said, "Mom was very selective about roles, and she often turned down offers she thought were not right for her. She was also quick to be generous on behalf of others"—as, for example, when she recommended Dorothy McGuire for *The Enchanted Cottage*. "This time," Teresa said, after rejecting the murder mystery, "I decided to wait."

She did not have to wait long. Her husband had recently completed a story and screenplay called *The Capture*; now he hoped to raise money for a production company, to turn it into a prestigious film. The plot concerned a former oil-rigger, haunted by guilt and remorse over the death of a man wrongly accused of robbery.

In March, the press announced that independent producer Niven Busch had signed Lew Ayres for the leading man in *The Capture*—and Niven expected Teresa Wright to play the leading lady, the dead man's widow. "He wanted her in this picture because they needed the money," according to Mary-Kelly; and if this became a successful venture, Niven reasoned, he would be set up for future productions. Teresa accepted the role, but with misgivings: she found the script underwritten, her role not

well constructed and the continuity agonizingly slow. When the picture
was released in April 1950, critics agreed with her reservations.

For the present, life at home continued in its quiet routine, much
of it focused on the children. Teresa and Niven spent considerable time
with Bea and Winston Miller and their daughters, Christine and Noelle.
"My father and Niven were both fascinated by the West and the cowboy
culture," recalled Christine, "and they often discussed sports news on
the phone. My mother was Niven's sister, after all, and he often stayed
with us. They were all very fond of each other." Meanwhile, *The Capture*
was being filmed in Pioneertown, a Western-movie location east of Los
Angeles in San Bernardino County.

At home, Niven and Teresa often dined with Dinah Shore and her
husband, George Montgomery, whose daughter Melissa was Mary-Kelly's age. Terry marked his sixth birthday in December 1950, and he had
some unpleasant recollections:

> I remember a lot of tension and unhappy scenes. My parents tried
> to keep them private, but they weren't entirely successful. I could
> often hear them arguing—loud voices in the night—and sometimes
> I tried to play the role of peacemaker. I remember on one occasion
> hearing them fight and going into their room bearing a bowl of
> ripe cherries [for them], my favorite. My mother, already greatly
> agitated, broke down sobbing, and I thought I had made a terrible
> mistake.

"My father was something of a bully with my mother," Mary-Kelly
added. "They were both very strong people, and Niven was driving her
a little crazy. He came from another era, and he had a wandering eye. It
was all very odd, because he needed her money but resented her greater
fame. He was used to getting his way, and he was impossible to negotiate
with during those years." Niven's niece Christine Miller added, "Niven
could be a rascal."

According to Terry, "My father, by his own later admission, had a lot
of lovers over the course of his life. I sometimes wondered if that were
not closer to being the *casus belli*." Terry was on the mark: Teresa found it
difficult—in fact, impossible—to ignore or to endure an unfaithful husband, then or later. The cold war that prevailed beginning in 1950 owed
to a complex of reasons that were especially difficult for the children to
witness, for they deeply loved and were loved by both Teresa and Niven.

⁊

They continued to work at their marriage, and that summer she accepted an offer from the independent producer Stanley Kramer—for a mere $25,000—to appear in a movie called *The Men*, to be directed by Fred Zinnemann. On paper, the project seemed a worthy one: the story of a paraplegic war veteran trying to adjust to civilian and to married life.

For the leading man, Kramer had secured Marlon Brando in his first film role; this augured well for the picture's commercial success, for Brando already had a national reputation as the bad boy of Broadway thanks to his celebrated performance in *A Streetcar Named Desire*.

Filmed in November and December 1949 and released in August 1950, *The Men* was a trial for everyone. "Marlon Brando was terribly insecure when we made this picture," recalled Zinnemann. "He had never been in front of a motion picture camera, and he didn't trust people. He was completely enclosed within himself. As a result, he approached the part of the paraplegic veteran as if the man was Stanley in *Streetcar*."

"He was a combination of a dynamic man and a twelve-year-old child who played jokes on people," Teresa recalled. "When he was working, he was completely serious, and he didn't want to make waves or cause any trouble. I wish I'd known him better, and I wish we'd had a longer rehearsal time. He was fascinating to work with. But I didn't like myself in *The Men*." In the final cut, she sometimes appeared overwhelmed and even out of place.

Her occasional awkwardness was not the reason why Teresa always described *The Men* as an unpleasant experience. To begin, she felt betrayed by her agent, who also represented Brando. To compensate for her low salary, Teresa was to have top billing, but that was changed for Brando's sake. Then there was the problem of the payment schedule, which had been fixed according to a so-called favored-nations clause: everyone was to be paid the same low salary for a small, independent picture with social significance. This, too, was a ruse to obtain Teresa's services: Brando received $40,000 for *The Men*, $15,000 more than Teresa's salary.

Worse still was Kramer's rank duplicity. She had accepted the part of Brando's steadfast fiancée and then his loyal wife because the original script by Carl Foreman described the woman as tough and persistent, and there were a number of strong, memorable scenes for her—all of this Kramer guaranteed. But by the time production began, her part had been as downgraded as her salary, and she was relegated to scenes of arch sentiment or stereotyped fortitude. *The Men* did nothing for her career.

"All I proved was that I was an actress who would work for $25,000 instead of $200,000," Teresa often admitted in the years to come. "Unfortunately, your importance in Hollywood is determined by how much money you were paid in your previous film. After *The Men*, I was never again offered good roles and good wages in quality films. I know that sounds crazy, but that's the way it worked in those days in Hollywood. I was never able to regain the kind of status I had with my first few films."

But as always she considered others who had contributed to *The Men*. To the editors of *Look*, she sent a telegram after they published a review in the magazine: "It was disappointing to find the names of director Fred Zinnemann and writer Carl Foreman omitted. I am sure you will agree that their understanding of the paraplegic and his problems is one of the outstanding contributions to the film."

∽

From 1950 onward, Teresa's movie performances were as finely wrought as before, but henceforth they were often supporting or minor roles in unexceptional pictures that she frequently had to accept for the sake of an income. Hollywood inexplicably considered that her star had dimmed—a conviction held for no reason other than her lower salary. "Hollywood understands only dollars and cents," she said. "You are what you are paid. It's odd—I seem to be so identified with films, but the truth is that I had only a span of about ten years in Hollywood. And four of the best movies I ever made were completed during my first two years there."

∽

The Men was a disappointing picture for Teresa, and the next projects were no less so. In *Something To Live For*, she received third billing after Joan Fontaine as a boozy actress and Ray Milland in a stoic portrayal of a recovering alcoholic that was a sequel to his Oscar-winning role in *The Lost Weekend*. Directed by George Stevens and produced from May to July 1950, the movie was the first to mention and describe the work of Alcoholics Anonymous; but unfortunately it is so gravid with clichés that some viewers may be tempted to run from the theatre and demand a stiff drink.

As in *The Men*, Teresa was cast in *Something To Live For* as a dutiful, honorable wife (this time with two rambunctious children already built into the script): she waits like the mythological Penelope for her husband to come home and be sensible after an interlude with a failing drunken actress he tries to reform. Although Teresa had nothing good to say about her own performance in the picture, the critics were kinder: she was, according to the *New York Times*, "marvelous."

Meanwhile, Niven worked on his novels and on yet another Western story and screenplay for Gary Cooper—*Distant Drums*.

∽

As *Something To Live For* drew to its damp conclusion, Teresa received an invitation from Dorothy McGuire, who was aware of her friend's predicament and unhappiness. In 1947, Dorothy, in consort with Gregory Peck and Mel Ferrer, had founded the La Jolla Playhouse, near San Diego; the company performed plays at the La Jolla High School during its summer recess.

The goal of the La Jolla Playhouse was to present nine plays every summer—one each week. From its first season, the company had extraordinary success despite its hectic schedule. A cast rehearsed a play for six days and then performed it eight times the following week. For each seven-day period, actors were paid $55 and given hotel accommodations and two meals daily.

The plays were presented before sold-out houses, and no wonder: among the many actors who were happy to work with their colleagues for a token stipend were Patricia Neal, Joan Bennett, Charlton Heston, Jennifer Jones, Raymond Massey, Beulah Bondi, Fay Wray, Groucho Marx, David Niven, Olivia de Havilland—and of course the three founders.

On Saturday, August 5, Teresa arrived in La Jolla, and the following Tuesday she began rehearsals under the direction of her co-star, José Ferrer, in *The Silver Whistle*, a sentimental but charming comedy by Robert E. McEnroe. After a week of rehearsals, the play was presented from August 15 to August 20, each performance entirely sold out. The play concerned a strange vagrant who spreads wisdom and good cheer in a home for senior citizens. In the role of Miss Tripp, the manager of the residence, Teresa had an opportunity to convey gentle, ironic humor and real passion; audiences enthusiastically applauded both her first entrance and her curtain call.

The play marked her return to the stage after a nine-year absence—since the ill-fated production of *The King's Maid*. "After all those years in Hollywood, I began to think that if I didn't do a play, eventually I'd never again be able to say a line onstage. Thanks to Dorothy, I went to La Jolla, and that one experience convinced me that my real interest is the stage." At the time, she said, "I am approaching a major change in my career, but this is not the moment for details. Certain adjustments have to be made in my family's way of living."

The adjustments were made soon enough.

"We were having a little trouble," Niven said later in a triumphant understatement. "I thought if we get away from this goddamned rat race, if we have a ranch, she'll stick to the ranch and we'll be all right."

He miscalculated, and to disastrous effect.

In January 1951, Teresa traveled briefly to New York, where she made her television debut in an episode of the *Lux Video Theatre* called "Manhattan Pastorale." Of her many TV appearances, Teresa said, "I do think that live television is a great school for teaching actors to cope with almost anything under any circumstances. You're working under so much tension in such a short time, and you've got to do the best job you can—just once—and then it's all over."

On her return, the complicated relocation of the Busch family to a ranch in Northern California began—the "adjustments" to which Teresa had enigmatically referred. The ranch Niven selected as an outlet to enlarge his cowboy capacities was a tract of undeveloped land in Hollister, California—350 miles north of Los Angeles. He paid for it with the joint savings accumulated since their marriage.

"Mom would never back out of a contract if she could avoid it," said her son Terry about his parents' marriage. "But the Hollister move was insane for poor Mom's career." Contrary to a news item in the Hollywood *Citizen-News* on June 26, 1951 ("Teresa will commute for her picture career"), it was clear that she could not travel for almost a day to work in Hollywood, to be available for meetings or readings and then travel for another day to return home. (The California freeway system was not developed until later in the 1950s, and so the only reasonable car route at the time was the old Route 101, at its best points a rough, two-lane roadway.)

"There was nothing in Hollister," added Mary-Kelly,

unless you needed Levi's, seed, fertilizer and irrigation pipes. The house was about twenty feet from the edge of a cliff; below was a winding road, banked by orchards and a narrow river. Imagine gravel, brush and heat. The only option for cooling off in the summer was water from a hose or a dip in the ankle-deep, mucky river. And there was no relief from the dry hills on all sides. The mountains were green and lush during some weeks of March and April, but for the rest of the year, they were dusty and dry.

When Niven announced his plans for the move, he made a declaration: he did not put forth an idea open for discussion. Teresa's first reaction was that she liked the notion of being a full-time mother, but very soon she realized the consequences. She did not appreciate being suddenly forced to accept the role of a farm-wife to the detriment of her career. But the ranch inspired Niven to fresh perspectives, and from his new life in Hollister, he wrote several of his finest novels, among them *The Actor*, *California Street* and *The San Franciscans*. For Teresa, however, it was impossible to work as an actress while living at the ranch, and this meant only loss for her.

She and her husband had a good joint income in Los Angeles. But Niven wanted something more, something like an investment for his future. It was tacitly understood, as the children came to realize, that the move necessitated Teresa abandoning her career—or at least interrupting it, which at that time meant virtually putting an end to it.

In Los Angeles, there were always opportunities for work, for shopping at a plethora of city stores, for visits with friends and parties. At the ranch there was not a single peer, no one who would understand her world of theatre and film, no one to see except her husband and children.

"Mom was not a snob," said Mary-Kelly. "She was able to befriend anyone and take an interest in all kinds of people. She had played cowgirls"—in *Pursued* and *The Capture*—"but she was not a horsewoman, a farm girl or a ranch hand. Was her life now supposed to be fulfilled by making stews and cakes, and watching her children play?"

Niven, however, loved riding horses—indeed, he loved everything about Western ranch life—and at the time of the move, he thought that it would benefit his children as much as himself, and his love for his children was never in doubt. But clearly he took no measure of the effect on his wife; if he did, the idea can only have had a strong ingredient of carelessness or even cruelty. "It seemed ruthless," said Mary-Kelly. "It was a brutal decision." Somehow, Niven failed to see that his decision was an act of downright sabotage against his wife's career. He also seemed to forget that if Teresa quit acting to live full-time at Hollister with him and their children, they would soon be short of money.

Niven also failed to consider the burdens of owning and maintaining a working ranch, although as Terry recalled, "the burdens were challenges, a part of the spice of country life. New irrigation systems had to be installed, and even more challenging and unpredictable were rapacious managers and unpredictable crop prices." A business had to be established and a life endured in a place that was, for Teresa, suffocating, lonely and hopeless. "Years later," Mary-Kelly continued, "I often wondered what might have happened if Dad had chosen land in or near Encino, had planted orchards there, bred cattle and done all the things he loved about ranching without that fateful move to the north."

The relocation to Hollister thus wrenched Teresa from everything she had worked to achieve. At Niven's behest, she tried to commute a few times, but that was completely unrealistic. "She was up on the ranch, coming and going," Niven recalled. "Then she was getting restless." Indeed.

"When she commuted, she could not come home to her kids in the evening after a day's work at the studio," Mary-Kelly recalled. "That was a heartache for her, and so eventually she agreed to move to Hollister full-time—for a while." Eventually, the situation tore her family apart.

Niven was a man of consummate charm, keen intelligence and considerable talent. "He was also an old-school macho guy," added Mary-Kelly. "He loved women, but he firmly believed that men are superior, and so he failed to recognize that Mom was in fact his intellectual equal."

First in Encino and then at Hollister, he wanted Teresa to give up her career and to stay at home caring for the house and the children. But when they were short of money, he sent her hurrying back to work—or he devised a project for her if none was on the horizon. "He was also bossy, even in unnecessary things. He liked to read a bedtime story to Terry—but Mom was forbidden to do that."

"The more I've thought of it," Terry reflected years later, "the more I've wondered how Niven ever persuaded Teresa to leave L.A. and go off to such a remote place as San Benito County. There was absolutely nothing for her there. It would have meant nothing less than giving up her career, for it was something like an all-day train ride or a seven-hour car drive to get down to L.A. from our ranch. And there she was, at the height of her powers. It was absolutely crazy."

Teresa's reticence and submission to her husband's demands followed a life-history pattern. Shuttled from place to place during her childhood and adolescence, she had been abandoned by her mother and grew up with a rootless, restless streak that was repeated time and again in her adult years. She considered herself unworthy of a permanent home because she never had one, and so a pattern of behavior was set down that was all but impossible to alter. It was as if Teresa had to follow an unstable path consistent with her poor self-estimation. Before she was married, she lived in at least four apartments during her first year in

Hollywood. Then she had another three addresses up to 1951, and even in her senior years, she often relocated without any good reason.

Throughout her life, Teresa felt unworthy of the rewards and accolades that came to her, and she was always uncomfortable with praise. Now, in 1951, she clearly believed that it was her duty to deny herself and her preferences for Niven's sake and for the children's: this is what a loving wife did. But she soon learned that such total self-abnegation could not compensate for so much loss.

In considering the arc of her entire lifetime, it was perhaps amazing that these traits never turned her into an unhappy, bitter, pessimistic woman, much less a gloomy Cassandra. She was always a person who rose to the challenges life dealt, who soldiered on, quietly using every experience to understand other lives—and thus to become an actress who was never anything but truthful in a role. She worked intensely and successfully according to her capacious gifts, and she attracted a wide array of friends throughout her lifetime—people to whom she was ever loyal, as they were to her. The difficulties and the eventual despondency of 1951 and 1952 did not destroy her, but many years intervened before she could regard that time of her life as a challenge and not an end to her career and her dignity.

But Teresa was no Pollyanna, smiling through her tears and looking for the silver lining in every dark cloud.

> Every now and then I reach a low point where I say or feel—what am I, really? What accomplishments am I making in the time I have to live, as a woman? as a mother? as a performer in the craft I've chosen to work in? The answer seems to be, not much! There once was a time when I was quite happy with myself on all these scores. Maybe that's the trouble—I was too pleased with myself, took it all too much for granted. Anyway, I've lost it all now, and in my worst moments of defeat I think it's not going to get any better—and then comes the thought that I keep pushing out of my mind: what if I just gave up, stopped trying? But I always know that I won't, at least not by choice, as I know "not trying anymore" can only mean one of two things—the end of life or the end of facing the struggles in life. Institutions throughout the world are filled with people who have given up struggling and just shut the door on living.

∽

The Hollywood gossips were intrigued by the family move to Hollister and launched a campaign to learn more. In response to a letter from columnist Hedda Hopper accompanying her long, laudatory article about Teresa, she replied, addressing other topics before making a statement about her present situation. Her return address was Box 289, Route 1, Hollister:

> Thank you for the wonderful Sunday story—I know it will help me and I'm sure that's why you wrote it. I know very well that I'm not "news" enough to rate a Sunday story by you right now, but I deeply and sincerely appreciate it.
>
> I've made a lot of mistakes career-wise since Mr. Goldwyn fired me but some day I hope to do an acting job that will justify your encouragement and may even make dear old Mr. Goldwyn happy that he gave me my start in pictures . . .
>
> Our ranch is really beautiful, and I love it. For the past two months, I've cooked three meals a day for seven people. We grow our own fruit and vegetables. Last week, I cooked venison one night and dove the next, brought home by my hunter-husband. I'm sending you some of my apricot jam.

All this was disingenuous. Teresa was unsuited for the role of a rural Fannie Farmer, and Hopper correctly sensed it. Indeed, she was convinced earlier, when Teresa wrote, "The ranch, 300 acres near Hollister, is literally out of this world."

Throughout 1951 and into early 1952, Teresa continued to defend Niven's idea. "He has always wanted a ranch—it's part of a hobby. Wait until you see our alfalfa and our tomatoes!"

But the house on the property required quick cash for basic improvements, and so Niven pitched his wife into a Western called *California Conquest*, her first Technicolor movie. "Niven Busch invests Teresa Wright's money," reported Sheila Graham in her *Variety* column. "He will make their ranch a paying proposition or go bust trying."

California Conquest was a story of the Mexican heritage in nineteenth-century California, and to make it relevant in 1951, when the so-called Red Scare spread like wildfire in America, the plot interwove a Russian plan to attack and assume control of the new territory. The movie was produced in four weeks, most of it in Sonora, a three-hour car drive from Hollister. "An actress must work," Teresa said gamely during filming. "You either create or wither."

She certainly tried to be creative, but mostly she withered in the uncomfortable, arid heat. Wearing trousers, riding horses, shooting rifles, setting out to avenge her father's killer, falling in love with a desperado played by Cornel Wilde, Teresa seemed far too clever for this pop-up book of a movie. "This was real, real action," she wrote in another letter to Hedda Hopper after filming was completed. "At first I was scared to death. Imagine shooting guns right at people. I had to go around killing men at the drop of a hat. I killed so many people in that picture—and the fight scenes! I thought those things were always faked, but some of the horses' hooves came right down on the men."

Only many years later was she candid about this picture. "I guess the lowest point in my career was when I played a lady outlaw in a terrible film with Cornel Wilde—for even less than $25,000."

"I remember seeing the filming," Terry recalled. "I was shocked to see her emerge from a dressing room in a pioneer-style dress, her hair in some antique arrangement, with a big pistol in a holster strapped around her waist. At that point, it might have begun to dawn on me that my mom was *not* like other moms. Before then, I don't think I had any realization as a little boy that my mother was in any way different from any other mom. She was gone a lot, working, but I didn't know that was unusual for the times."

Perhaps inevitably, the tension in the marriage increased. Mary-Kelly was not yet five, but Terry was seven and remembered an incident "involving a plate of food, flung at my father's head, sailing past him to collide with the dining room wall."

Acting in *California Conquest* was but the most recent disappointment for her, a tedious exercise for necessary cash. Combined with the crisis in her marriage, Teresa's attitude about her film career was perhaps inexorably affected, and she was not shy discussing it with a new forthrightness.

I have a new viewpoint about my career, which is that I have no viewpoint at all. What I may hold to be true today may not be true tomorrow. It may not even be true today, for all that hindsight may prove. If times change, I'm prepared to change my values. And what if my standards are too high? How do I know that my judgment is right? I'm certain of only one thing—I want to go on acting.

However—and here her aversion was clarified:

I have reached a state of complete frustration in films. One gets on a treadmill playing in pictures, living up to your star rating, doing more pictures to keep up your rising standard of living and doing other pictures to pay your income tax, until you feel like a squirrel in a cage. I want to become independent of all that.

⌀

A temporary escape from the doldrums of home and Hollywood came in an offer from the actor and director Alfred Drake, in early February 1952. Mary Drayton had completed her recent play *Salt of the Earth*, scheduled for a week at the Shubert Theatre, New Haven, before a Broadway run. Based on a novel by Ardyth Kennelly called *The Peaceable Kingdom*, *Salt of the Earth* was a gentle comedy about Mormons and their multiple marriages.

Arriving in New Haven for rehearsals, Teresa was introduced to Mary Drayton and her husband, the actor Tom Helmore, and to her co-star, Kent Smith, who was married to the actress Betty Gillette. From that time forward, they were all fast friends, their social and professional lives intersecting at several important points and their alliance uninterrupted.

Teresa was cast as the second wife of a devout Mormon, played by Smith. She has given him five children, but she no longer relishes the role of marital pinch-hitter. "Miss Wright does a remarkable job with a part that has her onstage continually," wrote the critic for *Billboard*, the trade weekly. "Her handling of comedy, [and] sentimental and dramatic lines, is superb. In both motivation and portrayal, she is able to bring a fine realism to a part that could escape a less capable performer."

But the play was not so well received: "lifeless and unfunny," proclaimed *The Playgoer*, "mere soap opera transferred to the stage"; and *Billboard* concurred, calling it "very flat . . . a waste of an exceptionally fine cast and a top-flight production." After a week of performances, the play closed and the Broadway booking was canceled. Happily, the friendships so easily formed endured much longer.

From New Haven, Teresa traveled by train to New York, where her old friends from *Our Town*, Tom Coley and Bill Roerick, had written a ten-minute two-hander, a sketch they sold to the producers of *The Kate Smith Hour* on television. They invited Teresa to co-star with John Hodiak in "The Luckiest Day of My Life," and she gladly accepted. The result was a touching piece, performed with great charm and simplicity by the two actors. Teresa appeared in at least five additional television dramas that year, all of them produced in New York studios, where virtually all television dramas originated in the early 1950s.

℘

Back home, the situation was reaching critical mass, especially because of Teresa's recent positive experiences on stage and television. Although *Salt of the Earth* was a failure, she was praised, as she had been in *The Silver Whistle*. The short episode Tom and Bill wrote for her television debut proved that the new medium had fascinating possibilities for her—even the fearfully earnest John Hodiak was surprised by that. Hence returning to the virtual enclosure of Hollister was a grim prospect she could no longer endure.

Before mid-year, Niven and Teresa were living apart. She found a place for rent in the San Fernando Valley of Los Angeles, and there she and Mary-Kelly set up house until all the formal details of divorce were settled. Terry remained with Niven, but the arrangement of two children in two distant homes was presumed to be temporary.

Living near the studios made it possible for Teresa to accept two movie roles that year. The first was *The Steel Trap*, a taut thriller with Joseph Cotten (ten years earlier her "Uncle Charlie" in *Shadow of a Doubt*): he played a larcenous bank employee who makes off with a million in cash on a Friday afternoon. Teresa played his wife, unaware of his crime until she learns that their trip to Brazil is part of his plan to disappear from America and live forever without penalty. Her anguish, and her refusal to go along with his crime, force him to return the loot before the bank opens on Monday morning.

Her role was unusual in two noteworthy aspects: she was a dazzling blonde, and she had one passionate love scene (in a bath towel) and several sequences requiring the full cycle of love-dismay-resentment-dejection. For once, Teresa had a picture that permitted her to convey intense sexuality, which she was rarely allowed onscreen.

The Steel Trap was also unusual for the wide use of locations in Los Angeles and New Orleans—in fact, there was only one studio set. Of her two pictures with Joe Cotten, she praised only the first: "the second one was terrible." This was a harsh judgment, perhaps due to her low spirits during production. *The Steel Trap* is no cinematic masterwork, but it was written and directed by Andrew Stone with a sure command of suspense, without a dull moment from first frame to last.

"All I did in that picture was constantly talk about the money [the Cotten character] was spending. I started off by exclaiming, 'Ten dollars!'

at the cash he hands a taxi-driver. Then we go on to something else, and I say, 'A hundred dollars!' Then the climax of my role was when I discover he stole a million dollars. And all the time in that picture, I had to be worried, and then worried some more. Most unsatisfactory."

ぐゆ

Someone in Hollywood probably saw Teresa reunited with Joe Cotten and at once had the idea to cast her in a thriller with yet another player from *Shadow of a Doubt*: Macdonald Carey, the detective-boyfriend in the Hitchcock picture. After *The Steel Trap*, Don Siegel, in merely nine days, directed them in *Count the Hours*. The movie was impressive more for the acting and atmosphere than for its somewhat disjointed story of a court-appointed lawyer racing the clock to exonerate an innocent man of a murder charge. Teresa had top billing as the wife of the wrongly accused chap, but it made little impression on her or audiences: "We shot it so quickly that I hardly remember it, but I'm told it was an effective little movie"—which for the most part it was, thanks to John Alton's angular, tenebrous photography and Siegel's brisk technique.

ぐゆ

On November 25, the Busch divorce became final. Niven's uncompromising attitude about the ranch, and his infidelities, were apparently the breaking points, but Teresa never mentioned these in her divorce complaint; instead, she claimed that her husband "made her feel useless by refusing me the right to have anything to say in the care and raising of my children and the running of our house." This was true, but it was not at the core of things: her words simply enabled them both to avoid the crush of gossipmongers and the concomitant scandal that Hollywood loved more than it condemned.

The settlement provided that Mary-Kelly would live with her mother and Terry with his father; the precise times for mutual visiting rights were to be arranged by the parents, and this was never a divisive issue between Niven and Teresa. Both parents loved both children, and over the years there were frequent travels to and from one home to the other. Niven, of course, could have had his ranch in Los Angeles County, where he would always have been closer to both children, but his commitment to Hollister precluded that.

"Being older, Niven was used to getting his way," said Mary-Kelly, and I think he was very difficult to negotiate with during those years. Mom explained to me that Dad had been so close to Terry that it would break the boy's heart to take him away from his father. It also broke *her* heart to leave Terry behind in Hollister, but she could not fight for herself—she thought that was too selfish, and finally she agreed that it was best for a boy to be with his father. She also knew that it would be hard for Niven to give up both children in a divorce settlement [an arrangement Teresa could easily have won for herself]. I always saw Mom's action toward Terry as a real sacrifice for his well-being.

But Teresa harbored a profound sense of guilt and loss:

> The main source of my happiness is my children, my friends and their children, and the pleasure I get out of observing or sharing their activities and pleasures, the love and response I give and receive from Mary-Kelly. Though I feel something of the same for my son, it is mostly tinged with regret for having failed him, if not really being a responsible, active mother to him, but having, for the sake of my own freedom, and what I believed to be his good, settled for a relationship of friendly interest but not a real mother's concern, responsibility or dependability. If he's ever sick or lonesome or afraid, he doesn't have me to turn to—so I can't really say I'm a mother to him.

In the years to come, continued Mary-Kelly,

> Terry and I were together for holidays and every summer, but we alternated Christmas and spring school holidays and split the summer with both parents. When Dad came to L.A. to take me to Hollister for a weekend or some longer visit, I remember Mom standing at the doorway to say goodbye. She and Dad were polite, but I knew it was an abnormal and uncomfortable situation, and I sensed that Mom was not as happy to see him as I was. I was *always* happy to see him, and the times I spent with him were always interesting, always lots of fun.

Very diplomatically, and without rancor or the desire to speak negatively of Niven, Teresa explained to both children that she and Niven were strong people, "and it was hard for a marriage to work because each had such different ideas about where to live and how to work."

As Terry recalled,

> Teresa was always very guarded when she spoke about the end of the marriage, and she tried hard not to disparage my Dad, whom I adored. But I could perceive her ongoing disapproval in the set of her mouth or the tone of her voice when speaking of him. For his part, Niven was always very wistful about Teresa, insisting that he loved her very much and wanted to stay married.

Years later, Niven said, "I hated to see the marriage break up. But the ranch thing worked out. I married again. I was happy on the ranch."

For him, it was as uncomplicated as that. Indeed, in his fashion he may have loved her very much and wanted to remain her husband, but other considerations prevailed, and other priorities and people won his allegiance. If he seems to have acted with monumental self-interest, he certainly did so without wishing to inflict any pain. At first, he was offended that his sister and brother-in-law, the Millers, maintained their close friendship with Teresa. But when he saw that they were firm in the matter, he accepted it.

Teresa knew that she ought not to ask for alimony: even with her reduced fees per picture, she was earning much more than Niven, and she very much wanted to support herself and Mary-Kelly. This at least partly explains her acceptance of three movie jobs in 1952—roles she also undertook, as she admitted, to remind producers that she was "still around, still working, still available."

Hedda Hopper maintained a discreet silence about the divorce, but her rival, the columnist and radio personality Louella Parsons, stepped in with a commentary:

> Efforts of their friends to get Teresa Wright and Niven Busch back together seemed doomed to failure. I hear Niven is willing and eager to get his wife and children back and he is carrying a great big torch. If Teresa is too, she is using it to burn her bridges behind her. She has moved into an apartment in Beverly Hills for two reasons. First, she wants to get away from memories of the past and second, the apartment is closer to MGM, where she is making a picture with Spencer Tracy.

After her brief time in the Valley, Teresa rented a house at 245 South Crescent Drive that belonged to Dorothy McGuire and John Swope, who were moving to their new home on Copley Place, Beverly Hills.

The picture Teresa began, just as the divorce decree was issued, was *The Actress*—based on Ruth Gordon's play about her youthful desire for a theatrical career in 1913, when she was seventeen. As Ruth's mother, who supports her daughter's ambition even to the point of confronting her husband (played by Spencer Tracy), Teresa eagerly assumed her first character role, a much older woman, and turned it into a comic and compassionate performance with uncommon skill.

At first, the MGM makeup department attempted to age her with the usual additions of lines and dark circles, which only made her look like a young woman with lines and dark circles. Teresa then told director George Cukor that she wanted to do a test with no makeup at all, just a dull matte finish, so that matronly pallor would pass for middle age. It worked brilliantly. But according to the contemporary notions of what constituted a wise career move, some colleagues (and her agent) thought it was supreme folly for Teresa to appear in such a role. She proved them wrong when the laudatory reviews were published.

The role of Annie Jones must be included among Teresa's finest achievements. She used not only the full range of a perfect Boston accent: she also knew, by a splendid instinct, that acting also meant a judicious use of her hands—and this she did with unalloyed accuracy and subtlety in each scene. Her gestures alternately invite or suppress a response, and in her many scenes with Spencer Tracy, she was never merely submissive, much less was she outranked by him. This was a performance worthy of awards, or at least nominations, but she received none—perhaps because she did not seem to act the role as much as inhabit it.

Her achievement was beyond mere imitative realism; like Tracy, she never had a false moment and they were so thoroughly involved in their roles that Cukor ordered several ten-minute takes. That might have been disastrous with less capable artists, but in this case they maintained an ideal rhythm and tone perfectly attuned to the alternately amusing and poignant dialogue.

The title character was played by Jean Simmons, who was twenty-three that season—only a bit more than ten years younger that Teresa. The two began a lifelong friendship that included a repetition of their on-screen mother-daughter roles years later. In this case, Jean was charming but Teresa was at the emotional center of the story. (*The Actress* also marked the movie debut of twenty-year-old Anthony Perkins.)

"Only one film was really interesting for me in the 1950s," Teresa said later, "and that was the dramatization of Ruth Gordon's play—and that was fun. It was my first real character role, a New England, small-town mother. I think it was an awfully good picture—one of those good films that MGM has a tendency to just throw out on the market because it's so good they don't know what to do with it. They really don't understand good pictures."

A congratulatory message was delivered to Teresa after a press preview:

"I saw The Actress last night and thought you gave a swell performance. You're better than ever, dear Teresa. Keep up the good work. With all best wishes for a Merry Christmas.—Sincerely, Sam Goldwyn."

Greatly touched by his gesture, she replied:

"Dear Sam, A word of praise from you is music to my ears. Thank you for your letter—and a very Merry Christmas. Most gratefully, Teresa."

From that Christmastime, the hostilities of 1948 faded into oblivion; henceforth, Mr. Goldwyn and Miss Wright had only good and true things to say about each other.

✎

CHAPTER NINE

1953–1957

AS SO OFTEN HAPPENS TO MOVIE STARS, TERESA WAS FREQUENTLY approached in America by strangers who were admirers or fans (the custom of waylaying a celebrity is far less frequent elsewhere): this usually happened when she was shopping or dining at a restaurant. "I remember that when we went out together, strangers often came up to gush over Mom," recalled Mary-Kelly. "She was always very pleasant, but later she said to me, 'People feel as if they know me, and this happens because my work keeps me in the public eye. But my work is no better or more important than anyone else's.' That was something Mom always repeated."

In February 1953, Teresa was in Phoenix, Arizona, rehearsing the leading role in John van Druten's comedy *Bell, Book and Candle* at the Sombrero Playhouse. Founded in 1949, this was a popular dinner-theatre venue for touring companies featuring prominent actors; it was also the major performing arts center between Dallas and Los Angeles.[1] Teresa had the leading role of Gillian Holroyd, the fey, free-spirited and barefoot witch with romantic fantasies as strong as her talents for magic. Her subtle and whimsical comic antics were so successful that the management tried to extend the sold-out one-week run of the play, but that was impossible as another production was scheduled.

Back in Los Angeles, she was grateful not to be part of the glamour set, always out and about to see and be seen. "My life has very little

---

1. Among the many performers in various plays at the Sombrero were Tallulah Bankhead, Ginger Rogers, Gloria Swanson, Shelley Winters, Walter Pidgeon and Groucho Marx.

connection to Hollywood," she said. "Socially it has a little bit, I suppose, but not much. I don't belong to a party-giving set, and I don't go to those things you often read about. Once in a while, I find myself at some big event, but it has no more effect on my life than if I lived in New York and had to go to the opening of a play or to a party where there are lots of other actors."

As for her friends: "Most of them are in the industry, but I have some who are not—like the writers I appreciate. Personally, I don't think that life in Hollywood touches you unless you're caught up with yourself and put your career first in your social life."

Teresa traveled several times to New York to appear in live television plays: there were five in 1953 and 1954, two of them produced by Martin Manulis, who had become an executive at CBS.

In the autumn of 1953, Teresa and her friend Betty Smith went to Italy, a holiday scheduled to include a visit with Dorothy McGuire, who was working in Rome on the film *Three Coins in the Fountain*. This trip marked Teresa's first true vacation since her honeymoon, and decades later she could recall her childlike excitement at everything: the charm of the Hotel de Ville, at the top of the Spanish steps; the usual tourist locations; the cafés in the squares, where they sipped drinks or coffee; and the shops, where they bought baubles and knickknacks for family and friends.

Martin Manulis wanted to employ Teresa's talents whenever he could and finally succeeded when he signed her to appear in two episodes of the popular *Climax!* television series. The first was "The Long Goodbye," produced by Bretaigne Windust, the director of *Life With Father*. "It was great fun," she recalled. "Windy always had a lot of faith in me professionally, and he wanted to see me do something different. This was a Raymond Chandler episode, and it was kooky but interesting. Windy had wonderful energy, and brought great excitement to the piece—that was his gift to us."

This live teleplay was infamous for a scene in which the actor Tristram Coffin, whose character had just died, wrongly believed that he was out of viewing range. With that, he rose, brushed himself off and walked briskly away, in full view of the television cameras and a nationwide audience. Such were the risks in the days of live television broadcasts.

⁓

"Live television got me back to the theatre," Teresa said years later. "When you've done enough live TV, you build up a certain professional feeling of being able to cope with any acting job. In my case, there were also very practical reasons. In the 1950s, I wasn't married and really needed to go out and work." And work she did, almost constantly.

Soon after they collaborated on "The Long Goodbye," Windust directed Teresa onstage in *The Heiress*, by Ruth and Augustus Goetz (based on the Henry James novella *Washington Square*). Catherine Sloper was a perfect role for her, but one, alas, that she never performed again. The character of the doctor's daughter, who moves from awkward shyness to bitter recrimination, is one of the theatre's great parts for women and was successfully undertaken by Peggy Ashcroft, Wendy Hiller and Margaret Phillips onstage, among others; Olivia de Havilland won her second Academy Award for the film version.

The Heiress was offered in an unfortunately rushed production at a tent theatre in Palm Springs. "I found it a terrific strain to do that with only five or six days of rehearsal," Teresa recalled. "Then it was opening night, and I thought, oh good—now I can spend the next six days [of the scheduled run] developing this role. I went into the dressing room for a change of costume, and there was another actor, learning lines for the next week's show. I was sure glad I didn't have to work that way in the theatre. I don't think it's good for anyone, and it's certainly not good for the play."

Things were far smoother after another television drama, and then she returned triumphantly to the La Jolla Playhouse in *The Rainmaker*, by N. Richard Nash. The sole female in a cast of seven, Teresa enlivened the role of Lizzie, a shy spinster unexpectedly redeemed by her love for a huckster. The play ran for two weeks, with standing room only; it was theatre at its best, she said later. It was also Teresa at hers, in a performance delicately counterpoising wistful yearning with a streak of self-preserving wit. These were, after all, among her own personality traits, and she instinctively understood every light and level of Lizzie's surprising soul.

∽

From 1953 through 1955, she was as active as she had been from 1939 through 1942. In Los Angeles between theatre, film and TV engagements, Teresa and Mary-Kelly moved again, this time to a snug house with great rustic charm. Located at 42 Haldeman Road, Santa Monica, it was close to the Pacific and, appropriately, in a neighborhood known as Rustic Canyon. She purchased it from Frances Pilchard at the time of her (second) divorce from Mel Ferrer.

The tasks of installing draperies and arranging furniture were interrupted when Teresa accepted an important role—the title character in a stage production of *The Country Girl*, by Clifford Odets. Uta Hagen and Paul Kelly had been the stars on Broadway in 1950, and the film version was in progress, with William Holden, Bing Crosby and Grace Kelly (who won her Oscar for it). In early April, when Teresa went to perform at the Avon Theatre, Vancouver, she anticipated the release of the picture and won extraordinary local reviews.[2]

By mid-April she was back home and at once began work at Warner Bros. in Burbank for her few scenes in a picture called *Track of the Cat*, produced by John Wayne and presented in widescreen and color, which did not help the production at all.

"It was not a good experience for me. I played a bitter old spinster with three brothers, a horrifying mother, an alcoholic father—and somewhere outside in the California wilderness, a panther just aching to get at the livestock and the family. I wish it had." The worst aspect of the movie, she added, was that "it didn't seem to make much sense. There was a dysfunctional family and a menace that was never shown [the panther], and a lot of it seemed like a poor version of a lost play by O'Neill or Strindberg. I don't think Bob [Mitchum, her co-star] knew what was going on, either." The movie was demolished by one fatal flaw: it was all talk and no action—and unfortunately the talk was achingly dull.

Teresa's character was incomprehensible, angry one moment and loyal and loving the next. When the movie came up in conversation twenty-five years later, she uttered her usual line about a picture she disdained: "Just forget about it."

Years later, *Track of the Cat* developed a strange cult following, a frequent occurrence with bad pictures rejected by both critics and audiences. Not even the director, William Wellman, understood the high-toned nonsense that was published about it years later.

For two months during 1954, there was an important interlude in her life, with a prospect but not the realization of a passionate emotional commitment. The circumstances of their meeting are impossible to

---

2. Many sources wrongly state that Teresa performed the role of Georgie Elgin in *The Country Girl* at the La Jolla Playhouse in August 1951. That possibility was discussed but it never materialized. The 1954 Vancouver production, from April 2 to 10, was her only appearance in this play.

establish—perhaps they were introduced at a party or through mutual friends; in any case, Teresa came to know a famous and popular actor.

Sterling Hayden was a handsome man, six-feet-five and, it seemed, always in demand as a star or co-star in Hollywood. Between 1952 and 1954, he appeared in no fewer than sixteen pictures, none of which he liked very much. He preferred to sail in his boats with his family or friends. On land and at sea, he worked on a book, eventually published, about his wartime experience as an undercover agent for what later became the CIA. For valorous deeds in dangerous missions abroad, he received several awards from the United States government.

Hayden was one of the tallest men in movies, often cast in Westerns or (as they were later called) *films noirs*, like John Huston's *The Asphalt Jungle*, or in offbeat romances, such as *The Star*, opposite Bette Davis. Taciturn and composed even in his violent roles, Hayden led a private life that was alarmingly unstable and often tempestuous. After a divorce from the English actress Madeleine Carroll, he married a comely blonde named Betty Ann de Noon, who gave him four children. He then divorced her, remarried her, then divorced her again and remarried her yet a third time, which led to a third divorce. The Hollywood press could not keep up.

When he met Teresa in 1954, Sterling Hayden had just been divorced from Betty Ann for the first time. He was two years older than Teresa, and he and his children frequently came to her home during that summer. He may have had all the characteristics of a love-struck suitor; on her side, she liked being with him socially and was fascinated by his tales of adventure, his travels and his espionage exploits. Even more, she admired his devotion to his four children. Her written account of their friendship, confided in a long letter four years later to the man who would be her second husband, tells of this time:

> I'm very proud of having known him. I saw a great deal of him for two happy months four summers ago. It was a happy time of lots of talk and watching our kids play together and swim together and doing things with them. Sterling is the greatest parent I have ever met and it was wonderful watching him with his own or anyone else's children. In that time, I learned to love him and do still, and perhaps will always love him in a way I doubt that someone other than myself could understand . . . It was so long ago, and so few people even knew we knew each other. Since Sterling is usually thought of, or at least used to be thought of, as just a beautiful

hunk of man (by me, too, before I met him), you may disbelieve this, but it was Sterling's mind that I loved—that wonderful, probing, questioning, seeking, tortured mind—always searching for the truth about everything he came in contact with . . .

After not seeing him for over two years, I went out to dinner with him [in February 1957] and then he asked me out again. I drove to his house to tell him about you and how much I loved you, and he said, "That's wonderful. If you haven't got that, you haven't got anything" . . . I understood [that he meant] "If you are unable to love and be loved, you haven't got anything." And he was right.

The brief relationship was tangled, with an admixture of conflicting emotions on both sides. Teresa was wary of Sterling. For one thing, his instability in relationships was all too obvious in his divorce that was about to be a remarriage. Intelligent, highly literate and generous, he nevertheless seemed to her more like an overgrown boy than a mature man. She felt that Sterling was too confused to understand his own emotions—"confused and deeply troubled"—and she later said that no words of endearment were ever exchanged.

When he subsequently invited her for dinner in 1957, she wrote, "I'm not quite sure why I accepted,

except that I'd enjoyed seeing and talking to him, and because of a certain stubbornness in me that hates to let go of a belief that caring about a person should be able to rise above pride or romantic failure. He never loved me, never said he did, in fact he said he had never loved anyone. That statement killed me and evokes my deepest sympathy now more than ever.

In the same letter, she reflected on the meaning of love for herself:

I was pleased about that evening, because I thought it proved that I was over being in love with him and had succeeded in having him for a friend. Then, when I heard no more from him, I knew I could still be hurt by the thought that he didn't like me enough to be a friend . . . I don't think I can ever stop loving someone just because they don't love me, and I had to get over being in love with them.

Do I seem to speak glibly of "being in love" and "getting over" being in love? Believe me it was not glib—it was accomplished both times [with Niven and with Sterling] with much pain. It's the kind of thing that can't happen to you when you are safely sheltered in a love that truly exists and is shared by you and someone you love. Which brings me to—what is being in love with someone? What does it really mean for me?

. . . To me, it's loving someone in a very special way. It's sharing and wanting to share a relationship with them that is different from your relationship with anyone else . . . We can love many things and many people in different ways and to different degrees. I can love my children, my family and friends. I can be interested in their ideas and thoughts and plans, enjoy discussing things with them, sharing some of my thoughts and plans with them. I can get great pleasure out of giving them my time, my interest, my sympathy or help if it's needed—in short, my love if and when they need it: the door is open. Catholics speak of a state of grace, and I can think of no better state of grace than being open, known, and accountable to and depended on by someone you love and is known to you.

Even later, Teresa denied that she and Sterling Hayden were ever lovers: "Many people think I had an affair with Sterling, but I never did." She had no reason to prevaricate.

✍

She continued to accumulate television credits each season—"Miracle on 34th Street," with Macdonald Carey (her co-star in *Shadow of a Doubt*); "Once to Every Woman," a romance about a spinster schoolteacher who falls in love with a married man; and perhaps most memorably, her role as a homely country girl in "The Enchanted Cottage," which she had been unable to perform a decade earlier, and which Dorothy McGuire had rendered in the 1945 feature film with poignant delicacy. The producers of this show had only one problem with Teresa: it was all but impossible to make her look plain, much less unattractive, as required by several sequences in the story.

In "No. 5 Checked Out," Teresa had the role of a young deaf woman unaware that the man she is drawn to is a crook on the run. This was an ultimately tragic story (written and directed by Ida Lupino), played by Teresa with affecting vulnerability.

Her brightly comic turn in "The Good Sister" was very different. As an American nun in charge of a German orphanage, Teresa portrayed an unorthodox sister who has a keen talent for romantic matchmaking among the local gentry. At the time, many viewers may have been surprised—or even shocked—to see that a devout lady was so in touch with ordinary life, and that she smiled readily at the happiness of young lovers. Teresa would, of course, never have played it for arch piety.

She had another rewarding comic television role in "Her Crowning Glory," a caper about a young woman who is told that she cannot be hired for a good job unless she wears a hat. The story follows her attempts to purchase the right one, which is accidentally crushed; another is lost and forgotten. Because Teresa acted with deadpan humor, as if wearing a hat was not only absurd but also farcical, the episode struck a gentle blow for a professional woman's independence.

When she was invited to portray the title character in "The Louella Parsons Story," she was at first hesitant. Because the powerful Hollywood columnist was still alive and working (and had more than 20 million readers worldwide), there were all kinds of red flags raised about the production. But the sparkling script by Whitfield Cook was reworked to lessen any critical comment about Louella; and director John Frankenheimer worked with Teresa to find a tone that was neither offensive nor reverential. "Her performance fairly dripped with lilac-scented venom," wrote television critic Jack Gould, and the show proved once again that Teresa's range of characters was never to be underestimated. Louella, who was known to appreciate strong drink, made no objections.

Prodigiously energetic, she completed major roles in three feature films and seven television dramas in 1956. The first picture, *The Search for Bridey Murphy*, was based on the best-selling book claiming to be the true story of an American housewife who, under hypnosis, tells the story of her past life as a nineteenth-century Irish girl. Produced hurriedly in late spring, the movie was like a docudrama: for most of the running time, Teresa had to lie on a sofa with her eyes closed, speaking long monologues in an Irish brogue. She was impressive in every sequence, but by its deferential adherence to the original monologues in the book, the final result was static and flat. She was glad to have an end of it.

That summer, she went into the production of *The Restless Years*, based on a fine play by Patricia Joudry. Teresa had the role of a woman who, abandoned in her youth by a boyfriend, then gave birth to a daughter out of wedlock. The child grows up to be a pretty, nubile young thing (played by Sandra Dee), overprotected by her mother, who has tipped over into a kind of sexual hysteria and fears that the girl is living a fast life. All but forgotten decades later, the movie gave Teresa an opportunity to break the general typecasting to which she was so often subjected: her performance is laced with nervous twitching and anxious, almost breathless patter. The film was completed in September, but for some mysterious reason Universal held it back for over two years.

From this story set in small-town America, Teresa went immediately to Tokyo. Winston Miller had written a story and screenplay called *Escapade in Japan*, and she was delighted to accept a role in it. She joined him and Bea for an Asian adventure and the making of a picture for which she always kept a special fondness.

The plot alone highlights Winston Miller's unique achievement. Teresa and Cameron Mitchell portrayed a couple attempting to heal their marriage (wounded by his infidelity) by taking a holiday in Japan. Their young son is on his way from America to join them, but his plane goes down in the ocean. Rescued by a fishing boat, the boy is taken in by a caring Japanese family whose son becomes his friend. The two boys run away for an adventure, and the film becomes a tour of Japan and a showcase for Japanese culture: the boys visit the Kiyomizu Temple, eat local food and attend a Kabuki performance.

Until the final sequence, Teresa had little to do but look anxious. But, as she said, "This was a very sweet picture, and people always seem to enjoy it." Smartly written and stylishly directed, *Escapade in Japan* was an unusual example of what is sometimes called a family movie. It was also a clear plea for international understanding and respect at a time when there was still considerable anti-Japanese sentiment in postwar America. This was Teresa's last appearance in a motion picture for thirteen years.

∽

She returned from Japan in time for Christmas. Refreshed and excited, she had stories about a culture she had come to admire, and she brought home some Japanese artwork.

Immediately after the holidays, she began rehearsals with director Arthur Penn for the television production of William Gibson's *The Miracle Worker*. This was an installment of the popular *Playhouse 90* series, under the aegis of Martin Manulis. Broadcast on February 2, 1957, this was first-rate drama brilliantly performed.

Teresa received an Emmy nomination for her performance in the challenging role of Annie Sullivan, the strong and inventive teacher of young Helen Keller, played by eleven-year-old Patty McCormack; Katie

Bard had the role of Helen's mother. Few television dramas won such undiluted praise, and the success of the broadcast made it possible for Gibson to revise his play for Broadway and then for a feature film (but with other actors).

∽

On the afternoon of Sunday, March 3, 1957, Teresa arrived, late and harried, at Katie and Martin's home, high up a winding road in the section of Los Angeles known as Bel-Air, between Beverly Hills and Brentwood. The occasion was the christening of their infant son, John Bard Manulis, and Teresa had been asked to stand as godmother in place of another woman who had died a few months earlier. After apologies and embraces, Teresa took her place beside the appointed godfather, a respected playwright and screenwriter.

Robert Anderson was born in New York on April 28, 1917—a year and a half before Teresa. His father, James Anderson, had successfully moved up from near-poverty to considerable commercial success as a businessman and later as an executive with an insurance company. His work ethic led him to revere the American virtues of ambitious self-reliance, constant competitiveness and stern, virile courage.

James married a New Jersey woman named Myra Grigg. Their first child, Donald, was born in 1913 and became a celebrated physician and educator. The second son arrived four years later and was christened Robert Woodruff Anderson, the second name honoring his maternal grandmother.

When the boys were still young, James moved his family from New York City to a spacious home on Elm Street in suburban New Rochelle. There, Donald excelled in sports, while Robert learned from his mother the value of intellectual pursuits. Myra, who held a master's degree in humanities, had worked with several authors as the editor of their academic dissertations. She introduced Bob to the theatre, world literature and the fine arts. From the start, James Anderson favored Don for his muscular athleticism; Myra, however, thought that the more sensitive Bob "was the sun, moon and stars."

Bob followed his older brother to the cloistered world of Phillips Exeter Academy in New Hampshire, a private secondary school that had catered to the sons of the wealthy since the eighteenth century. But James did not pay the hefty tuition for his second son: "I worked my way through Exeter as a janitor and waited on tables," Bob recalled. "And I was a proctor in the dorm, so I got my room free."

Bob followed his brother again—to Harvard University and graduated *magna cum laude* in 1939 with a degree in English. Donald suggested to their father that he might give Bob some gift to honor his admirable academic achievement, but James Anderson replied that Bob had only done what was expected of him, and that was that. This was but one example of how Robert suffered trying to please his implacable father.

While at Harvard, Bob wrote and acted in school plays. He also volunteered to join the casts in the drama club at the Erskine School in downtown Boston, an academy for girls that needed young men for their productions.

The plays at Erskine were directed by a slender, bright and energetic lady named Phyllis Stohl; she was ten years older than Bob, who at the time hoped for a career as an actor and singer. Born in 1907 in Utah, Phyllis read his prolific output of skits and short plays and persuaded him that his true vocation was as a playwright. Then completing his master's degree in literature at Harvard, Bob duly altered his focus. He also fell passionately in love with his mentor, and on June 24, 1940, Robert Anderson married Phyllis Stohl.

They continued to work together in and on plays while Bob subsequently enrolled in Harvard's doctoral program. He had completed all but the dissertation for his Ph.D. when he went to war in 1942. Phyllis continued to work at Erskine during his absence; she also had considerable success as a radio scriptwriter and director and later as a theatrical agent.

While serving in the South Pacific as a communications officer aboard battleships, Bob wrote several plays. One of them, *Come Marching Home*, won the National Theater Conference Prize, an award given for the best dramatic work by a man in the service; after the war, it had a brief run in New York. The prize, along with a scholarship, enabled him to study playwriting when he returned home to Phyllis.

The marriage continued, but with some bartering about priorities and schedules. Phyllis knew that Bob would be a good man to live with, to help as a young writer and to guide as a somewhat insecure but amorous lover. While he worked on plays in the late 1940s, Phyllis maintained her long hours at the school office, and he was often anxious and upset if she was late for dinner. "I tried to make her my whole life, and me, hers," he wrote later. "I had very little life aside from her, and therefore resented overmuch any slight inattention on her part. I had no real men friends and so would wait for Phyllis and mope if she couldn't see me."

Her absences were frequent. Many times, he answered the telephone to hear his wife's voice: "Bob, I'm going out with the kids [i.e., the drama students]. Don't wait for me." Alternatively, she often unexpectedly brought a crowd of young people back to their apartment for an impromptu supper. This made for some domestic tension, for which Phyllis had a ready reply: "Well, Bob, if I'm too busy, you'll just have to have an affair."

That statement came as a terrific shock to him, and only later did he realize that it was her way of sometimes pushing him away: he could be just too much for a woman long accustomed to independence at work and at home. As for Bob, he tried not to sulk like a schoolboy and went, bruised but determined, back to work.

Early in their marriage, Bob and Phyllis sat down and composed a list of goals for themselves and their marriage. Not only did they aspire to work intensely in their craft and to achieve success. They also wanted the lifestyle that attended that success: together, they were climbing the ladder to the top. Everything was subservient to work, and Bob—rather melodramatically—was convinced that his dedication would lead to his martyrdom for art's sake, and that he would be dead by the age of fifty.

By 1950, the Andersons had moved to a garden apartment at 14 West Eleventh Street, Manhattan, where Bob worked on a play he called *Tea and Sympathy*. Phyllis, meanwhile, had become one of the theatre's most respected agents, much in demand for her literary judgments, her editing and her formidable negotiating skills. *Come Back, Little Sheba*, the prize-winning play by William Inge, was co-produced by Phyllis (with the Theatre Guild, whose play department she headed); Inge dedicated the published text to her.

In the absence of steady income, Bob found continual employment as a radio and television writer while he worked on *Tea and Sympathy*. He contributed scripts for dozens of radio plays and for television dramas— several of them produced by Martin Manulis. He also wrote sketches for a musical revue called *Dance Me a Song* and two plays: *Love Revisited* was briefly staged at the Westport Country Playhouse during the tenure of Manulis as artistic director; and *The Eden Rose* was performed for three nights at the Theatre Workshop of Ridgefield, Connecticut. Both works seem to have vanished. By then, perhaps only Phyllis believed that a major success was on the horizon.

◊

"Every play I've ever written is me," Bob said years later. "And no play is as autobiographical as *Tea and Sympathy*," which opened on Broadway in September 1953 and ran for almost two years. "Like the character of Tom, I had problems with my father. I had also been very lonely at school, and I fell in love with an older woman." In the dedication of the published play, he wrote: "To Phyllis, whose spirit is everywhere in this play and in my life."

Bob was also fortunate that Elia Kazan, regarded as one of the great theatre and film directors, had agreed to stage *Tea and Sympathy*. But during the casting process in 1953, Kazan was in Hollywood, selecting actors and preparing to direct *On the Waterfront*. He asked his friend and colleague Karl Malden to supervise the casting in New York; Karl had already worked several times with Kazan in plays and movies and had earned an Academy Award for his supporting role in the film of *A Streetcar Named Desire*, which he had also played onstage.

Karl's part in supervising auditions and recommending the final list of players to Kazan and Anderson was a major factor in the play's ultimate success and was gratefully acknowledged in the playbill and the published text. "Casting the play seemed easy at the time," Karl said years later. "Along came Deborah Kerr and John Kerr and Leif Erickson and John McGovern—well, all you have to do is say, 'Thank you very much' and call their agents." The circumstances were not that simple, but Karl's unpretentiousness always minimized his many varied achievements on stage and screen. When his task in New York was completed, Karl departed for Hollywood and his historic role in *On the Waterfront*.

After it opened on Broadway, *Tea and Sympathy* became an enormous hit, thanks not only to Bob's allusive and empathetic writing but also to Kazan's direction and the performances by Deborah Kerr and John Kerr (who were unrelated and pronounced their surnames differently). From that time, Robert Anderson was considered an important new American playwright—and soon a screenwriter, as offers from Hollywood came tumbling into the office of his agent, Audrey Wood. While *Tea and Sympathy* was running, Bob had another work on Broadway—*All Summer Long*; at his suggestion, John Kerr left *Tea and Sympathy* to accept a role in it, but even his talent could not save the play from an early closing.

Just as Bob had publicly acknowledged his debt to Phyllis when *Tea and Sympathy* was presented and published, there was in fact another woman whose spirit was everywhere in his life in 1953—Deborah Kerr. Known for her beauty, poise and elegance, she was not only a sensitive, skilled actress: she was also remarkable for kindness and empathy in her private life, and she was very attentive to Bob.

"That period," he wrote later in a typed journal, "was a chaos of emotions." The cause of the chaos was the illness of Phyllis. Just when the success of *Tea and Sympathy* pitched Bob into the throes of fame and fortune, there came sobering, sad news. Phyllis had felt increasingly unwell, and finally the doctors diagnosed cancer. Thus began her inexorable decline.

When Deborah left the play to fulfill a Hollywood contract, she told Bob that she was going to attempt a reconciliation with her husband, Anthony Bartley, with whom she had a strained, distant marriage. Bob begged her to remain in New York, to provide emotional support for him during the trauma of his wife's increasing suffering. "But," she said, "I would ruin your marriage." Once she arrived in Hollywood, Bob recalled, there were unceasing "tears, letters [and] phone calls." Their intimacy was to continue sporadically for several years—an intimacy Bob detailed in his diary and in conversations over many years.

After a long struggle, Phyllis Stohl Anderson died at the age of forty-nine in New York, on November 28, 1956. But in a disturbing sense, she never died—not merely because she was liked and admired by many in the theatre world, nor because Bob kept her memory alive with a scholarship for young playwrights. Something else happened. He was not only a grief-stricken widower at the age of thirty-nine: he also became obsessed with Phyllis and was never able to come to terms with her death. As long as he lived, she was the unseen presence and the ultimate influence in every place and every room of his life: neither a day nor a deed excluded a discussion of Phyllis in his conversations with friends, reporters, writers, students and audiences. No one who knew Bob was unaware of Phyllis.

Those who loved him—and they were many, and for good reasons—knew to expect the frequent reiteration of her name: "Phyllis, my wife . . . As Phyllis, my first wife, said . . . Phyllis used to say . . . When Phyllis and I . . ." At first, this was taken as a natural consequence of loss and heartache. But with the passage of time, it became a disturbing trait, dreary to some, alarming to others, offensive to those close to him. "As he internalized his father's extreme expectations," reflected Mary-Kelly Busch, "Bob tried to be the best person he could be, and part of this meant talking about Phyllis to keep her memory alive. As he often said, he felt guilty for his inability to save her"—but along with this unfortunate misplacement of good sense, Bob somehow remained (thus Mary-Kelly) "a truly good, wise, kind and loving person."

Friends rallied to Bob in the immediate aftermath of Phyllis's death—none more persuasively than Ingrid Bergman, who was about to perform in *Tea and Sympathy* in the Paris production. "I think you belong over here," she told Bob in a phone call. "It's Christmas, and the play will supply you with a purpose and a family." Earlier, they had met briefly in New York to discuss the play, and Bob felt comfortable with Ingrid, who now booked a room for him at the Hotel Raphael, where she lived during the run of the play. On December 10—twelve days after his wife's death—Bob arrived in Paris. He and Ingrid consoled each other, for her marriage to Roberto Rossellini was effectively over, and Bob seemed a lost soul.

Within days, they were ardent lovers. "One critic liked Ingrid more than the play," Bob recalled, "and he wrote, 'Ingrid Bergman saves the play.'"

"She really dedicated her time to me," Bob said forty years later, "and she never made plans until she knew I was taken care of." According to Ingrid: "He was very close to me in those days. Maybe I was in need, too. I knew it was important perhaps to both of us." But she saw that Bob's need was too deep, his attachment to Phyllis too conflicting, his life too confused: "I realized very quickly that he was a man who couldn't cope any longer with anything, and I did all I could to help him survive." She, too, was in a dark time: her marriage had collapsed, her children required support and attention, and she had to continue working.

Before Bob returned to New York, he went to Cartier's, where he bought a silver plate for Ingrid, and on it he ordered the engraving: "Ingrid Bergman saves a play—and a playwright." Her gift to him was a scarf she knitted during his time in Paris; this he kept and wore each winter, proudly extolling its origin to anyone who would listen.

In January, Bob returned to New York. Four days later, Ingrid (for whom the Paris producer temporarily suspended performances of *Tea and Sympathy*) arrived in New York to accept a major award for her role in the film *Anastasia*. During the few days of her visit, she was shuttled from ceremonies to interviews to celebratory dinners—always in the company of studio chaperones—and so she had but a few moments to meet with Bob casually, in the presence of others.

In a letter Ingrid wrote to Bob on her return flight to Paris, she explained her feelings, why she urged him to move on with his life and why she felt that a certain realism—no matter how harsh it might sound—ought to determine the course of their lives:

Dear Bob,

The plane has just taken off. I cried. I turned my face [toward] the window so no one would see it. I am so tired, Bob . . . [and] I have so much to be grateful for . . . You asked me so many times when you could return to me in Paris, and I said, "Wait." It is not that I don't want you to. I want you to get hold of yourself, alone. I can't help you. Right now, you must fight it out alone. To be in Paris again would just be to hide away with one person. But you know it would only be worse for you afterwards. There will always come the time when you have to face the loneliness. I'll be thinking of you tomorrow as the curtain goes up and I count the house. Goodnight—Ingrid.

So ended an intense but brief intimacy—but not their friendship, which endured until Ingrid's death in 1982.

After her departure, and all during January and February 1957, Bob was occupied with the details following Phyllis's death—"endless stuff on probating a will," as he wrote to his brother on January 23, "and appraising clothes and jewels. And I still cannot allow myself time to think. If I am alone too long, all the images of the last nine months gather round, and I begin to go over them with anguish and remorse—little pointless things, like why didn't I spend the last night at the hospital . . . I wish I had made her happier for the twenty years [sic] I was with her."

Some distraction from grief came when Bob traveled to Los Angeles for meetings with director Robert Wise, who was preparing to film *Until They Sail*, for which Bob had written the screenplay. His work coincided with the christening of the Manulis baby, whose godparents were to have been both Bob and Phyllis. Katie and Martin therefore invited Teresa to stand as replacement godmother.

Bob was staying at the Beverly Hills Hotel, and he invited Teresa to an early supper two days later, on Tuesday, March 5. Later that evening, they went to an advance screening of Robert Wise's latest picture, *This Could Be the Night*. The stars of that movie were there—among them, Teresa's friends Jean Simmons, with her husband, Stewart Granger, and Tom Helmore, with his wife, Mary Drayton. On Thursday, March 7—"that first wonderful Thursday," as Teresa later wrote to Bob—she prepared dinner for them at Haldeman Road, but it was (as Bob wrote in his diary) "a dinner we never ate." He did not leave the house until the small hours.

They met on several more occasions—but not every day, nor every evening. Teresa perhaps believed that Bob was busy working with Wise, or at the studio. Whatever her thoughts and his explanations may have been, Teresa apparently did not know that Bob had other female companions in Hollywood that month. "I hope that no matter what happens in the future," he wrote to her that month, "we will not look back on this time with anything but happiness and a sense of wonder."

CHAPTER TEN

1957–1959

AT THIRTY-NINE, ROBERT ANDERSON WAS SIX FEET TALL, LEAN, AGILE and an avid tennis player. Courtly and handsome, he sometimes seemed like a university professor with his horn-rimmed eyeglasses and authoritative manner. There was something melancholy and tentative in his nature, but he was a welcome presence at any social gathering. He had a fund of anecdotes about his early years, his first marriage and his success on Broadway; about the movie version of *Tea and Sympathy*, which greatly disappointed him; and about the several stage and screen projects completed or in process. He was also, like Niven Busch, something of a chauvinist: he adored women but rarely accepted them as intellectual equals. Still, they found him fascinating.

For one thing, Bob was an attentive listener and obviously well educated. He quickly and sincerely recognized people's emotional backgrounds and temperaments; he empathized with their struggles; he condoled and encouraged them in their sorrows. He was also generous with his time and resources, and in later years he became a valuable teacher and mentor to apprentice writers. Often at his own inconvenience, he supported an event or sprang to a need in a friend's life. I was very often the recipient of his kindness and his wholehearted endorsement of my career, and I was but one of many to be offered the long arm of his friendship—in my case, for thirty-five years.

Bob Anderson was highly literate and talented; more important, he was a good and decent man who never hurt anyone—at least not intentionally. He was frank about himself and did not have to be asked to discuss his sexual exploits, often to the point of providing too much information. He was a jumble of unsorted feelings, and although he understood the dark corners in other lives and enabled people to laugh at their faults, he was for the most part imperceptive about himself and slow to mock his own foibles.

Despite all that, he evoked the love and loyalty of an intimate circle over his long lifetime. And not incidentally, he was unfailingly courteous, the living embodiment of the ideal of the respectable, socially presentable gentleman.

Just days after the passionate rapport with Teresa began, Bob met and charmed young Mary-Kelly, who thought that he was "terrifically nice not only to Mom but also to me. He didn't condescend to me, and he was sincerely interested in my school activities, my interests and my friends. He seemed to know just how to make a nine-year-old feel special."

Whatever professional duties Bob had to dispatch during March 1957, he found ample time for romance, or at least for its facsimile; in fact, he was a busy bee, buzzing from one pretty flower to another.

Before he arrived in Los Angeles on February 18, Bob had arranged a date with Deborah Kerr, who was working with Cary Grant on the film *An Affair to Remember*; as he noted in his diary, Bob was pining for her—and her husband was now in London. But after one or two assignations, Deborah gently but astutely dismissed Bob: "You don't want contentment," she told him. "You thrive on discontent."

At the same time, he also cleared some hours for Jean Simmons during the production of *Until They Sail*, in which she co-starred. They met several times in February and March for a day at the beach, a dinner to mark the first day of filming and for dinners *à deux* at her home. Jean's husband had fortuitously departed to work on a film in Rome, and Bob stepped into the breach.

If these multiple pursuits—like his involvement with Ingrid just days after Phyllis's death—were an effort to channel his passion away from grief, the strategy was markedly unsuccessful. This was a period of his life, and others were to come, about which Bob confided to his brother, "It's pleasant to be free, but promiscuity becomes rather tiresome and you feel a loss of dignity after a while."

∽

Bob learned from Teresa that Niven Busch had remarried. His fourth wife was Carmencita Baker, a young woman from an old, established San Francisco family. She was very good to Mary-Kelly and Terry; she never tried to replace Teresa as their mother; she loved them; and her generosity and good spirit elicited their love in return. Mary-Kelly gained another new friend in Mila Malden, the elder daughter of Karl and Mona; Mila was exactly Mary-Kelly's age and had a younger sister named Carla.

"I remember the house in Rustic Canyon," Mila recalled. "There was a huge avocado tree in the front, the inside was very warm and welcoming—and the living room was crammed with books and magazines." Mila and Mary-Kelly, lifelong friends from that time, spent much of every summer together for five years, with Mary-Kelly alternating time with her mother and time with Niven and Carmencita in Hollister. Topo Swope, the daughter of Dorothy McGuire and John Swope, was also a good friend during Mary-Kelly's childhood.

As for Terry: "He is in great form," Teresa wrote to Bob on April 13 during her son's visit to Los Angeles. "Mary-Kelly is ecstatic over his being here, though he is already off with his buddies. Kit Helmore, Tom and Mary's daughter, and Topo are both coming down for the day." Soon after, Teresa had more to say about her son: "I am proud of Terry, he's a remarkable boy, so independent and interested in everything happening to and around him."

Terry spent half of every summer at Haldeman Road with Teresa and Mary-Kelly before proceeding to Hollister for the remainder of his school holiday. "Bob looked like a scholar or a college professor," Terry recalled years later.

> I liked him from the first. He didn't speak down to me or put on any sort of false front. He treated me like another adult, more or less. His wonderful manners—his courtesy and consideration for what I was thinking or might need—were front and center. He was, then and always, incredibly generous, probably spoiling us a bit when he had some suitable occasion. Bob took the trouble to teach me a bit how to play a guitar. He loved to sing and had a rudimentary knowledge of guitar tuning and chords. From the first, Bob found a way to be a parent without trying to be my father. He tended to leave matters of correction and discipline to my mother, and he never ordered me about or pushed me for any response to him that did not come to me naturally.

✍

"He had a captivating charm," said Christine Miller, who met him that year. Bob sent a bouquet to Teresa after their second meeting; she responded in kind, ordering a spring bouquet to be sent to him at the hotel:

"If receiving flowers embarrasses you with your friends at the front desk, you'll just have to rise above it because I just *must* send them.—Love, T."

When Bob returned to New York, he sent affectionate cards and notes, always adding details of his professional activities. Teresa was equally attentive, but she withheld news of her career, believing as always that her accomplishments were neither interesting to anyone nor in any way significant. "Darling," she wrote on March 21, while he was still in Los Angeles, "I've never been aware of the first day of spring before, and now I'll never be unaware. Thank you for a lovely day and the lovely warm feelings of happiness I shared with you."

Five days later, Bob was on his way to Salt Lake City to visit Phyllis's family, and then he returned to New York, where serious work awaited. While in Los Angeles, he had been invited to a meeting with Teresa's former director Fred Zinnemann, who was planning a film based on the best-selling book of 1956, *The Nun's Story*, by Kathryn Hulme. Fred and Warner Bros. producer Henry Blanke quickly determined that Bob was the right one to contribute the screenplay, and he signed on for the job.

Published as a novel, *The Nun's Story* was based on the true story of a Belgian nun, daughter of a prominent surgeon, who had joined a religious congregation in the 1920s. She worked with the sick and the poor in her native country and in the Belgian Congo before leaving the religious life to join the underground Resistance at the start of World War II.

In Los Angeles, Bob also met Audrey Hepburn, who was to play the leading role, and there were meetings with Fred, Audrey, Kathryn Hulme and Marie-Louise Habets, the real-life former nun (called Gabrielle van der Mal/Sister Luke in the book and movie); by this time, Marie-Louise was Kathryn Hulme's lifelong companion. Kate and Lou were then living in Los Angeles.

Audrey Hepburn was in a troubled marriage to Mel Ferrer, whom at this time she saw but rarely. Very soon after Bob left Los Angeles at the end of March, Audrey departed for Europe. She and Bob were soon reunited for further research and filming in London, Paris, Bruges, Rome and the Belgian Congo. Although Bob was avidly courting Teresa by post and by phone, he and Audrey became lovers, and so they would remain for the next two years. Of this, Teresa knew nothing at the time, and there is no allusion to the affair in any letters to and from Bob from 1957 to 1959.[1] She wrote only of her longing to be with him again, her

---

1. For a full treatment of the Anderson-Hepburn relationship, see *Enchantment: The Life of Audrey Hepburn*.

concern for the success of his work, and (as in her letters of June 12 and 16, for example), of her love for him: "I miss you very very much . . . I feel a big love inside of me for you, and I wish I could give it to you right now." At other times that year, she reminded him, "I miss you more and more each day."

Bob's trips for preproduction and the filming of *The Nun's Story* occupied almost all his time and energies for two years. The result was a hugely successful, award-winning film, magnificent in every detail; it remains Bob's finest work, as it is Audrey Hepburn's and Fred Zinnemann's.

Teresa wrote to him almost every day from March to June, and Bob replied often, but not daily: he preferred to make long-distance phone calls from New York to Los Angeles, a costly indulgence in 1957. In one letter, he mentioned that he would like to return soon to Los Angeles, to be with her and to see other actresses he knew—among them, Deborah Kerr, who now lived in Pacific Palisades, near the ocean. "Remember," Teresa wrote afterwards, "*I* live in Santa Monica. Just the same—Love, T." But Bob had no time for another personal journey to California. As for the phone conversations, she wrote to him on April 15 that she thought his voice was "sweet, and sexy, too—or does my mind just turn to such thoughts when I talk to you?" As she had written three days earlier, "You make everything look so beautiful to me, and I sing inside and smile outside."

She also had a keen sense of humor. When Bob had to return briefly to Los Angeles during preproduction for a conference with Zinnemann and the Warner executives, he told Teresa that he had asked the studio for a hotel suite or an apartment with a double bed. Replied Teresa: "You *can't* ask Warners to get you an apartment that has privacy and a *double bed*, in which to write *The Nun's Story*—now really!! Love, you just can't. It sounds like something for The New Yorker!"

Bob replied by sending her several photos of himself with Phyllis. "I love your wanting to share some of the past with me, but I do long for a snap or a picture of you alone . . . Of course I'm not fed up with that [with the photos, as he had asked], it's just that I'd like to have a little snapshot of you alone—that's natural, isn't it?" But he continued to send pictures of his former wife, along with anecdotes of his marriage. Conversely, he was cross and withdrawn if Teresa mentioned Niven's name or told of innocuous events during her marriage.

✍

She was kept busy during the first half of 1957, rehearsing and appearing in half a dozen television dramas—among them, "The Edge of Innocence," with her old friend Joseph Cotten, and a new friend, Maureen O'Sullivan. She was also mulling an offer to appear on Broadway in *The Dark at the Top of the Stairs*, a new play by William Inge, author of *Come Back, Little Sheba* and *Picnic*. In addition, she was constantly involved in Mary-Kelly's school life and routinely welcomed her daughter's friends to Haldeman Road.

Teresa too had a growing cadre of good friends: in addition to the Maldens, the Manulises and the Swopes, there were also parties and visits with people like John Forsythe and his wife, Julie; Nedda and Josh Logan (who was directing the film of *South Pacific*, with John Kerr in a major role); the actress Maggie Hayes—and, as it happened, Deborah Kerr.

"As I spoke to Deborah," Teresa wrote to Bob on April 3, "I was dying to say something about you, but she said to me, 'We share the same dentist'—which you must admit is a funny greeting. I wanted to say, 'Yes, and I talked to Bob Anderson this morning,' which would have been sillier."

There was one memorable evening in the absence of her cook-housekeeper when Teresa prepared a gourmet veal recipe that everyone appreciatively devoured. Her guests were her friends Tom and Mary Helmore, Bill Roerick (Tom Coley was working out of town) and Boris and Evie Karloff.[2] "Boris is such a lamb," Teresa wrote to Bob on April 10, "and no one on earth can assume his look of injured dignity as he carried a dirty plate into the kitchen, saying in his slow British drawl, 'What's to be done with this?'"

That season, Teresa was invited to a formal dinner at the home of Sam Goldwyn and his wife, Frances: it was, she reported to Bob, a thoroughly warm and friendly evening, the first time she had been reunited with Goldwyn in almost ten years.

At another party, she saw two old friends—Dinah Shore and William Wyler, both with their spouses. Dinah had been a neighbor in Encino and had become close to Teresa during the time of the Sterling Hayden friendship; Dinah was, as Teresa wrote to Bob on April 12, "aware of the

---

2. Evie Karloff, the actress Evelyn Hope, was married to Tom Helmore from 1931 to 1945. They divorced; she married Boris Karloff, and Tom married Mary Drayton. The Helmores and the Karloffs remained staunch friends forever. Evie was married to Karloff until his death in 1969. Many sources state that Evie died in 1966, but in fact she died in 1993; I met her several times during the 1980s.

love and hurt I experienced at that time. She knew and liked the boy [!] but disapproved of him for me (friends are often overprotective in a funny sort of way). Well, last night she looked at me and said, 'Teresa, you're looking wonderful. Is there someone special in your life now?' . . . I could have hugged her, and I would love to have sat right down and told her all about you but didn't. I just said, 'Yes, Dinah, there is.' She said, 'Who? Tell me about him!' and I said, 'I'd love to, but not now. I hope you'll meet him someday.'"

✍

By early April, before departing for Europe, Bob was working in his New York apartment on East Seventy-ninth Street when a telegram arrived from Teresa: "Don't know if it's goodnight or good morning but hello. The blue Ford [her car] and I miss you." Sometimes he wrote letters from Manhattan or from the house in Roxbury, Connecticut, that he had purchased with his royalties from *Tea and Sympathy*.

One theme in Bob's letters caused Teresa some dismay: he continually wrote and spoke about Phyllis and the emptiness of his life without her. "I'm grateful for the brief happiness I've shared with you," she wrote on March 30,

> [and I'm] hopeful that it will be there again but aware that it might not. Whatever else I may also feel about it at any time, that sense of wonder and happiness will always be there, as will my thanks and my love . . . I'm afraid you may be hurting with unhappiness and I wish I could hold you in my arms and absorb some of your hurt—but it isn't that simple, is it?
>
> Maybe the only cure for a long accumulated sadness is a slow burning out. Anne Morrow [Lindbergh] seems to be speaking of this in a poem called "No Harvest Ripening," on page 40 of her book The Unicorn and in "Second Sowing."
>
> I look at the picture of you and it's quite smiley and happy. Please be that way again.

Bob replied, suggesting that in their letters they initiate a "dialogue" about one another—perhaps not an odd idea for a playwright, but one Teresa found peculiar: "Why should either of us want that?" she answered on April 3.

Both of us know enough to know [what] we don't know, so let's just be happy about what we felt, and forget about it until we see each other again. You know, because of the little we really know about each other, even if you were not a writer to whom words and thoughts were precious, [then] long letters, struggling to say things we're uncertain of, trying to recapture feelings that can't possibly be there all the time, would not be wise—we'd be trying to bridge a gap we have no right to bridge, and our letters could be a kind of fudging on the truth.

She then wrote how happy she had been at a recent party with friends they had in common: "I felt that I had a perfectly wonderful secret inside of me that they could see if they looked close enough." At a Sunday luncheon at the Swopes, she had met Jo Mielziner (who had designed the sets and lighting for *Tea and Sympathy*), "and I wanted to lean over the coffee table and say, 'I'm in love with a friend of yours who says you are a sweet man and I should talk to you.'"

But over and above everything, in the surprise that was her love for Bob, she had "a disbelief that you have existed for me at all, that strange feeling that you had just been a dream . . . and then, suddenly and sweetly, you are real to me, and I feel a warm rush of happiness inside of me and a joy of being aware of someone I love." And her need was all too evident when Bob was in the Congo working with Hepburn and Zinnemann: "Oh, love," she wrote on May 30, "I envy this letter because you will be holding it soon, and it will be so long before you do the same for me." But Bob had another woman in his arms, and her name was Audrey.

In the same twenty-two-page handwritten letter, Teresa told Bob her memories of their meeting, and again described feelings of inadequacy, even over the slight matter of tardiness:

The first day you met me, I had become *unglued* to the point of almost becoming a basket case, and all because one more little responsibility (that of being a stand-in godmother) had been added to that day, and I had failed to meet it. Being late for the christening that day was a lot more than being late for a christening—it was being late, inadequate, failing my friends and myself, my responsibilities . . .

She knew of Bob's continuing heartache over Phyllis—"a true and honest tragedy," as she wrote to him on May 30. "But I have known sorrow, too, and my insides are just mashed to a pulp by personal failure. There's a great difference: no shame with yours, plenty with mine." This sense of "failure" was surely the result of the awful experiences she endured in childhood and the abandonment by her mother, although her many achievements and deep friendships remain the strongest contradiction that she was ever "a personal failure." But she believed differently.

The more Bob wrote about the chores he had to dispatch after his wife's death, the hundreds of condolence letters he had to acknowledge, and his remorse and grief about Phyllis, the more unworthy Teresa felt. He had sent her a small piece of jewelry as a present, and with her thanks she wrote:

> Why should happiness and gratitude for someone's lovely thought of me lead me to tears? I partly understand it. I know I've never developed a capacity for receiving. I can't accept "gifts" of any kind graciously, without feelings of guilt—"I haven't earned this . . . It may be a mistake . . . Did I seem to ask for this? . . . I don't deserve it . . ." Of course that's neurotic and part of the deep trouble of me.

She added a remarkably self-aware statement, connecting the motif of a profound, continuing sadness in her life to the terrible experiences of childhood that she had already confided to Bob:

> Maybe my attraction to Niven was the intuitive knowledge that here was someone to whom I could give without having to receive too much. Fortunately, the healthy side of me finally rebelled . . . [But] whenever I feel deeply happy, I'm bound to touch that sadness that's been pushed down deep inside of me.

Although Bob was known for his sympathy with his friends, he did not respond kindly to Teresa's description of her complicated, now long past relationship with Sterling Hayden. He was frankly jealous of her affections, past or present, and he tended to see passionate involvement with any man in her life where there was only friendship.

Nor could he accept that Teresa had an emotional intelligence that made her wiser about intimacies and marriage than Bob ever was. In those matters, he considered her foolish or immature or both. "He was so charming with women," as Christine Miller said, "and their attraction to him was understandable. But he was very patronizing about them, and as society evolved, he did not. Bob liked accomplished women, but not independent women. He was so successful at charming women that it was perhaps inevitable that he became a womanizer."

Bob was jealous of Teresa's feelings but reticent about his own: she was disappointed (as she wrote to him on August 3, 1958) that after sixteen months of their intense relationship, he had said "I love you" only once. She did not require constant verbal protestations, but surely anyone in her circumstances may have appreciated an occasional expression of endearment. Perhaps his blandishments were reserved for Audrey.

In April, Bob sent her the manuscript of his play *The Eden Rose*, which had failed in its 1951 staging and which he was trying to revise; he also hoped to cast her in a production of it, as the character named Nan. Her response reveals not only the depth of her understanding of him, but also her ability to parse a drama critically in the most acute terms:

It has some lovely things to say about the relationship between a man and a woman that should be heard by an audience . . . [but] as an actress, I have reservations about it. The end of Act 1 and the show-down scenes with Roger and Ted are, I think, only action scenes—the ones that make an audience tense a little, wondering what will happen next—as compared with the quiet, thought-provoking interest of the rest of the play . . . The conversation between Nan and the three men is always honest and revealing, giving you insight into the lives of intelligent people, capable of tenderness and passion and loneliness, fear and courage . . .

But to have two people onstage just talking about themselves might tire an audience after a while, and since Nan is almost always on stage, it might be important that she be a strong personality, which I am not, nor a great beauty, which I am not . . .

I don't believe I'm visually right [for the role]. The big scene is based on Nan's appearing a great beauty in Acts 2 and 3 and exposing herself in Act 3. Since I could not appear beautiful in the first two acts, there would be no shock value in my not being beautiful in Act 3.

The danger of redoing an old play is that [you] have grown away from it . . . Also, I think the last of Act 3, leading up to the [final] curtain is unsatisfactory. To me, what happens after Ted leaves the room is not an honest or at least a natural sequence of events, but a contrivance leading up to an end-of-play curtain . . .

Teresa's remarks were both specific and accurate: she could have been a professional play reader and editor, as savvy as Phyllis. But Bob could not accept Teresa's comments, and many years intervened before he sent another of his efforts for her consideration. He never quite believed in her judgment, and this lack of appreciation for her insights frequently worked to his own disadvantage.

"When Bob met my mother," said Mary-Kelly, "she was already a famous Oscar-winning actress with a long list of impressive credits. She did not need Bob as a mentor—quite the contrary, she could critique one of his works with remarkable sensitivity, and that must have come as a big and not always a welcome surprise to him." As for *The Eden Rose*, it is impossible to find a record of its production anywhere.

∽

At last the contracts were settled for William Inge's *The Dark at the Top of the Stairs*. It was not an entirely new play: its first incarnation was an early Inge work called *Farther Off From Heaven*, staged in 1947 in Dallas. Now, Elia Kazan was to be the director and Teresa the leading lady; both director and playwright considered no other actress for the role. As rehearsals began, Teresa and her director became good friends. Joining Teresa in leading roles were Pat Hingle and Eileen Heckart.

"I have noticed about people with mysterious gifts," Kazan reflected.

In many cases, a wound has been inflicted early in life, which impels the person to strive harder or makes him or her extra-sensitive. The talent, the genius, is the scab on the wound, there to protect a weak place . . . When I've worked with men and women who came successfully out of misfortune, I've found that they have strength that is extraordinary, and their strength is a gift to me. So it's been particularly with the actresses I've worked with. Their precious gifts, for which they paid in pain, have made me successful when I was successful. I've relied on their talent; it's the essence of what I've needed most.

After more than sixteen years, Teresa was eager to be back on Broadway. She had left as a pretty ingénue of twenty-two and was returning as a thirty-nine-year-old Academy Award-winning actress with two children.

She needed a home in New York for herself and Mary-Kelly, and for Terry's visits. By a fortunate coincidence, Tom and Mary Helmore had to move to Hollywood for an unspecified long period. (At the top of Tom's projects was a major role in *Vertigo*, his third collaboration with Alfred Hitchcock.) And so an exchange was easily negotiated: the Helmores moved into Teresa's house on Haldeman Road, and she took over the spacious Helmore apartment at the Dakota, on Central Park West. Both families maintained these temporary residences until 1959. Soon, a full-time, live-in maid and housekeeper named Annie Lee Claxton joined Teresa and her daughter.

Now ten, Mary-Kelly was a bright and energetic achiever with broad interests and many talents. She was enrolled at the prestigious Dalton School, an academy known for eliciting from students a high degree of individual creativity. "Mom was a very fair and reasonable mother," said Mary-Kelly. "She gave me freedom, she didn't meddle, and she was always involved in my schoolwork and my outside activities."

∽

The Dark at the Top of the Stairs was a challenge for everyone in the cast, but especially for Teresa, who was onstage for all but a few moments of the three acts (comprising nearly three hours). As a bossy but loving wife to a blustery but needy husband, and the possessive but protective mother to a teenage daughter and a preteen son, she had to play the part of Cora Flood with a delicate alchemy. "Cora tries to dictate to her husband," Teresa said at the time. "She spoils both her children. She is much too closely attached to her son." This was a role that would have been easy for an actress to misconstrue—to overplay either as merely sympathetic or as terrifyingly managerial.

The play opened on December 5, 1957, at the Music Box Theatre and ran for 468 performances, until January 17, 1959. Critics noted Teresa's acute ability to counterpoise the jumble of human emotions Cora feels and cannot quite control. "As the petulant, frustrated mother and wife, Kazan has made a flawless choice in Teresa Wright," wrote one typical reviewer. And the biographer and historian Bernard Dick, who saw the play that season, recalled, "What I admired about Teresa's performance is that she imbued Cora with such warmth"—a quality implied in the text but not always evident onstage.

"The part of Cora had very little lightness in it," Teresa said years later. "But I got a great deal of satisfaction in doing that role, even though, night after night for over a year and more than 450 performances, it sometimes became a burden. I think all actors are affected by the parts we play. The more we learn about minds and emotions in a role, the more you have to believe those emotions onstage. You have to believe in what you're saying. In this case, I had to go on every night believing what Cora was saying—and I had a feeling of identifying with this woman who had a lot of troubles. She was a difficult, confusing lady, and sometimes it got to be closer to home than I wanted!"

During rehearsals that autumn, and for the tryouts in Boston and Philadelphia, the cast and the playwright depended on Elia Kazan to bring credible life to a play that might have been presented merely as a study of family neuroses. "No one came anywhere near [Kazan] as a director," she continued.[3]

> I felt in a way that I'd never been directed before—by directed, I don't mean that he told me what to do. It was a question of bringing something out of you, but he didn't sit back and wait for the right thing to emerge—as [William] Wyler did, for example. No, Kazan guided and talked about the character so much that you began to see insights into both yourself and the character that you just weren't aware of before. I've never known anyone who had the knowledge of human nature that he had—he was keenly aware and articulate—and spontaneous when he talked about it. He approached every character by first opening himself up completely—and then he shared this tremendous insight and knowledge and compassion.

When Teresa spoke of this to Bob (who had benefited from Kazan's direction of *Tea and Sympathy*), he had to admit that she expressed the matter perfectly.

"I work rather slowly," she continued, "and I find things in the character as I go. I let the character teach me what to feel—I try not to impose myself on the character. That's where Kazan was such a help. He was experiencing the discovery with you—he wasn't coldly sitting back and analyzing. You never once felt his theatrical knowledge imposed on you. I used to sit and listen during rehearsals as he spoke to each character in the play. Everything that came up for discussion he explored and explored some more."

After so many years of movie and television work, Teresa was at first concerned about returning to the Broadway stage.

3. Kazan had directed plays by Thornton Wilder, Tennessee Williams, Arthur Miller and Robert Anderson, and he was considered one of the two or three most important people in the theatre.

There's a difference between working in a rehearsal hall, then going to an empty theatre for full dress [rehearsal], and then playing to a full house—you have to adjust your voice to every situation. At first you feel as if you're speaking too softly—then you're shouting too loudly. But that really was not a problem for me. I felt that I grew in the part as time went on, and [Kazan] told me that I did. The more stage experience you have in a play, the more likely you are to take command and hold [the role onstage]. I think I was much better in *Dark at the Top of the Stairs* at the end of the run than I was at the beginning. I grew in the part, as certainly anyone ought to in a year's run!

For all the gravity with which Teresa approached her career and all the pleasure she derived from it, she was (like many performers) ambivalent. "I love acting but it has never meant much to me personally," she wrote to Bob on February 4, 1958. "I'd never sacrifice anything important to it, let alone my life."

In her career, she gave far more prodigally than she received. Of this she was unaware, but her inability to believe in her own essential worth and her own prodigious talent prevented her from thinking that she had ever done anything of enduring value. Bob, for one, knew the first consequence: "I never met a girl to whom fame meant less," he wrote to her on February 28, 1959. That was throwing the emphasis elsewhere, but it was a sturdy compliment; on the other hand, fame meant a great deal to Bob.

꩜

By early 1958, Bob's base was at 48 Berkeley Square, London, where he rented a flat; went forth for and returned from the filming of *The Nun's Story*; and worked on a new play called *Silent Night, Lonely Night,* and on a screenplay he hoped to sell as another project for Audrey. In this last ambition he was eventually stymied.

But perhaps because of his intimacy with Audrey and his inability to commit to Teresa, Bob had fallen into fits of terrible depression, and Teresa was the recipient of numerous letters and phone calls in which he repeated his feelings of failure and his profound self-doubts about his career. "I am being very cruel to Teresa," Bob wrote to his brother in January without exaggeration. But he concluded the same letter with a telling coda: "Audrey is a wonderful girl, full of laughs and gentleness."

"I wish I had some brilliant words of wisdom to send you," Teresa
wrote on February 4,

> something profound that would fill you with self-love and faith.
> Faith in yourself—in your ideas, principles, your talent. But since
> I don't possess these myself, it's futile to wish I could give [them]
> to someone else.

And then, for the first time, she expressed doubts about their respective capacities to develop a mutually rewarding relationship. He had spoken of his love for her only once, and now in his absence, she revaluated
her side of the equation. "I love you, Bob—not deeply or profoundly,
I'm afraid," she wrote on February 4. "My feelings and my knowledge of
both you and myself are too squeezed, too boxed up for that—it's probably just a little love I have, but I feel the knot of it inside of me, and I
send it to you—such as it is."

She explicated one of the key reasons for her doubts: "I don't think I
really wish you [were] back here in the same state you were in before—
living in the past and so unhappy with everything around you in the
present. It seems to me I love you very much, but if I'm honest, I think I
have to admit I don't love you enough—for if I did, then my just loving
you would be enough—and it is not." With the letter, she sent a copy of
Harold Brodkey's new book, *First Love and Other Sorrows* (with comments
on much of the contents). These she had studied intensely, along with
Erich Fromm's *The Art of Loving*.

Teresa was weary of Bob's ceaseless complaints that no one understood him, he was not appreciated, he could not work well anywhere.
"Really, Bob, you do make working impossible for yourself—you cannot
work at home, cannot work at your office, cannot move to another office
because of the rent . . . Good Lord, man, it makes me mad to think of it.
Maybe you make all these obstacles for yourself." When he replied with
a description of his writing life during the time of his marriage to Phyllis,
Teresa sent back a gentle warning on February 21: "I can't live in the past
and I don't hold much hope for the future." On August 5, she was more
explicit:

> I love our moments or days together, [but] I can't think of them
> growing into weeks or months or years. I have a lot of responsibili-
> ties and have been very busy the last six years [since her divorce]
> building new foundations. I've built them alone.

With her mother, Martha Espy Wright, 1918

With her father, Arthur Wright, 1923

Arthur Wright, about 1935

About age three

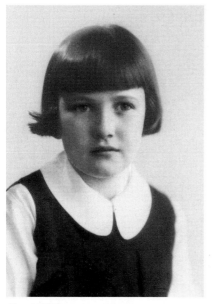

About 1927

Age ten, in the play *Butterfly Wings* at the Rose Haven School for Girls, June 1929

Age 18, at the Wharf Theatre, Provincetown, August 1937

In front row, center—Graduation Day at Columbia High
School, 1938. Hitchcock used this photo in *Shadow of a Doubt*

On Broadway, as Mary Skinner, in *Life With Father*, 1939

In Hollywood, 1941

Niven Busch, 1941

With Carl Benton Reid and Dan Duryea, off-camera during *The Little Foxes*

In the final scene
of *The Little Foxes*

Wedding Day: May 23, 1942

Teresa and Niven

With Greer Garson, in *Mrs. Miniver*

With Hitchcock, on the set of *Shadow of a Doubt*

With Patricia Collinge in *Shadow of a Doubt*

In *Shadow of a Doubt*

With Fredric March, Myrna Loy, Dana Andrews and (at the piano) Hoagy Carmichael, during production of *The Best Years of Our Lives* (1946)

1947

With Jayne Meadows and David Niven, in *Enchantment* (1949)

Niven and Teresa, with Terry and Mary-Kelly, at Hollister, about 1951

Christmas portrait, 1953, with Mary-Kelly and Terry

Robert Anderson, age
thirty-seven (1954)

With Eileen Heckart, Pat Hingle and (standing) playwright William Inge: *The Dark at the Top of the Stairs*, 1957

Wedding Day: December 11, 1959

Bob and Teresa
with Mary-Kelly
and Terry, 1962

Terry Busch, 1961

Mary-Kelly Busch, 1986

With Tom Helmore and Scott McKay, during the tour of *Mary, Mary* (1962)

As the tortured farmwife, with Bruce Dern, in the episode "Lonely Place" (*The Alfred Hitchcock Hour*, 1964)

In Connecticut, 1965

In Hollywood, 1969

At the publication party for *The Art of Alfred Hitchcock* (1976), photo by Donald Spoto

On Broadway, in
Morning's at Seven (1980)

At the marriage of
Francesca Jegge to Terry
Busch, August 1982

Bob and Teresa,
about 1985

Mary-Kelly Busch, with her husband, Daniel Picchioni, 1991

With Maryann Plunkett, in *The Road to Mecca*, 1990

With Matt Damon, in *The Rainmaker* (1996)

The ultimate New York Yankees fan, 1998

With Donald Spoto, 2004, photo by Ole Flemming Larsen

I long for the solace and protection and the special delight that the marriage relationship can have above all others, but I would never dream of just settling for marriage for its own sake—it would have to be something I would reach for and rise to with the strongest desire and hope and faith, and the two of us are very short on hope and faith in that direction.

She concluded wisely: "None of us has a right to expect any more from a loved one than the joy we experience in loving them."

Soon after, Teresa wrote to Bob that she was reviewing the names of a few psychiatrists in order to begin some form of counseling. She liked Dr. Janet Rioch, and eventually she was able to "turn on a light in a dark corner and see something for the first time that had been very closed to me"—her reference to those childhood traumas when her mother brought men into bed, frightened her—and then abandoned her. Confronting and articulating terrible memories is a part of the process of healing, but is it ever possible to banish forever the effects of such dark clouds as these that hung over her entire lifetime?

The underlying sadness in Teresa's life, the source of her poor self-image and lifelong lack of healthy self-esteem, were caused by a mother who never said goodbye, never returned, never wrote her a letter. Martha had not died—there was no final event to overcome. She simply withdrew from young Muriel's life, leaving an emptiness the child could only interpret as her own unworthiness: she must have done something wicked to drive away her own mother.

Perhaps in therapy Teresa could understand intellectually the chain of cause and effect, but that took her only so far, and it was not far enough. Emotionally, her life had been forever deprived of a primal nurturing. It is almost impossible to calculate the kind of concomitant psychological wounding that haunted her throughout her life. But despite that, she grew up not as a bitter, cold, emotionally sterile woman incapable of giving what she had not received. To the contrary, she became a woman with deep empathy for others—capable of nurturing as a parent, devotion as a wife, caring as a friend and perceptive of a wide range of human experiences and characters.

⁓

As if she were not busy enough, Teresa had to discount rumors that she and Bob were about to marry. In the New York *Journal American*, Dorothy Kilgallen—a columnist not known for discretion—reported:

"Intimate friends of Teresa Wright and Robert Anderson are expecting a June marriage." This was nonsense: there were no friends with such expectations. Teresa sprang into action. In a handwritten letter dated February 16, she set Kilgallen straight, concluding, "I would like it to be known that the speculations are unfounded and untrue."

Ironically, by the end of the year Bob was intimating the notion of marriage, but Teresa was more than hesitant, perhaps because the small world of film and theatre had become smaller and informed her about Bob and Audrey. "I know for sure now that having me near you is not important to you, nor am I an important part of your life. But I beg you to seek help for your own happiness, just for your own future . . . It's hard for me to believe that you have really shaken that depression of yours that so disturbs and depresses me." As she said, she had been thrown into confusion by so many things, not least his present to her of a ring "that was just for laughs," as he said. "I love you, but I'm confused," she concluded on November 24.

Bob was no less puzzled. "*If* I should think about getting married again—and I am getting very tired with living alone," he wrote to his brother on November 19, "there is the problem of where I might live . . . My thoughts are still very confused on the matter. I haven't talked with Teresa about where she might want to live, as I haven't opened up the question of marriage at all—or if so, only in the negative sense that I have not been ready for marriage and might never be."

Bob was, as Mary-Kelly said many years later, "more lost than he led people to believe. I saw this heaviness in Bob, this negativity and under-tow. He could be gallant and giving and attentive and commending on the surface, but there was this darkness that was almost incapacitating for those around him. Mom knew this from the start and told him she found his depression hard to live with. He could laugh at Mom's quirky habits and those of others, but he had no sense of humor about life, no sense of irony." Christine Miller was on the mark when she said, "For a man who wrote so well about intimacy, it was startling and confusing and perplexing to all of us that he was unaware of what he was doing in his own personal relationships."

∽

By November 1958, *The Dark at the Top of the Stairs* was close to marking a year since its premiere. That is always a doubtful time for any play, as a cast invariably needs time with their director to sharpen, to refine, to re-consider, to keep everything from becoming stale. In this case, two things happened that were greatly disturbing for the cast: first, Kazan withdrew his attention from them as he began rehearsals for a new play—*J.B.*, by Archibald MacLeish—and took Pat Hingle with him from the cast of *Dark*; second, the actor replacing Hingle, George L. Smith, went into the play "cold," without rehearsals, without preparation. Teresa and her friend Eileen Heckart (who played her sister) were thrust into an impossible situation as actor after actor in the play submitted a notice of resignation.

"Being onstage with an undirected actor is tough," Teresa wrote to Bob on November 18,

> and it's impossible for me to be out there and not *care*—and not suffer for what's happening to the play during the first act. I am now in a state of panic, of not being able to pronounce words and almost forgetting lines, and it's plain HELL every night. It's a terrible thing to watch a good play and good company disintegrate. Ever since Pat left, who was such a strong, forceful, happy spirit among us, a terrible change has taken place not only because Pat was Pat, but because the original "inner circle"—the *family* [in the play] was broken . . . Eileen [Heckart] says it's been torture for her ever since November 7, but of course she's such a pro, she's the only one I can count on to be the same onstage, no matter how she feels—though she is convinced that she is now very bad in the part and that the audience hates her. Judy, on the other hand [Judith Robinson, in the important role of Cora's daughter], had real hysterics one night two weeks ago at the end of Act I. I had to bring her up to my room and quiet her and take care of her and get her back down for Act II . . . The company is just falling apart—no director, no producer, no playwright to help keep things up.

Somehow, the play limped along toward its closing on January 17, 1959—but by this time Teresa despaired: "There are as many different kinds of performances of this play now as there are actors in the play—and you know the great *unity* Gadge [Kazan] gives his productions. Well, I feel we could now be billed as 'Bill Inge's Variety Show.' It's awful, and the depressing part is that I know Gadge could pull us all together in just one day." For Teresa, the play's final curtain could not come down soon enough.

✑

CHAPTER ELEVEN

1959–1965

WHEN *THE DARK AT THE TOP OF THE STAIRS* CLOSED, TERESA WAS FI-
nally free of the strict and strenuous schedule of eight performances a
week. Now she had the opportunity to enjoy living in New York, and she
had more time for her daughter. They remained in the city until June so
that Mary-Kelly could finish the academic year at Dalton. "Mom had offers that year to star in movies that would have meant going to Europe,
but she turned them down to stay at home with me."

Mary-Kelly's class was studying the culture of ancient Greece that
semester, and when a friend threw a Greek-themed birthday party, Teresa cut a sheet to make a costume for Mary-Kelly to wear. Because the
weather was quite cold, Teresa also sacrificed a wool blanket to make a
cloak to fit over the chiton. "Mom enjoyed the project as much as I did—
perhaps even more."

Teresa's children were not relegated to the sidelines of her life. During
the summer of 1958, she had rented a house in Greenwich, Connecticut.
"It was mainly for the benefit of Mary-Kelly and me," recalled Terry, "so
that we would have more chances for kid encounters than we might
have had staying with her in the city. I often went into New York and
backstage [during performances of *The Dark at the Top of the Stairs*], which
was very exciting for me." He and his sister also recalled dinners with
both Teresa and Bob. During that summer, Teresa commuted, driving
herself to and from the theatre, and occasionally traveling by train.

Niven, who considered his son's education a priority, had realized that
Terry was deprived of solid learning in the two-room country school-
house in Hollister. He therefore moved the family to San Francisco for
a year, from 1958 to 1959, so that fourteen-year-old Terry could attend

144

the Town School for Boys, a private academy that was effectively a prep school for prep school. Terry was subsequently enrolled as a boarding student at the Bellarmine College Preparatory School in San Jose, about fifty miles from Hollister.

Terry endured the usual pangs of teenage romantic disappointment, and when he came to New York for visits with his mother, he recalled Bob's comfort and attention "when my first serious love came to its inevitable end. I was despondent. All the adults in my life were dutifully sympathetic, but none took it really seriously. None but Bob. He talked to me at length about it, listening, understanding, empathizing. He alone seemed to understand that my pain was real pain."

Even as a student, Terry showed a talent for writing, as did Mary-Kelly. "Bob didn't have to be supportive of me," Terry added, "and yet he was. He read everything I wrote, he talked to me about it in serious terms, he told me what he liked and what might make the writing better." When Terry was an undergraduate at the University of California, Berkeley, he began writing short stories, and Bob encouraged him to submit them for publication. "He was always my key mentor and advocate, an important and encouraging influence in my formative years— and more than anyone, he made me believe in myself as a writer."

Niven was alert and sensitive to Terry's abilities: "He always let me know he thought I had a serious talent, but he didn't want me to feel pressure to follow in his footsteps or define myself in his mirror. Once, I brought him the story of [the musician] Huddie Ledbetter (known as "Lead Belly"), and he tried to sell it as a movie project that both of us could work on. He did sell a treatment, but that version was never made. I loved the chance to work with my father on that and other projects, and I learned a lot from him."

The support and confidence offered by Niven and Bob were well founded as Terry's career went from strength to strength. After earning his Ph.D. in Rhetoric at Berkeley, he taught, lectured at several business schools, became a corporate communications director and speechwriter for several large companies and published widely in several fields.

After secondary school, Mary-Kelly graduated from Mary Baldwin College, in Staunton, Virginia. Later, she studied English at Wesleyan University in Connecticut, where she earned a Master of Arts in Liberal Studies. She then became a writer of books for children and young adults and also led drama workshops.

✑

Throughout 1959, Teresa and Bob (who maintained separate addresses) divided their time between New York and Los Angeles. As a writer, Bob could write anywhere, and that year he was mostly in London, occupied with revisions to his play *Silent Night, Lonely Night*—and waiting for Henry Fonda to be available for the Broadway production.

For Teresa and Mary-Kelly, life continued with no upset when they returned to Haldeman Road that year—an event celebrated by friends and colleagues at several parties. During his holidays, Terry was often present for the social gatherings, where a number of the sons and daughters of Teresa's friends became his friends, too:

> The most important were those in the Swope family, the Helmores, the Kazans, the Maldens and the Widmarks, among others. I recall one party when I was fifteen. The house was crammed with the A-list names, but the only person I wanted to meet was the guest of honor, Dr. Tom Dooley, home from one of his amazing tours in Southeast Asia. I was never much impressed by actors, but this guy was something else—a national hero. I was shocked when he died of cancer a few months later.

Terry later recalled one of Bob Anderson's finest traits. "Everyone praised him as the perfect gentleman, and that was clearly part of his own self-image—something he took pride in. And it was really something to admire. Where it really showed and taught lessons was not in how he treated his peers, but in how he treated doormen and cabbies and waiters—with courtesy and consideration, not condescension."

But parties did not lift Bob's depression. In January, he considered psychiatric help—a step he had already enjoined on Teresa, whom he regarded as far more in need of professional counseling, which was perhaps a classic case of projection on his part. "It is so hard to know what to do," he wrote to his brother, detailing his confusion about several matters. "When I shift into neutral and just allow myself to enjoy the day to day pleasures of contact with a lovely and warm person, everything seems all right for getting married [to Teresa?]. But then I get a letter from someone else [Audrey?] which suddenly quickens my pulse, or I go to a party with old friends and suddenly feel that I am there with the wrong person, and then I have serious doubts."

Bob's search for the right therapist was interrupted when his mother died on April 2, 1959. Attention to his father and to legal matters kept him occupied—chores he had to dispatch alone, because his brother lived far from New York City. Eventually, Bob found a doctor he could trust, and from that time he spoke often and in surprising detail to almost anyone about his therapy sessions: "Oh, I had such an interesting session with Dr. Portnoy," or "Well, I thought I had the same problem until I told Dr. Portnoy, and he said . . ."

This therapist, as Mary-Kelly soon learned, "adored Bob and his writing, and he got Bob to talk about his work—what writer wouldn't like that? Their meetings turned out to be more like ego-sessions for both men." Eventually, Bob withdrew from therapy, citing as his reasons travel and the demands of work. He wrote about these things to his brother and then turned to the subject of Teresa:

"I don't know what will come of it, but I feel sorry for her. She is a lovely and gallant and tender little creature. I am afraid that her terrible anxiety about rejection, which she has had all her life, would make it impossible for me to function normally."

This is not difficult to understand. Bob knew that his serial and sometimes simultaneous liaisons were part of his "normal function," and that if Teresa knew about those affairs, she would feel rejected, which would not be an irrational reaction. At the time, and despite her occasional disinclination to continue the relationship, she hoped that solid mutual love would set the balance right for both of them.

To complicate the situation, Phyllis was still the unseen ghost in Bob's life, a formidable figure causing him enormous guilt. Just before New Year's Day, he wrote a letter to his dead wife:

The ache in me is that we never made our marriage what we wanted it to be. It was always just about to begin. Four years of war, five years of cancer, with a few struggling years thrown in-between, when we both worked our energies out and had so little left for each other. There was never time just for us, or so rarely. Yet I adored you, but hated the terrible things we did to each other. Does it make any sense to say that I was unhappily married to a woman I adored and continue to adore?

∾

The demand for constant companionship overcame Bob's often-stated preference for complete freedom and independence. Thus, after more than two years of courtship, he finally asked Teresa to marry him. "She doesn't think it would work," he noted in his diary on August 30,

1959—but within days she recanted. Doubtless she saw their respective needs as symbiotic; certainly, she wanted to love him, to appease his loneliness and to support his talent, which she valued highly. In any case, she did not want to lose him. A wedding date was set for December in Los Angeles.

Meanwhile, Teresa traveled several times to New York in preparation for her television role in a dramatic retelling of the life of Margaret Bourke-White, the first American female photojournalist in wartime and a celebrated documentary photographer. Bourke-White recently had brain surgery to reduce her tremors for Parkinson's Disease, and she met several times with Teresa. Present to document the preparation and the production was Alfred Eisenstaedt, whose photograph of Teresa had been on the cover of *Life* magazine in December 1946; in the television drama, he was also a character, portrayed by Eli Wallach.

With Margaret, Teresa carefully studied and imitated the developing symptoms of Parkinsonism—the slow movements, the shuffling gait and the facial rigidity, which was especially challenging for an actor. *The Margaret Bourke-White Story* was broadcast on January 3, 1960, and Teresa's performance won her an Emmy nomination as the best actress in a television drama.

✎

Finally, Henry Fonda committed to Bob's play, joining Barbara Bel Geddes. *Silent Night, Lonely Night* is the story of a couple who meet at a New England inn on Christmas Eve, each of them with marital difficulties they discuss . . . and discuss . . . and discuss. His wife is in a mental asylum; her husband is unfaithful. On this night, after prolonged talk, they make love—and in the morning, refreshed, each returns to marital commitment. The play opened in Boston that November before a Broadway premiere on December 3.

On opening night at the Morosco Theater in New York, Bob's father sat with Teresa. As the houselights dimmed and the curtain rose, he whispered to her, "No matter how bad this is, I'm going to tell the poor boy I liked it." The critics offered almost unanimously negative reviews: "excessively verbose," wrote Brooks Atkinson in the *Times*, adding that the silent and lonely night was also a very long one indeed. There was also wide critical rejection of Bob's thesis, introduced six years earlier in *Tea and Sympathy*: that sex is the great healer.

But perhaps the major problem with the play is that once again Bob allowed his autobiography to control what there was of plot. "I might have written too personally about my own life," he said later. That assessment was on the mark.

"There was a great deal of pressure for *Silent Night, Lonely Night* to succeed," recalled Bob, "but the experience was very hard for me. Fonda was not directable—even though he was almost desperate for a strong play with a long run. To tell the truth, I suffered through it all."

In addition, Bob felt keenly the successes of other playwrights: in the 1950s, there were prize-winning plays by Arthur Miller, Tennessee Williams and William Inge, and revivals of major works by O'Neill. These were his competition, and he felt that he deserved to be ranked among them. He earned a substantial income from his screenplays, but his works for the stage after *Tea and Sympathy* were few and unsuccessful critically and commercially. This failure deepened his sense of insecurity, for Bob judged himself as he judged others—on the basis of achievements and credentials. *Silent Night, Lonely Night* closed after 124 performances, and seven years intervened before another play by Robert Anderson reached Broadway.

Three days after the premiere, Bob and Teresa left New York for Los Angeles, where they were married on December 11. As Bea Miller had done when Teresa married her brother Niven Busch seventeen years earlier, she now helped her select a wedding outfit again. "Very often, when Teresa was in Los Angeles over the years, my mother asked her what she was going to wear for this or that occasion," recalled Bea's daughter Christine. "Teresa replied something about a particular dress, or a blouse and a skirt—but Bea saw that sometimes Teresa's choices were unsuitable for the occasion. So she took Teresa shopping and got her ready."

This was virtually a tradition, as Bea invariably supervised such details with sisterly warmth and zeal. "Teresa was always sweet and funny, but she was also slightly scattered," Christine continued. "Her family and friends always knew that she was thrown into confusion by the details of everyday life—as she was not by the requirements of her career, which she fulfilled with alert preparation and keen professionalism."

In deference to Bob's family tradition, the wedding was held at the Beverly Hills Presbyterian Church, and a reception followed at the Manulis home. Karl and Mona Malden attended along with other friends of the bride and groom—and Audrey Hepburn, whom Bob had especially invited.

⁂

The new year began with a flurry of activity—but not for Teresa. She had felt unwell during the final weeks of the Inge play and continued to suffer gastric distress into 1960. At first, doctors believed that she would have to have surgery for gallstones, or for the removal of her gall bladder. But the situation was less drastic: tests revealed a benign gall bladder polyp, and with rest and a careful diet, she was able to avoid surgery and fully recovered.

As for her career, there were no movie offers: a new era with new kinds of stories was opening for stars like Sophia Loren, Natalie Wood, Lee Remick, Piper Laurie—and even for Audrey Hepburn, who exchanged the costume of a nun's habit for the fashions of a high-priced call girl (in *Breakfast at Tiffany's*). At the age of forty-two, Teresa was told by her agents that good roles were hard to find—by which they meant good roles for women over forty.

In addition, only two offers for television dramas followed in the next two years. Because she did not want to take Mary-Kelly out of school or to leave her with Bob and a housekeeper, Teresa rejected offers to travel abroad in American plays sponsored by the State Department. Instead, she became, by agreeable default, a full-time homemaker and housewife.

Bob was more occupied in the business. He was nominated for an Academy Award for his screenplay for *The Nun's Story*, and as a result several producers and directors invited him to business meetings. There was a verbal agreement for him to work again with Robert Wise, this time on a project called *The Sand Pebbles*—but that required a long gestation period.[1]

Bob and Teresa returned to New York immediately after the marriage, and Mary-Kelly (who went to school in California for the autumn 1959 semester), returned to the Dalton School. Bob gave up his apartment on East Seventy-ninth Street after he found a spacious two-bedroom, three-bathroom residence with a fireplace and maid's quarters, at 1172 Park Avenue. After some redecorating, the three moved in on May 1, and this was Mary-Kelly's address, too, during her final years at Dalton. "We shudder at having a Park Avenue address," Bob wrote to his brother on February 10, "but we'll try to live it down."

While Teresa was settling in and arranging a home for three, she also had room to augment and expand her collection of newspaper and magazine clippings—recipes, articles about politics, education, travel and

1. Bob Wise had several productions on the docket, among them *The Haunting* and *The Sound of Music*, before he could direct *The Sand Pebbles*, and the logistics of filming the last one in Taiwan and Hong Kong required protracted and delicate political negotiations.

entertainment. The usual storage place for many little piles of clippings was atop the master bed, which was, according to Teresa, "the bane of my husband's existence." Clipping and keeping were the dual points of a hobby and a habit that Teresa never broke.

"I helped Teresa pack things up when they moved from Haldeman Road to New York," recalled Mila Malden. "I never saw such an accumulation of things in my life! She never threw anything away. It wasn't because of acquisitiveness—there simply might have been a recipe she wanted to try, or an interview with someone she admired."

Bob's grumbling about the cache of Teresa's clippings was as nothing compared to a more frequent and sometimes more public kind of criticism.

"In my late teens," said Terry, "I began to see a slightly unpleasant seam in Bob's character—his tendency to tease with a rather heavy hand. At dinners with the family or at a party, he noted just how much meat I could eat and began to spin a repeated story that 'We have to buy two big steaks—one for Terry and one for the rest of us.' The joke per se didn't offend me, but the repetition of it got a bit tiresome."

That was criticism enough, but soon Bob turned toward Teresa, whom he teased for her foibles. In addition, the mention of Phyllis became a constant, as Mary-Kelly recalled, "and the balance of all fairness was off. If he complimented her on something well done—which he certainly did, and often—she could not believe him."

"I was embarrassed and then angered by Bob's criticism of Teresa," Christine Miller remembered; she saw them more frequently when she came east to study at Wellesley College. "He was very passive-aggressive with her—polite but critical. Terry and Mary-Kelly were upset by it, too. Eventually, it was very difficult to be with Bob and Teresa, because his manner was so hurtful to her."

Why did Teresa submit so meekly to these reproaches and words of disparagement? Very likely because she wrongly believed she was indeed inferior to Phyllis. Her strong sense of what was correct in performing in a play or a movie did not extend to her sense of herself, which was always fragile and even deeply negative.

Even apart from the inappropriate comparison of Teresa to the late Phyllis, Bob had what Terry regarded as "obsessive recall of his life with Phyllis, the stories he told and repeated, anywhere and to anyone. This pattern was wearing for my Mom, but I had no idea what I might do to make him desist."

If conversations did not refer to Phyllis, Bob too often focused on the high estimation offered to him by this or that critic or director. This was, Terry considered, rather like a sports hero taking people on a tour of his own trophy case. Why did Bob feel it was necessary to do this? Certainly his family and friends and people familiar with theatre and film knew of his accomplishments. Why, then, did he constantly assume the role of his own press agent?

Bob tried to answer this question in a journal he began to keep in 1990. First, he remembered that his father had the same habit: "Isn't that a nice tribute?" James Anderson said, speaking of an honor tendered to himself. From that Bob extrapolated to his own tendency to the same kind of self-glorification: "Are we all so hungry for nice things said about us—or do they bolster an otherwise shaky image?" That was a shrewd self-assessment, posed as a hypothetical question.

These habits and traits were paradoxical because they emerged from a man who was consistently generous, caring and empathetic—supporting his friends in need, condoling those who grieved and rejoicing in the good fortune of others. From the start, these were qualities that touched the lives of Terry, Mary-Kelly and Chris Miller. Later, professional colleagues knew that they, too, could count on Bob for advice and a good heart.

✍

For the summer of 1960, Bob and Teresa fled the heat of New York for Haldeman Road and the nearby ocean. Eventually, as their careers kept them more often in New York, Teresa decided to sell the Santa Monica house. With the proceeds, she paid her half ($22,500) of the price for their new home on Curtis Road in Bridgewater, Connecticut—"a lovely old farmhouse," as Bob described it, but a place that wanted considerable refitting and upgrading before their 1965 move-in. For writing, Bob kept his small cottage in Roxbury, seven minutes away. Over the years, neighbors included Arthur Miller, William Styron, Richard Widmark, Sylvia Sidney, Frank McCourt and Dustin Hoffman. "Many theatre friends lived there," said Bob. "I stay because I'm happy with my little place, isolated on nine acres of woods, with privacy for writing, yet near friends, tennis courts and three of the best regional theatres in the country."

Bob and Teresa had times and moments of undiluted pleasure and great fun together, as they did with Terry and Mary-Kelly. During one of their sojourns in Los Angeles, for example, Bob and Teresa attended a party for Audrey Hepburn that (as he wrote to his brother on July 11,

1961) "turned out to be a welcome home for Teresa, [with] so many people she hadn't seen for so long: Samuel Goldwyn, Willie Wyler, Louella Parsons . . . It was fun having so many people treat her so affectionately."

At the end of 1961, Teresa was invited to recreate the title role in Jean Kerr's comedy *Mary, Mary*, which had opened on Broadway in March, was still running, and would continue for 1,572 performances and almost four years. Barbara Bel Geddes was having a great success with it in New York, and Mrs. Kerr, producer Roger Stevens and director Joseph Anthony believed that the national road tour would benefit from Teresa as the leading lady; Barbara had other commitments.

The play concerns Mary McKellaway, a sharply witty, independent divorcée. Because she must meet with her ex-husband over a complicated tax matter, she arrives at their former New York home, only to find that he now has a much younger fiancée. There is very little action, but the dialogue sparkles as the characters—including an elderly accountant and a Hollywood roué—banter about marriage, divorce, alimony, affairs, exercise and everything contemporary and problematic.

"In order to be an actress, you have to keep at it," Teresa told Bob when she agreed to star in the national tour of *Mary, Mary*. "You have to act every chance you get, so that when the big chance comes, you're ready. Otherwise you're scared and out of training." About her intentions and planning, Bob was accurate: "She has no big ambition, but a play like this will be fun for her. I think she would rather putter around the apartment and jog in and out of junk stores trying to decorate the bedroom. I think she thrills to a real challenge in a part—but just to act doesn't seem to give her much of a boot. Once she gets going and starts getting those laughs, everything will be better."

The play was presented for six weeks in Los Angeles and six weeks in San Francisco before going on a nationwide tour. Bob was at the opening night: "She is lovely in it," he wrote to his brother on June 22. "It's a delightful change of pace, and she is enjoying it all." Much of the pleasure derived from acting and traveling with her co-star and friend Tom Helmore, who was also in the cast. Weeks later, Bob summed up the reaction of critics and audiences around the country: "Teresa continues to do very well in the play, and everyone is delighted with her."

As for Bob, he was working on an original screenplay with the provisional title *The Tiger*: "It concerns my struggle with Dad at the time of Mother's death," he wrote to his brother in two letters (on June 22 and July 9, 1962), "[which is] the really core unsatisfactory relationship of my life. It is written in anger, but also in bewilderment and in pity . . .

[about] a father and son who never got along being left together [after the mother's death]. Naturally, much of it is fiction, but much of it is not." Six years later, he turned the unproduced screenplay into the Broadway play *I Never Sang for My Father*, an even more patently autobiographical work than *Tea and Sympathy*. *Father* was later a successful movie that earned several Oscar nominations—including one for Bob's screenplay.

"What depresses me most," Bob said, "is that nobody [i.e., neither his producer or director at that time] seems to do any work on it except me. I have to scout around for moneymaking possibilities. This is the big risk in this business, and the advanced writer is in no better position at times than the beginner—and usually worse, because he has family and responsibilities."

~

The tour of *Mary, Mary* was so successful that Teresa was asked to do another comedy in 1963. *Tchin-Tchin*, after the French original by François Billetdoux, had enjoyed a healthy run on Broadway with Margaret Leighton and Anthony Quinn, but they did not want to continue in a work that required them to be onstage for almost three hours. Teresa accepted the challenge and toured with Dane Clark as her co-star; they portrayed an Englishwoman and an Italian-American man who learn that their spouses are having an affair with each other. The cuckolded couple meet, have a drink, talk—and then they drink and talk some more, and some more . . . and finally they fall in love. The performances were by common consent superior to the play. According to Bob, audiences were both delighted and shocked to see Teresa in the role of a tippling English lady who throws moral caution to the winds.

Her reviews were more than gratifying: "Miss Wright displays the essence of her great ability as an actress as well as her beauty and charm, which have enchanted movie audiences around the world since the beginning of her film-making career," wrote a representative critic. "In the role of Pamela, the cheated-on wife, her performance as first the sober and then the pixilated middle-aged spouse was a delightfully rewarding experience in the theatre."

Meanwhile, Bob was back to work on the screenplay for *The Sand Pebbles* for Robert Wise, who planned to direct it after completing *The Sound of Music*. Writing and revising *The Sand Pebbles* was a healthy distraction for Bob, who was lonely and depressed during Teresa's absence. In a letter to his brother on July 10, 1963, he cited an amusing and poignant line from *Tchin-Tchin*: "I've got that lousy free feeling."

But Bob was briefly encouraged when his play *The Days Between* was revived nationwide to excellent reviews. This was another of his lightly veiled autobiographies, this time the story of a writer who cannot repeat the one success of a decade ago and so makes his wife and son miserable with his dreams of freedom and fortune. Successful in the provinces, the play never reached New York.

∽

During 1964, Teresa was engaged for two hour-long episodes of *The Alfred Hitchcock Hour* that have become television classics. In the first, "Three Wives Too Many," she was reunited with Dan Duryea, her old friend and co-star in *The Little Foxes*. He had the role of Raymond Brown, a traveling salesman and bigamist with four wives in four cities; his legal wife, Marion (Teresa), decides to track down and kill her three rivals—not in jealous rage, but to turn Ray into an attentive, stay-at-home husband.

"Three Wives Too Many" is a rarity in the Hitchcock series—a flippant, funny satire on murder as a fine art. Teresa as Marion goes about her killing spree with a perfect Baltimore-Southern accent, a fine tailored wardrobe and great warmth and dignity—a polite lady, putting poison in her rivals' drinks as if she was gathering posies for a nosegay. The script and the actress wisely went for black comedy, and the result was a darkly witty teleplay worthy of Saki. With *Mary, Mary* and *Tchin-Tchin* behind her, Teresa continued an era in which she favored comedy—not only as a refuge from previous dark stories, but because she was really very good at it, mining its subtleties and never playing to the gallery.

The second episode in the Hitchcock series in 1964 could not have been more different from "Three Wives Too Many." As Stella, a Southerner in "Lonely Place," Teresa portrayed a countrywoman married to a dim-witted, selfish peach farmer (played by Pat Buttram). Desperate for love and attention, she is shadowed by a psychotic hired hand (Bruce Dern) who teases, then attacks and nearly rapes her, in one of the most violent and harrowing dramas broadcast standards permitted in the 1960s.

Teresa's performance, with a pitch-perfect Southern drawl and the dry mouth of a terrorized woman, is a sharp amalgam of loneliness, terror, shock and heartache—all of it played out on her features with a slow glance, a change of tone and the slightest alteration of expression. She had to coddle a wild squirrel in this episode; to run a long distance; and to spar with Dern while wielding a knife. With her plain, matted hair, her sagging housedress and her face a mask of hopelessness, Teresa gave one of the memorable performances in television history. There was considerable consternation in some Hollywood circles that year when she was not nominated for an Emmy award.

An anticipated highlight of autumn 1965 was a three-week staging of *Tea and Sympathy* at the Pheasant Run Playhouse, in St. Charles, Illinois. Bob and Teresa wanted to learn if they could collaborate compatibly on one of his plays—he as director, she as the star. Audiences and local critics were not disappointed, but the Andersons were: the experiment was unsuccessful. "Teresa would rather have the marriage than the part," Bob told a reporter. "We don't really want to work together."

∽

CHAPTER TWELVE

1966–1973

IN THE EARLY 1960S, TERESA HAD CONSIDERABLE SUCCESS WITH road-tour comedies, and she delivered memorable performances on television. But by 1966, a decade had intervened since her last feature film, *Escapade in Japan*, and since that time her agents had received no offers from Hollywood. Audrey Hepburn, Julie Andrews, Barbra Streisand and Elizabeth Taylor were major stars then, and the decade introduced a new wave of actresses—among them, Simone Signoret, Geraldine Page, Sophia Loren, Shirley MacLaine and Anne Bancroft. As Teresa approached her fiftieth birthday, the types of roles for which she was most remembered were no longer being written.

From 1964 to 1973, she appeared in nine television shows, one made-for-TV full-length drama—but only two motion pictures. Both features, made in 1969, were unfortunate: she had negligible roles in them, parts that seem pointless. In *Hail, Hero!*, she popped in and out of two sequences as the mother of Michael Douglas (in his movie debut); in *The Happy Ending*, she portrayed the mother of a bored alcoholic housewife—a role she accepted only for the chance to work again with her friend Jean Simmons. Three additional movies employed her over the next thirty years, but nothing remotely worthy was on offer from Hollywood until a few years before she died. "So I went back to the stage as often as I could. I was always more comfortable in the theatre." In fact, the stage was the place of the triumphant third act of her career.

∽

She never retreated into dreamy solipsism, yearning for the good old days. Nor, despite the offers, did she play a gruesome crank in a horror movie. For a time, Teresa settled quite contentedly into the routines of a Connecticut housewife, the partner of a respected playwright. Their home, on Curtis Road in Bridgewater, was a large nineteenth-century farmhouse with a yellow door. Inside, there were always pots of fresh flowers; shelves of books old and new; and antiques of varying value that Teresa had found here and there, and which she was always trying to repair or refinish. Wooden beams supported the ceilings, and the place was cozily cluttered with farmhouse furniture and warmed by the glow from fireplaces.

Teresa's love for Bob was undiluted, never less than ardent, loyal, reassuring and empathetic—and never more so than when his father died in May 1966. That milestone apparently freed him to complete *I Never Sang for My Father*, with Bob's alter ego as (thus the dialogue) "the eternally bereaved husband [and] dutiful son." The play finally reached Broadway for a moderate run in 1968: it may have been cathartic for the writer, but it did not free him from the heavy chains of the past.

On her side of the family equation, and however much she loved her father, Arthur was more and more a financial burden to Teresa: she paid for the house he shared with his wife, Edy, and for most of their needs and caprices.

Left to herself, Teresa took special pleasure in her gardens. "I had a fine day planting," she wrote in a letter one springtime, "covered up to my ears to protect me from the sun. I must have been a funny sight, with my stockings, boots, pants, shirt, long blue French smock." Her efforts were rewarded: "Teresa is bustling around in her garden," Bob wrote to his brother in July 1967. "Last night we ate our own celery, broccoli and lettuce—it only took 100 hours of work!"

Teresa also derived a great deal of pleasure scouring rural areas and farmhouses in the Connecticut countryside, exploring new routes to a friend's house and stopping here and there if she saw something beautiful or an item on sale at a roadside stand or in an open barn. There was always an apple or a piece of cheese in the glove compartment in case of a hunger emergency.

"She spent a good deal of her time and money making the rounds of tag sales in the country towns, filling their two-car garage with furniture to repair or refinish," Terry recalled. "Every project she tried to undertake seemed to blossom in complexity, causing her to move one step forward, two steps back, muttering and sighing all the while at what Mark Twain called 'the conspiracy of inanimate objects.'"

In addition, Teresa now had more time for reading—an enterprise she always undertook with considerable seriousness. Neither pretentious, boastful nor intellectual about her choices of books, she confided her thoughts to Bob and very few others. Her letters reveal an admirable breadth of interest—from the works of Viktor Frankl and Erich Fromm (whom she termed "profoundly wise and truly informative") to the fiction of Katherine Mansfield.

"I've read a great many of Mansfield's stories as well as her journal and her letters to J[ohn] M[iddleton] Murry," she wrote to Bob, who was in London preparing the British premiere of one of his plays. "I first became interested in Mansfield through an essay Katherine Anne Porter wrote about her." Teresa rated one of Mansfield's best-known stories ("Marriage à la Mode") as "very touching: poor William, and poor, poor, stupid Isabel, who gave up her life, her love and probably her sanity when she rejected her one good and honest impulse to write to William." Teresa was no imperceptive, shallow reader.

⟋⟍

"I haven't had a hit for fourteen years," said Bob in the spring of 1967, when he finally had one. He completed *You Know I Can't Hear You When the Water's Running*, four one-act plays about sex (spoken, not shown) in its various permutations; it opened on Broadway in March 1967 and ran for 771 performances, until January 1969.

As usual, each of the short plays has strong elements of autobiography—especially "I'm Herbert," the last of the quartet, a two-hander in which the female character is named Muriel. "It's not a play about senile old people," Bob told a visitor from the *New York Times*. "It's about Teresa and me. We make dates to meet for a movie and she turns up at the wrong theatre, or if I'm supposed to meet her at 53rd and Fifth, she'll turn up at 63rd and Park." This was not an unwarranted grievance, and it sometimes drove Bob to quiet distraction—as, on the other hand, his autobiographical writings frequently betrayed the intimacy of their marriage and hurt Teresa.

As always, she was the epitome of professional order: she memorized lines meticulously; she researched with single-minded preparation; she worked efficiently and generously with other players. But her organizational abilities, insights and inspirations rarely extended into the realities of daily life. What family and friends often called her scatterbrained lack of focus was perhaps the worst failing in her life.

Bob loved Teresa despite her occasional confusions and habitual dis-
order; more to the point, he needed her (and he needed her need of
him), and this was something he never admitted. If he sometimes loved
her less than wholly or, in the years to come, less faithfully, it is also true
that his devotion sprang from his admiration of her strength and independence—the qualities he paradoxically resented because they meant
that she could survive without him.

∽

In 1967 and 1968, Bob's batteries were well charged. While *Water* was
running, *I Never Sang for My Father* opened on Broadway in January
1968, for a three-month engagement. Thus, for a time Robert Anderson
had two plays on Broadway simultaneously. Against her better judgment—unspoken until years later—Teresa agreed to perform the brief,
unsatisfying role of the leading character's sister. This was a sketchy part,
and she identified several problems with both the construction of the
play and her role in it. But, as Mary-Kelly recalled, "She was unsure
where her loyalties should be—to Bob as her husband or to the integrity
of the play. She took the part for his sake, but the actress playing the
waitress in the restaurant scene was more fortunate in her job than Mom
was in hers."

With their professional lives centered in Manhattan, the Andersons
required a residence there. In 1966, when Mary-Kelly graduated from
the Dalton School and prepared to depart for college, Bob and Teresa left
the Park Avenue apartment and decided to live full-time in Bridgewater.
But that was an ill-considered notion, for the house was an inconve-
nient, two-hour drive from the city and they often had to rent various
places in New York. And so, early in 1968, they purchased a two-bedroom apartment at 14 Sutton Place South.

The address was more fashionable than the living space, which was
both modest and not updated since its 1929 construction; for that reason,
it was not highly priced. A cozy living room had two windows facing
blandly south, toward the buildings across East Fifty-sixth Street; there
were two bedrooms, each with bath; and a compact kitchen was just off
a small foyer. For Bob's workspace, they also purchased a small maid's
room on a lower floor. None of the rooms offered a pleasant view.

∽

In addition to the manifold challenges before his Broadway premieres,
negotiating for screenwriting and fielding offers for lectures and teaching

seasons, Bob always welcomed young apprentice writers. Apparently he never turned away a request for help or advice; he read the plays, stories and novels of strangers carefully, as if he were their dedicated friend or agent; and he sat down with hopeful authors and—tactfully and kindly but with the full force of his impressive erudition—he made cogent suggestions as to how a work might be improved. His comments were never less than valuable.

In this regard, Bob's generosity and guidance are remembered by a cadre of writers (this one included) who frequently turned to him and were always warmly assisted. Among those grateful for his mentorship was the Pulitzer Prize-winning playwright Donald Margulies, who as a student met Bob and began an enduring friendship that, Margulies reiterated, benefited his career.

But the first object of Bob's kindness and generosity was always Teresa's family. "Bob was the only person in my family to actually read my doctoral dissertation," said Terry. Eager to hear about the interests and professional aspirations of both Terry and Mary-Kelly, and always encouraging their talents, Bob was also attentive to their cousin Christine Miller.

After graduating from Wellesley, she lived and worked in Manhattan, where she often visited Bob and Teresa. "Bob could be so courtly and generous," Chris recalled. "I was his guest for dinner at the Harvard Club more than once, and he was always cheerful, full of news and stories and sincerely interested in my work."

But Chris found the marriage of Bob and Teresa problematic. "Bob was always charming, wonderful and literate. He and Teresa were so drawn to each other, but sometimes I thought that maybe they should have remained friends from the start and not married. They didn't live well together, and Bob was very critical of her and never refrained from criticism in the presence of others. He always complained that she drove him mad with her sense of clutter. Their ordinary styles of life were very different. On the other hand, Teresa was really much more stable emotionally than Bob—she was very grounded."

Bob's open criticism of his wife, which increased exponentially with time, also upset friends like Karl and Mona Malden, Jean and Richard Widmark, and Molly and A.R. ("Pete") Gurney. "I remember Bob being so critical of Teresa," Mona Malden recalled. "It's one thing to be critical of someone in private, but he was constantly critical of her in public. He walked into our home more than once with her and said aloud, 'Why doesn't *our* house look this clean, Teresa?' I loved Bob, but this was impossible. She was very quiet when this happened. She took it, which I thought was a big mistake."

∽

Although movie rights to *Father* were snapped up and the 1970 film version was successful, critics did not approve of the play, the playwright or the playwright's wife. "I stopped reading reviews after *Father*," Teresa said years later. "There was one particularly devastating review for both Bob and myself which quite destroyed me."[1]

After *Father* closed in May 1968, Teresa helped Mary-Kelly prepare for her August wedding to Rodney Smith, a photographer. That same season, deeply affected by the nation's traumas, Teresa pitched herself into a variety of efforts to counter them. A month after the assassination of Dr. Martin Luther King Jr. in 1968, she was among a representative group of people in the arts invited to visit King's widow. She continued her frequent donations to the Southern Christian Leadership Conference, headed by Dr. King from its founding in 1957 until his death. She was also a generous contributor to other civil rights organizations and humanitarian causes.

"Mom wanted to help everyone," according to Mary-Kelly. "She was very outspoken against nuclear weapons, she was strongly opposed to the Vietnam conflict and supported the antiwar movement. To name just one cause that touched her, she gave to the Southern Poverty Law Center for years." Years later, Mary-Kelly's second husband, Daniel Picchioni, remembered: "When we helped Teresa sort through her collection of old articles, we found box after box of clippings she had kept. You could follow the course of liberal causes and the slow progress of social justice in those clippings."

She was also roused to political action. With increasing apprehension, she was moved by the murders of Dr. King and of Robert Kennedy that April and June; by the racial violence that erupted in cities; and by the widespread confrontations between police and protesters in major cities. The idea of Hubert Humphrey as president was unacceptable to her, as were both Richard Nixon and Ronald Reagan. Temporarily setting aside her credentials as a lifelong liberal Democrat, she worked on behalf of the progressive Republican presidential candidate, Nelson Rockefeller.

---

1. In the New York *Times*, critic Clive Barnes called the play "sentimental soap opera" and dismissed Teresa's "lack of technique" and her "monotonous voice" (Jan. 26, 1968). Then and later, these were not widely shared reactions to the play or the actress.

"We're never going to solve any of our problems domestically until we really observe civil rights," she said. "Somehow we have to come to terms with our affluent society. All this talk about 'The Beautiful People'—it makes me angry to see an ad for a trinket costing $25,000 or someone wearing a $25,000 gown to a charity event. It's all out of balance, and it's fodder for a revolution. There is such a sense of hate in the air. We have to work very hard to eliminate the things that cause such hatred."

And so, during the summer of 1968, Teresa swung into action, joining the Rockefeller campaign in the hope that he was the most likely to effect positive change. "Teresa is going to Miami for Rockefeller, to help Happy [Rockefeller's wife] greet delegates from August 3rd to 6th," Bob wrote to his brother on July 29. "I suppose he hasn't a chance." But Bob was indulgent of what he considered his wife's quixotic activity. "I sure hope Rockefeller makes it," Teresa told Bob. "Otherwise it's Humphrey and Nixon [as opposing candidates]—and what a choice *that* is!"

From Miami, she telephoned Bob in New York on August 6. "Apparently she had a fine time greeting the delegates for Rocky," he wrote to Don the same day. "But she was appalled by the cynicism of it all. So many delegates told her that they wanted to vote for Rocky, but they depended on the [Republican] machine for their jobs, and they'd be fired if they didn't vote as ordered"—that is, for Nixon. As for Bob, he, too, was a liberal Democrat: "I think if we get Nixon or Humphrey at this crucial time when hopes and sights are high," he wrote in the same letter, "that we'll be in for unheard of trouble from the young and disadvantaged."

∽

In the winter of 1969, Teresa received an urgent call from her friend Jean Simmons in Los Angeles. Divorced from Stewart Granger and now married to the daunting, difficult writer-director Richard Brooks, Jean had spiraled into chronic alcoholism. Her husband may have believed that shock therapy was the best antidote—in this case, a movie called *The Happy Ending*, starring Jean in an obvious and cruel exposé of her troubled life.

"It was just a terribly painful experience," Jean said years later. "To be honest, I had the problem the character had, and it was tough for me to get through the picture." Ironically, Jean was nominated for the best actress Oscar that year, but Teresa provided emotional support during production, once again (as in *The Actress*) playing Jean's mother.

For the first half of 1969, Teresa commuted from New York to California, where she completed her absurdly small role in *The Happy Ending*;

tried to help Jean find the right path to sobriety; and made her small contribution to *Hail, Hero!* The real-life happy ending was achieved when Jean finally and successfully dealt with her addictions, living and working soberly and maintaining the loyalty and affection of many.

Teresa supported her friends professionally whenever she could. William Roerick and Tom Coley, for example, composed a tribute to their friend E.M. Forster, who died in June 1970. In August, Teresa joined Bill, Tom, Peggy Wood and Robert Dryden at the Berkshire Festival, Stockbridge, and then, in October, at the Theatre de Lys, Greenwich Village, where they read selections from Forster's work "with the naturalness of human conversation," as one critic reported.

"Most of the time I don't know what I'm going to do next," Teresa said soon after. "I'd love to do Shaw and Restoration comedy—almost any comedy." An opportunity arose when she returned to New York: the role of a betrayed but acerbically feisty Texas wife and mother in Oliver Hailey's Off-Broadway comedy *Who's Happy Now?* Unfortunately, there were but thirty-two performances, and after a November premiere, the play closed before Christmas.

∽

As for his own playwriting, Bob attempted to repeat his successful format of one-act plays (*You Know I Can't Hear You When the Water's Running*) with a far darker set of two: *Solitaire/Double Solitaire*, on which he worked for most of 1970. "Solitaire" is set in a computerized future in which marriage has been eradicated and human relations reduced to transient meetings and ultimate destruction. The action of "Double Solitaire" occurs in the present and is a series of marital arguments, mostly about sexual compatibility. The two plays, presented in one evening, continued Bob's preoccupation with sex as the glue that holds a marriage together. They also strongly suggest that Bob had seen and hoped to benefit from the success of *Oh! Calcutta!*, a series of sketches about sex that had a long run beginning in 1969.

The language of "Double Solitaire" pushed the boundaries of frank talk about sex in the theatre. "Teresa loathed it," Bob wrote in a letter to Eva Marie Saint, whom he had hoped to cast in another of his plays. "My producer [Gilbert Cates] says, 'How could you expect your wife to feel any differently?' . . . We are still married, [but] our lovely farm only *looks* peaceful . . . I had to escape to Europe and live with the quiet and calm of hotel rooms."

Bob decided to give *Solitaire/Double Solitaire* for production to the eminent Long Wharf Theatre in New Haven, Connecticut, a highly respected nonprofit company founded in 1965. The double bill opened there in February 1971, staged by Arvin Brown, the company's artistic director. He and his wife, the actress Joyce Ebert, were frequent visitors to the house on Curtis Road, and Bob trusted Arvin's talent and instincts.

"Bob was very generous to me," Arvin recalled. "He was determined to take a chance with a young director. But with all his kindness and talent, he had blind spots. At that time, he felt ignored and underappreciated, and paradoxically this led him to some stubborn moments when revisions were in order. He might have had more recognition and produced some better work if he had been willing to do more re-writes. 'Double Solitaire,' for example, had the most blatant and explicit discussion of sex that had ever been heard onstage. But Bob was adamant in keeping almost every word of it."

From their social evenings, Arvin recalled that "Teresa had a really sly sense of humor, compassionate but genuinely funny. She was also extremely intelligent—and as an actress, I don't think she ever got her due." That assessment was shared by all her directors.

Bob's friend and occasional producer Gil Cates, like Teresa, also suggested some alterations in the play's dialogue—not from oversensitivity to the language, but to ensure that audiences would hear the emotional subtexts and not merely be shocked by the explicit dialogue. But Bob remained inflexible and the Long Wharf audience was lukewarm. This was not, however, the end of the double bill.

Just when Bob's two plays were being presented, Teresa resumed her series of remarkable theatrical accomplishments and even surpassed them. Her first achievement—considered a landmark portrayal—was in O'Neill's *Long Day's Journey Into Night*, presented at the Hartford Stage Company in February and March 1971. As the addled, drug-addicted Mary Tyrone, Teresa undertook one of the greatest and most challenging roles in American drama.

"I never dreamed of playing this part," she said that year. "People always have to send a role to me, and then I know within myself whether I can do it. I made up my mind on this part overnight." Rehearsals lasted for long, intense hours, but the cast worked efficiently and collegially.

"At first I almost went mad," she recalled, "because it is an awful lot [to learn] in a short time without a long, long schedule of working on it." Most of all, she was initially disoriented by enacting the character's addiction, but very quickly she decided to learn the lines first, to fix her stage movements, to understand what she was saying and to whom—and then to add the effects of the drugs. "First I had to have all the foundations firm, because if you're thinking of everything in a forced haze from the start, you can't think of anything else." There was nothing mystical or self-referential about her preparation. "I don't do a lot of backstage walking and muttering and that sort of thing. It's more interior. It's quiet." She had no more to say, and no desire to deliver a self-conscious performance.

Reviewers visited from all over the Northeast, ransacking their vocabularies for words of praise. "Wraithlike and lost," wrote the critic of the *New York Times*, "Teresa Wright makes Mary into a figure of infinite pity, taking refuge in drugs and the past, mourning her lost son, the lost hopes of a career as a concert pianist, and the days when she loved her husband and was happy. Miss Wright glides through the play like a visitor, which is precisely right for Mary."

The review in the *Hartford Courant* called her performance "wonderfully low-key, wistful, almost ethereal." And according to Brian Dennehy, who later undertook the role of James Tyrone on Broadway, his first choice of actress to play Mary would have been Teresa. The secret to the role, Dennehy insisted, was that all three men in the play love Mary, the former convent girl, and that adoration was believable when Teresa played the part.

Among a platoon of friends who saw her performance were Fredric March and his wife Florence Eldridge, who also lived in Connecticut and often socialized with Bob and Teresa. In 1956, the Marches had created the leading roles in the Broadway premiere of *Long Day's Journey*—but Teresa's reviews were far more complimentary than Florence's, and now several critics made just that point. When Teresa was told that Freddy and Florence were coming backstage after her performance, she was horrified to think of the potential embarrassment, and so she hurried to clear from her dressing room the published critiques that had praised her at Florence's expense.

∞

That spring of 1971, the Edinburgh Festival invited Arvin Brown and the Long Wharf Theatre Company to bring two plays to Scotland the following summer—the only American regional drama group to receive such an honor. Bob's double bill was selected for its darkly avant-garde style and, for a classic American comedy, *You Can't Take It With You*, which had won the Pulitzer Prize in 1937. Arvin suggested that Teresa take the role of Penny Sycamore in the second play as a refreshing antidote after Mary Tyrone. She accepted at once.

On August 27, Arvin, Bob, Teresa and the casts and crews of *Solitaire/Double Solitaire* and *You Can't Take It With You* arrived in Edinburgh, where their repertory performances began on September 6. According to Arvin, "Bob's play caused quite a stir," and the playwright gloomily undertook further revisions before the Broadway premiere, already booked for a few weeks later. While he worked at their hotel, Teresa explored Edinburgh.

Her role in the comedy by George S. Kaufman and Moss Hart was a lark for her and the audiences. As Penny Sycamore (a role performed earlier by Josephine Hull and Spring Byington, among others), Teresa played a daffy wife and mother, a lovably eccentric dilettante who writes plays with titles like *Sex Takes a Holiday*. Penny pursues this avocation not from artistic ambition but because one day a typewriter was delivered by mistake to her home.

The comedy was repeated, again with Teresa, at Long Wharf that autumn—and once more to enthusiastic notices. She was now where she most wanted to be—firmly in the theatre—and she was not offstage for long during the entire decade to come. Apart from two television roles filmed in California, Hollywood faded easily into the background of Teresa's life.

The New York production of *Solitaire/Double Solitaire* arrived uneasily soon after, on September 30—eighteen years to the day after the first night of *Tea and Sympathy*, whose success it did not repeat: *Solitaire* closed four weeks later.[2] And with that, Robert Anderson, at the age of fifty-four, saw the last Broadway production of his work. Six plays in eighteen years is certainly a respectable legacy, but Bob should perhaps be more remembered for his screenplays—especially *The Nun's Story* and *The Sand Pebbles*—than for his theatre achievements.

Teresa duly noted his "disgust," as she called it, at Broadway's rejection of his double bill. She encouraged him not to retreat into self-pity, but he always felt as if he had been denied a place among the major playwrights—O'Neill, Williams, Miller and Inge. The failure of his recent plays fed his profound sense of insecurity.

---

2. I attended the second performance and noted that the evening seemed confusing and monotonous rather than powerful or shocking.

On the other hand, Bob was soon much in demand as a teacher and lecturer at places like Harvard and the University of California—tasks for which he was brilliantly suited and much admired; indeed, he became an energetic mentor and *éminence grise* to an entire generation of young playwrights. Later, he edited an important and widely used series of literature textbooks for students (which, ironically, brought the most substantial income of his career). Until the late 1980s, he was always busy with one project or another, and his services on the Boards of the Dramatists Guild, the Authors League, the American Playwrights Theatre and other professional societies provide an impressive record of his work in support of the theatre. Was he one of America's great playwrights, in the league of O'Neill, Williams, Miller and Inge? Perhaps not. But as a craftsman, teacher and screenwriter, he had few equals, and that was no small bequest to the cultural life of the twentieth century.

Nor was Bob humiliated by the reaction to *Solitaire*. "They didn't like all the explicit talk about sex," he told me a few years later. "And when I thought about it, I realized—well, maybe I should be writing *novels* about sex, where I can have as many interior monologues and exterior dialogues on the page as I want. Novels will give me more freedom." And so he began to write a book called *After*, which was to have dire personal consequences.

෨

Friends and colleagues often met socially with Bob and Teresa in the writers' community in Litchfield County, Connecticut. Among them were, as always, the Gurneys. "We became very good friends," Pete recalled years later, "and when I first came to New York and began to write plays and have some success, Bob was very supportive. He read my plays and wrote long essays and letters to me about them." Bob also applauded Pete's later, great successes with plays like *The Dining Room, The Cocktail Hour* and perhaps his best-known work, *Love Letters*, which seems to be performed somewhere in the world every night before delighted audiences.

Gurney recalled Teresa with great fondness. "Everybody adored her. Of course she could be very vague, and Bob became impatient with her at dinner parties they gave—she wasn't quite clear about when to serve the meal, for example. He wanted everything done to perfection.

"And Teresa was a great collector. She cut out almost every article of interest to her from newspapers and magazines, and they just piled up in the house. Bob was much more organized and discriminating, but Teresa wanted to gather life around her—and if you talked about a book, she wrote down the details. 'I've got to read that,' she said, and she had lists of things to read in order to improve herself."

Gurney often played tennis with Bob, Elia Kazan and Elia's son Nick. After one game, the Gurneys and Kazan went to dinner at Curtis Road, and (thus Pete) "Bob started in on Teresa—'Phyllis could do thus-and-such the way Teresa can't.' Kazan jumped in and said, 'Now, Bob, cut that out.'"

∽

One of Teresa's finest performances was filmed in the late autumn of 1971 and televised the following February 11; she accepted the offer because once again, the role was a departure from anything she had recently undertaken. *Crawlspace*, based on a recently published novel and directed by John Newland, was a smartly crafted and superbly acted thriller, subtle and intensely disturbing. The story concerns a childless middle-aged couple (Teresa and co-star Arthur Kennedy) who take in a young drifter (played by Tom Happer) whom they find living in their basement crawlspace; he turns out to be a paranoid psychopath. Teresa offered one of her most affecting portrayals, limned with small gestures of empathy, love, confusion, anger, fear and pity.

Continuing to try for wildly different roles, Teresa agreed to a strenuous national tour in Paul Zindel's play *The Effect of Gamma Rays on Man-in-the-Moon Marigolds*, which had recently won the Pulitzer Prize. This was certainly a change of pace: as a single mother whose life has become tangled and confused, she abuses both drugs and her children. Selfish, domineering and prone to sudden rages, she is a terrifying character—but, finally, not completely unsympathetic.

"It's a marvelous work," Teresa told a reporter. "I play a perfectly dreadful person. I told my husband that Beatrice was awful, but I love her. She's so touching and sad. She's a woman without much education, but she has some sort of artistic awareness, although she doesn't know how to use it. She launches terribly sarcastic attacks against her two daughters, but it's a fascinating play because it has a marvelous element of hope. And the play is funny, too."

She began the exhausting tour in the fall of 1972, immediately after Mary-Kelly gave birth to a son she and her husband Roddy named Jonah.

Teresa received $2,000 weekly for the tour of *Gamma Rays*: acting in Equity-approved road companies was more lucrative than performing on Broadway. But Teresa was not overpaid: the schedule of eight performances a week was grueling. She then had to move to another city and another hotel, and learn the layout of a new performance space. In addition, the configurations of theatres and auditoriums vary widely, the dimensions are unpredictable, the backstage areas dark and dusty, the dressing rooms cramped and cold, and not all stage managers are on their cues. These issues routinely create discomfort, confusion and sometimes risks for visiting players. Traveling with the cast from city to city in an airport limousine, Teresa performed in venues from New Jersey to Pennsylvania to Indiana to Missouri to Ohio to northern New York State. "The worst travel schedule is this tour," she said. "I think mad men made it up."

In Durham, North Carolina, she had a close call. "Did I tell you about my misadventure?" she asked in a letter to her brother-in-law, Donald Anderson, on November 10.

> On the opening night, I failed to receive the call to places, and in order to be onstage at the appointed moment, I had to run down a long hall, up two flights of stairs, across the back of the stage and up another flight of stairs [onstage] for my first entrance, in time to gasp my first line—and then it was down a flight of stairs [again onstage] to the telephone and my opening monologue—a nonstop stream of talk that takes all the breath and energy I have, even under the best of circumstances. But in spite of this bad beginning and some terrible lighting goofs, the audience response was great and the second night was much better.

There was a more serious setback in Davenport, Iowa, where Teresa developed a troublesome cough that advanced to bronchitis and a high fever; she was forced to miss a performance. "I've had flu and sore throat six times on this tour," she told a reporter, "and I've been fighting it with vitamin C and rest. You can go on when you're not feeling well, but not without a voice, and not with a cough. I've gone onstage feeling sick, but this is the first time I've missed a performance." She insisted on playing the next performance, but a physician, fearing pneumonia, remained backstage. For the remainder of the tour, until the spring of 1973, she felt constantly exhausted, and the cough persisted for many months.

But waiting for her at home was something far more alarming and depressing than backstage discomforts or respiratory ailments.

Bob had completed his novel *After*, and during Teresa's short break from the tour at Christmastime, he handed her the page proofs to read. "I'm a bit apprehensive about the effect of the material on Teresa," he had written to his brother on September 11. "If she attacks it, which she well might for many reasons, it would be difficult on all scores. But now that I know that the publisher is very high on it, I think I can withstand her quite understandable reactions. I knew that parts of it would hurt her." His expectations and predictions were entirely accurate.

Published in 1973, *After* is a novel about a writer who nurses his cancer-stricken wife until her death. He then meets a young actress with whom he has a fierce, passionate affair that is frequently treated in clinical anatomical detail. When she read the book, Teresa was irrevocably hurt—not because of the book's sexual candor, and not (as Bob maintained for years) because she saw herself on the pages. Her reaction was caused by something very different, for she at once realized what Bob later admitted: *After* was the lightly fictionalized account of his relationship with Audrey Hepburn, who was clearly identified by virtually every description of the character in the book, and as well by those among Bob's friends and colleagues who knew of that intimacy years earlier.[3]

"Writers can only use their own histories," Bob told me in 1984, "and my novel *After* really tells the whole story of my affair with Audrey." At that time, everyone kept a discreet silence, mostly in deference to Teresa. To no one's surprise, Hepburn kept her own dignified counsel.

Teresa had apparently known of the affair that ended before her marriage to Bob; she did not, however, expect it to be so clearly and bluntly documented and publicized. The novel was so adoring a portrait of a writer's impassioned love for a much younger actress after his first wife's death, and so plainly a portion of his own life story before and after Phyllis, that perhaps any woman would have felt less confident of her place in her husband's heart. For someone with Teresa's fragile self-image, the episode was catastrophic. She felt deeply betrayed, but Bob never understood this.

The marriage, then fourteen years on, was forever changed by Bob's need once again to write about himself and those in his past. "If my mother had really felt secure in her marriage," said Mary-Kelly, "she and

---

3. For a complete treatment of *After* in this regard, see *Enchantment: The Life of Audrey Hepburn*, pages 126–28.

Bob could have worked out this problem. But she knew what was going on, and she felt that she wasn't loved."

Teresa resumed the tour of *Marigolds*, performing with her usual single-mindedness, force and humor, but privately she nursed an incurable wound.

∽

CHAPTER THIRTEEN

1974–1978

"WE OBSERVED A TRUCE," BOB SAID OF HIS MARRIAGE FOLLOWING the publication of *After*. He and Teresa temporized about a separation, and he visited her during the tour of *Marigolds*. "I told her that I thought we should try to stay together," he wrote to his attorney, "but that I could not be castrated in terms of my writing." His use of such a violent metaphor suggests that, absurdly, he regarded Teresa as the major adversary, the threat to his success as a novelist.

In January 1974, a three-month run of *Death of a Salesman* began at the Philadelphia Drama Guild. George C. Scott was signed to direct, but he and Arthur Miller loudly disagreed on many aspects of the production. Finally, after disruptive arguments resounded in the auditorium, Miller took over the direction of his own play. Martin Balsam played the hapless Willy Loman, and Teresa was Linda, Willy's long-suffering wife. The engagement was so popular and critically successful that at once there were plans for a major Broadway revival.

Returning to New York in March, Teresa resumed discussions with Bob about their future together. She found him greatly depressed: he had written a screenplay based on *After* and sent it to Paramount Studios, where it was rejected speedily "and insultingly," as he told his attorney.

Teresa was not surprised to hear this news, but she remained silent and changed the subject. "I think you want a separation or divorce," she said. Bob, now fearful that she would leave his life forever, replied that he believed their marriage was "as good as ninety percent of the marriages we knew." But he also said that he thought "both of us wanted something more." His letters and conversations from 1974 to 1978 reveal a man in a state of suppressed panic that he would lose his wife: "I found it inconceivable that we wouldn't go on together." But she felt quite differently, and before the end of 1974 they had agreed on a one-year trial separation.

The troubled marriage soon became evident to Teresa's son and daughter. After earning his doctorate at Berkeley, Terry accepted a teaching assignment at the State University of New York, which made possible more frequent visits with his mother and Bob. "I began to see more clearly some of the distressing patterns in their relationship: Bob's tendency toward heavy-handed teasing, for example—and the Phyllis memories never abated."

But now there was an additional topic that intruded into Bob's conversations: "He tended to dwell far more often than seemed appropriate on sex and sexuality," according to Terry.

> The occasion didn't seem to matter—[it could occur at] a private chat or among a group of guests at dinner. He followed any hint of the topic or introduced it out of nowhere, to the point that we began to tease him about developing into a dirty old man. Sometimes Mom would just roll her eyes, and sometimes she would take serious issue with him, and he made a serious defense of himself, saying that sex was one of the great drives behind human actions and thus the proper study of a dramatist. I know that some of his friends, behind his back, were puzzled and even worried about this fascination. All of these issues lay behind Mom's eventual decision to divorce him.

Mary-Kelly believed that Bob was having a true midlife crisis, that he was anxious about his attractiveness to women and consequently about his sexual competence. Her concern was made more poignant by the fact that (thus Terry) Bob was still "the kind Bob, the gentleman Bob [who] had not disappeared."

౭౦

Notwithstanding all her anxieties and activities, Teresa (like Bob) made time to help others, even strangers. In 1974, I was living in New York, beginning the research for my first book, *The Art of Alfred Hitchcock*, a critical appreciation of the director's motion pictures. I thought it essential to speak with a few of Hitchcock's leading players, and I telephoned Teresa Wright's New York agent at the time, a man named Stark Hesseltine. Without any publishing credentials or personal recommendations (or even, at that time, a publisher for the book), I expected to be turned away. I was wrong. Hesseltine gave me a phone number to call.

When I rang the number, a man's voice replied that Miss Wright was not at home at the moment, but that he would pass along a message to her. Presuming that I was speaking with a secretary or another agent, I said that I would also like to extend my respects to her husband, whose screenplay for *The Nun's Story* I much admired. Did the man know how I might also contact Mr. Anderson? There was a slight pause, and I heard a chuckle: "This is Robert Anderson. Thank you for your nice words about my work."

Later that day, my phone rang, and Teresa Wright invited me to meet her at 14 Sutton Place South, Apartment 8-F, on the afternoon of June 26. She was the first interview I conducted among hundreds for many books in my subsequent career, and she set a high standard for a warm welcome, a generous allotment of her time to help me and an invaluable contribution to the work in progress. We met for over two hours that day, discussing *Shadow of a Doubt* and Hitchcock; her memory was prodigious as she recalled specific moments during preproduction and filming.

My notes for that interview also indicate that she referred to a scene or two from the Hitchcock movie and then explained how other directors might have filmed it—William Wyler, for example, and Fred Zinnemann and George Cukor. Teresa was a first-rate, highly engaging storyteller, and when I departed that afternoon and thanked "Miss Wright," she corrected me: "Teresa," she said.

Within the week, she called me again, to offer a few more anecdotes she thought might be helpful. I invited her to tea, and she accepted. A friendship had quickly been formed, and for the rest of her life we remained in contact by phone calls, letters and visits past counting. And as friends will do, we shared confidences.

As it happened, Bob had departed for a summer of teaching at Harvard. I wrote to him in July, asking to borrow a copy of his script for *The Nun's Story* for my own study. He replied at length on August 6, explaining in courteous detail the reasons for his delay in answering my letter:

Apologies for not getting back to you sooner. Your letter arrived the morning I was taking off for Cambridge for the summer, to be a kind of unofficial writer in residence at the Loeb Drama Center.

Immediately after my arrival, my brother's wife had an unsuccessful operation for a brain tumor, and so I have spent a lot of time with him in Rochester. She died last Tuesday, and I have just returned to Cambridge to take up where I left off.

Thank you for your good letter about THE NUN'S STORY. I know that Teresa enjoyed her talk with you, and she did attest to the fact that you knew much of the script [of *Shadow of a Doubt*] by heart.

I would like to loan you a copy of the script, but I can't at the moment. I had to send my only copy to a man at Purdue who is writing a book on me. He has the use of it until the fall. When he sends it back, I shall get it to you.[1]

Thanks for your enthusiasm, and if you don't hear from me by mid-fall, please drop me a note and remind me. I shall be moving around a good deal (publicizing the paperback of AFTER and lecturing), so I may lose track of things. Don't hesitate to jog my memory.

Bob and I finally met in New York early that autumn. I was at once struck by his kind concern for my inchoate career as a writer and by his generous endorsement of my friendship with Teresa, which he complemented by the tacit offer of his own. Another letter followed, dated November 23, when he returned to Cambridge:

The screenplay of *The Nun's Story* is on its way to you! I am teaching a playwriting seminar here at Harvard, and Teresa is acting at the Long Wharf Theatre in New Haven. Hope all is well with you and your research for your book.[2]

At Long Wharf from December 20, 1974, to January 17, 1975, Teresa appeared as Lily Miller in O'Neill's *Ah, Wilderness!*, again under Arvin Brown's direction. At first, he hoped that she would play the leading role of the mother, Essie, but Teresa declined: "I was emotionally upset [over Bob] and just did not feel up to doing the mother. I suggested Geraldine Fitzgerald, and she was wonderful in it. Besides, I loved the part of Aunt Lily—it's a wonderful role, and I was grateful to Arvin for letting me play her. He is a very loving director—very loving. He loves the characters and he enjoys seeing you bring them to life."

1. The professor at Purdue was Thomas P. Adler, whose book about Bob was published in 1978. See the Bibliography.
2. My lengthy appreciation of The Nun's Story is included in *Enchantment: The Life of Audrey Hepburn*.

On his side, as Arvin said years later, "I speak of Teresa often to those who knew her work and even to those who didn't—and I stress her quality of listening. She was totally present in a scene, and that had to do with her capacity to listen. She listened to other actors onstage the way very few actors do." That habit of attention may also be observed in each of her movie and television performances.

Bob, meanwhile, had frequently commuted from Harvard to New York during the summer and autumn terms, but not for business. While Teresa was rehearsing and then performing at Long Wharf, he began a long-term affair with a well-known lady, married and with children. Because he and she were both married and careful to avoid any adverse publicity, the affair was conducted in guarded secrecy, and they rarely met more often than once weekly. But in Manhattan's small literary world, it was risky.

Although Bob felt that his marriage was now only a formality, he was a jumble of mixed emotions and frequently expressed the hope that he and Teresa would be reconciled. "My life remains complicated," he wrote to his brother.

> The woman from New York has filled my room with flowers, the air with telephone calls [and] the mailbox with desperate letters. It is confusing. Meanwhile, things have been moving very comfortingly with [Teresa]. But still, the woman in New York is extraordinary, and it was and is a great love—and so we are meeting again this weekend . . . If she were available, there is no question of what would happen. But I don't think she should leave her husband, and I know that now that I am free, I couldn't subsist on once a week in the afternoon.

Was Teresa aware of this liaison at the time? It is impossible to say for certain. But from 1975, her trust in Bob diminished even as her enduring love for him survived, despite *After*.

"What a complicated and tortured man he was," said Mary-Kelly. "We loved him despite the way he undercut his great heart. I suspect that underlying all of his divided allegiances was his inability to value himself enough—a flaw he accused Mom of having. He was stuck in a mode of perpetual longing. He had so much to set him at ease and be truly happy about, not least of which was Mom's undying love for him." But Bob was never at ease, never truly happy. Teresa did not know what more she could do for him; she was also aware that she had to be alert, energetic and optimistic for her work.

∽

In January 1975, as I continued to work on *The Art of Alfred Hitchcock*, I was invited to conduct a course on the director at the New School for Social Research, in Greenwich Village. In addition to lectures, discussions and screenings of Hitchcock's major works, I thought it would be enriching for the students to learn directly from those who worked with Hitchcock. The first person I contacted was Teresa, who visited my class on March 24, gave a brief presentation on working with Hitchcock, and then fielded questions for over an hour. She took to the role of ersatz visiting professor with relaxed good humor and a natural ability to reach students of all ages. Similarly, a few days after my first meeting with Teresa, I interviewed Tippi Hedren, who also became a close friend. She, too, often visited the Hitchcock classes to discuss her experiences on *The Birds* and *Marnie*.

On April 6, Teresa invited me to dinner at Sutton Place, from which she had not yet moved, and where we were both surprised to find Bob, whose out-of-town speaking engagement had been suddenly canceled. According to my diary, the evening passed pleasantly, but at one point he unfavorably compared something Teresa said or did to the customs of "Phyllis-my-first-wife."

But Bob was as ever the generous advocate of another's work. That spring, Ingrid Bergman was in New York, appearing on Broadway in John Gielgud's production of Maugham's *The Constant Wife*. Bob very kindly asked me if I would like to interview her for my Hitchcock book, and he rang her at once. And so it was that, on May 8, Ingrid invited me to be her guest for a performance of the play at the Shubert Theatre, and to join her for dinner at Sardi's, just across the street. The taped interview, which covered her three performances for Hitchcock (in *Spellbound*, *Notorious* and *Under Capricorn*) was another rich contribution to the book. That was the first of many meetings with Ingrid, who also became a good friend to me, thanks to Bob's intercession.

∽

Also in May, plans were finalized for the revival of *Death of a Salesman* at the Circle in the Square, located on Fiftieth Street at Broadway. Arthur Miller had other commitments and reluctantly turned the direction back to George C. Scott. "Linda is an exhausting role to play," said Teresa, "but ah! to get another chance to play it. As an actress you like to do all the great roles more than once, especially when one works as slowly as I do in developing a character."

Arthur and Edna Wright were in the audience one evening. "He certainly was affected by it," Teresa said. "He's 84 and hasn't been selling insurance for years now, but he still has a salesman's view of life—the [desire for] success, the American dream, being well liked and getting life's tiger by the tail." Arthur was unwell that season, and soon his health began to fail, slowly and irreversibly. He died at his home in Chatham, New Jersey, in December 1978 at the age of eighty-seven; Edy's death followed in July 1989.

After the stormy time in Philadelphia, Teresa hoped for smoother waters in New York, but she was disappointed. Constantly anxious about Scott's chronic heavy drinking, she saw its increasingly harmful effect not only on his performance and direction but also on other cast members, whom he often dragooned to join him at local watering holes. Scott was not completely out of control until one night when, by an unfortunate coincidence, Teresa had arranged for her son and a few of his academic colleagues to see the show.

"We never got to see it," Terry recalled. "At the theatre door, we were handed a notice that the evening's performance would be canceled owing to Mr. Scott's 'grave illness.' Mom was furious with Scott, with her fellow actors who had been out drinking with him and with the craven manager of the theatre who had canceled the show. She thought they should have told the audience the truth and let the understudy play the part that night to show Scott up. Never before and never afterward did I see her in such a rage."[3]

Teresa received reviews that ranged from fervent to downright worshipful. Her Linda was "a woman of grave charm," according to *The New Yorker*. "Face severely in repose, voice rarely raised, Teresa Wright is both patient and rock-hard in her steadfast coping," wrote Walter Kerr in the *Times*. "She is so poignant that one wan smile tells encyclopedias of pain and survival," observed the *Daily News*. Nothing less than superb notices described her performance.

A few days after the formal premiere, Teresa composed her thoughts in a calm, reasoned letter to Bob, dated July 2; the content may indicate her awareness of his extramarital wandering.

3. At the performance I attended at the end of June, Scott seemed unusually wild, but I took that for the role. When I visited Teresa backstage later that evening, she said she was relieved that there had been no cancellation. Only later did I understand her meaning.

We have tried our year's separation, and I think it must be clear to both of us that though we have love and concern for each other, we no longer have a marriage.

You have said, "I can't imagine going on without you," or words to that effect—but unless we can both say "I love you, I need you, I desire you, I am happiest when I am sharing a life and a home with you," we should not try to be together—and hard as it is for both of us to face this right now, I think we must meet to discuss taking the next step in a separation or divorce.

I am most anxious to do my best to start supporting myself. Obviously, I would like to support my father as well, but as I said last March or April when we first discussed all this, I don't know how I'll ever do it.[4] As for me, I will trust you to help me to the extent that I may need it, and I think you should trust me to take care of myself when I can.[5] I hate for you to be put in the position of just paying for my support, but I can tell you I find it devastatingly destructive to just take without being able to give and to share. So please, dear, help me to help myself. I will do "Ah, Wilderness!" so that will insure my earning money through November.

Let us both try to find ourselves—and if we do, perhaps there is a chance that we can get together in some different relationship in the future . . .

There is more to be said—much more—but [it is] too late and too heartbreaking. I love you, Bob, but not enough to be just tolerated, or just taken care of financially. There *is* joy in life and one must try to find it, or make it or *be* it.

Love, Teresa

Three days later, the telephone rang in my apartment on East Sixty-ninth Street: Teresa was calling from an outdoor pay phone on Third Avenue to ask if I would offer her a cup of tea. I heard anxiety in her voice and told her to come at once. On arriving, she seemed unusually weary, and even before she dropped into a chair, she said, "I'm going to divorce Bob."

Up to this time, I had no idea that her marriage was in such dire straits. She had told me nothing about *After* since we had met a year earlier, and nothing about her emotional estrangement from Bob. By this

4. Over the past decade, Bob had been sending $250 each month to Arthur and Edy.

5. Since 1960, Teresa's salary had ranged from $7,000 to $65,000 annually—before taxes. But from 1970 to 1975, her income had remained at the lower end of that scale.

time, I felt that he was as much my friend as Teresa was, and this posed a dilemma for me: I am ashamed to remember that I asked myself what this news would mean for *me*. Would I have to choose between them, give up one friendship to keep the other?

At the moment, I saw only a forlorn friend to whom (I recall thinking) I could offer only tea and sympathy. But, as Teresa told me how betrayed she felt by Bob's book, clearly there was an unspoken subtext, and I wondered but did not inquire if there was another woman in Bob's life; she volunteered only that there was no other man in hers. That afternoon, she asked me more than once, "Do you think I am acting too quickly? Am I making a mistake?" I told her that I did not think so. I was unutterably sad for both of them. As she departed hours later, she managed a smile and a line she knew I recognized: "Well," she said, "after all, a girl's got to breathe."

Teresa's letter of July 2 elicited an immediate reply from Bob. On July 7, she received his four-page, single-spaced typewritten letter, a long and labored self-defense. After rehearsing the history of their last year, he made a startling comment:

> I don't think you can begin to know what a devastating effect your reaction to my book [*After*] had on me as a person and as a writer. And I know the book itself had a terrible effect on you . . . I have come to feel that I could live with it as far as it affects my life, but I don't think you realize how it affects your life and your mood. You said that you didn't feel "loved or cherished," and I asked you, if this were true, didn't you feel in any way responsible.

Bob's letter rambled on. He accused Teresa of insensitivity to his emotional and professional needs, and was apprehensive that she would begin divorce proceedings. He seemed unable to understand that his love for her was simultaneously diluted by his cagey infidelities and diminished by her independence. Many times that year and in the decades to come, Bob told me that he hoped he would die before Teresa, "because she can't live without me." I believe he was very wrong indeed: it was he who could not live without her, although that would have been intolerable for him to accept.

Weeks later, perhaps because Bob was as always unable to keep his private life private, the press became aware of the troubled marriage. "We decided on a year's separation," Teresa told a reporter who had heard the news and now put a blunt question to her. "And now that the year is up we're caught in indecision. What will happen, I just don't know. Everything is in the air right now. It has all been very difficult."

∽

Her refuge was her work. In September, Arvin Brown's Long Wharf production of *Ah, Wilderness!* transferred to the Circle in the Square for a three-month run. Once again, she was the darling of the critics: reviews of her performances were spiced with adjectives like "delicate and moving . . . ideal . . . splendid." Tom and Mary Helmore, who had taken an apartment on East Fifty-second Street, gave a reception for Teresa, who included me on the guest list that included Brian Aherne, Mildred Natwick, Janet Perkins and Whitfield Cook. Like Teresa, each guest had a connection to Alfred Hitchcock, who was the recurring subject of our conversations that afternoon.[6]

After the play closed in November, Teresa remained at Sutton Place South, reading scripts for stage and screen that had been submitted for her consideration, while Bob stayed mostly in Bridgewater, working on a new novel. They met frequently for dinner, for continuing discussions about a divorce, and for visits with Mary-Kelly, Terry and Chris Miller. In the spring of 1976, Teresa began a tour in the deft, serious and sophisticated one-act comedies "Come Into the Garden Maud" and "A Song at Twilight," which comprised *Noël Coward in Two Keys*. She and her co-star Richard Kiley performed to capacity audiences in several cities through the summer.

During the tour, Teresa's agents sent her the script for *Flood!*, a television project that took her to the Warner Bros. Studios in Burbank. As the title indicates, this was another so-called disaster movie from Irwin Allen, following his productions of *The Poseidon Adventure* and *The Towering Inferno*. But underneath the typical exigencies of the genre, there was an affecting story of a married couple (Teresa and Richard Basehart) whose relationship had lost any semblance of trust and confidence. Teresa may have drawn on her emotions at the time for her portrait of a woman whose husband can only condescend to her but never confides in her. Her character, Alice Cutler, drowns in the floodwaters while trying to save a life.

That autumn, my book *The Art of Alfred Hitchcock* was published, and the New School was host for a reception to mark the event. During one

6. Brian Aherne had appeared in Hitchcock's movie *I Confess*; Mildred Natwick was in *The Trouble With Harry*; Anthony Perkins, Janet's son, played Norman Bates in *Psycho*; Whitfield Cook wrote the screenplay for *Stage Fright*; and Tom Helmore had a key role in *Vertigo*.

of my visits with Hitchcock earlier that year, he had offered to record a droll audiotape endorsing the book; it was played at the celebration on November 18 to everyone's delight. Tom Helmore joined Teresa as my honored guests, and each of them stepped up to speak engagingly about their work with Hitchcock. Bob escorted Teresa, and later we dined at a Greenwich Village bistro after the reception. I noted that nothing seemed amiss in the Anderson marriage, which was turning out to be an unpredictable roller-coaster ride, with meetings that were warmly companionate one day and laced with recriminations the next.

That same year, Bob, like Teresa, made the first of many visits to my classes at the New School. I regularly offered screenings of *The Nun's Story* as part of a series on director Fred Zinnemann, or on the subject of religion in films. Bob's remarks were important for the students, whom he addressed with friendly cordiality. I also invited another, even more personal specialist on the subject to join us—Sister Irene Mahoney, an Ursuline nun for many years who was also a university professor of literature with a Ph.D. and the author of several superb historical biographies. She had been a close friend to me for many years, and she and Bob made the seminar discussions of *The Nun's Story* rich beyond anyone's expectations.

After Bob's first visits to the New School, and when I was in a position to hire a variety of experts to join the faculty, I thought first of him—after all, who better to offer a course on screenwriting? He sent his regrets:

> Thanks for offering the screenwriting course, but I'm in a writing year. As you know, I like teaching and usually manage to do some each year. But I'm finishing a second draft of a play, and then I move directly to a TV movie . . . When I get out from under that, let's get together, and you can tell me how your novel is going.

That novel was an ill-advised venture on my part, one never to be completed, for which the world of letters can be forever grateful. But Bob took my efforts seriously, sending me detailed suggestions for revision and expansion and inviting me for meals to discuss the book's ill-fated structure, style and characters. I learned a great deal, not least that fiction would never be my strong suit. But Bob was never less than my loyal advocate and champion.

᪥

The new year 1977 was full of constant activity for Teresa, a time in which she completed her first feature film in eight years; another television drama; and two memorable stage performances. Her crowded schedule was undertaken not only because she wanted to earn and save as much as possible but also because work gave her a sense of purpose that her private life did not.

She began with a role in the Merchant-Ivory movie *Roseland*, a three-part anthology about the denizens of the famous dance club on West Fifty-second Street in Manhattan. Given star billing and working at Roseland during a bitter, snowy January, Teresa appeared in the first tale as a woman so confined by memories of her late husband and their past (which she repeatedly sees in a mirror at Roseland) that she almost alienates a suitor, affectingly played by Lou Jacobi. With a perfectly pitched Brooklyn-Irish accent and a sense of muted melancholy, Teresa created in a half-hour a full portrait of a brave and sad woman who finally comes to terms with the present and waltzes her way back into real life. Her entire segment, dance numbers included, was filmed in four days.

Writing of her achievement in *Roseland*, Stephan Talty accurately celebrated Teresa's "luminous and totally unspoken feeling for a past innocence. The surpassing gentleness of thirty years ago had returned, untoughened and without bitterness. She could not become a Norma Desmond [in *Sunset Boulevard*] because she had not lost her great qualities."

After that production, Teresa began rehearsals for an important revival of Ibsen's *The Master Builder*, in which she assumed the difficult role of the title character's wife, Aline Solness. This was a thorny challenge, for the past tragedies in Aline's life, which we do not see, have overwhelmed her present and rendered her marriage as drab and colorless as her unchanging black wardrobe.

When I traveled to the Kennedy Center in Washington, D.C., to see the production that June, I noted the remarkable stillness in Teresa's performance—a vivid counterpoise to Aline's inner hysteria. She held the stage throughout but never overshadowed her co-stars, Jane Alexander and Richard Kiley. Late that evening, I accompanied Teresa for a drink at her hotel nearby. The play had somehow both wearied and refreshed her, but it was a dark and unhappy drama, and she was unsure about continuing in it through mid-July at the Westport Country Playhouse. But Jane and Richard—and Jane's husband, Edwin Sherin, who was directing—persuaded her.

After a brief summer interval, Teresa was again in the thick of rehearsals—this time as the subdued but strong matriarch Aunt Hannah in Tad Mosel's play *All the Way Home*, based on James Agee's novel *A Death in the Family*. She received $285 a week for two months, almost exactly her stipend for the Ibsen play.

Acting was her refuge, but Teresa could not escape making a final decision about her divorce, and to Bob's astonishment, she insisted on proceeding. On December 11, 1977, she sent him an art card with a reproduction of the Matisse *Pot of Geraniums* in memory of their flowers at Bridgewater. On the reverse she wrote:

Not exactly a happy anniversary, but since it's our last one, I just want to remember that happy day 18 years ago—and once again, some of the many happy days that followed for the next 12 or 13 years. So with thanks for the past and hopes of a happier future for us both,
All my love, T.

It was, as she indicated, their "last anniversary" because the divorce papers were on the lawyers' desks. And the last three words before her signature were never truer. She would forever after offer him all her love, even though she knew he could not respond in kind. "Bob was in love with someone before me," Teresa told her daughter, referring to Audrey Hepburn. "I thought he was over it, but he wasn't." Audrey and Phyllis, the two women most alive in Bob's every day even in their different absences, claimed his deepest devotion. He was the prototype of the romantic fantasist: Phyllis was long dead; and Audrey, who had divorced Mel Ferrer, had remarried and was living in Rome.

In February 1978, a document issued by the Superior Court of Litchfield County, Connecticut, stipulated that the dissolution of the marriage between Plaintiff Teresa W. Anderson and Defendant Robert Anderson owed simply to the fact that "the marriage has broken down irretrievably." She did not provide the court with details, nor did she list any grievances. Not long after, Teresa Wright Anderson legally modified her name—for the first time—to Teresa Wright.

"People used to say 'You talk a lot about Phyllis,'" Bob wrote in a letter to Teresa that accompanied his signature on the divorce decree. "I don't intend to change. Why should I? I am what all the years and relationships have made me. My cherishing of the past does not threaten whatever might be in the present. So now people say, 'You talk a lot about Teresa.'" He did indeed, but always to say how he could not comprehend the divorce.

∽

From that time, Bob sent her money to supplement her income; there was no schedule for alimony payments, which she declined. "Take the money," he added.

> You have not worked these first two months [of 1978]. The Settlement provides that the amounts can be changed to fulfill the intention of the Agreement. Since that depends on a combination of what you earn and what I earn, we'll know more later. But you need the money now, so take it. I have been nibbling away at capital for the last two years, trying to hold inviolate my basic investment in stocks and bonds (which goes up and down with the market). If we were together, I could convert all this to bonds now, and as a couple we would have a very nice retirement fund.

That carrot did not persuade her, nor did the elaboration of his financial status:

> I am very depressed about the work outlook. I am hoping for the success of the book [his forthcoming second novel]. If it does not succeed, and if no real movie money is coming through, I will have to alter my life drastically. I am already trying to be as careful as I can be. I want to try to give you whatever "extra" I can, if I can.

Bob had recently sent her a check for $800, but such an amount was irregular. He then turned the issue of money over to her, adding an implicit complaint: "You know your problem with money—if it is available, you will spend it." He concluded by urging Teresa to return to counseling, this time under the care of a woman named Dr. Helen De Rosis, who had written about women and anxiety (the three-word title of a book she later published).

In April, Simon & Schuster published Bob's new novel, *Getting Up and Going Home*; years later, it was adapted by another writer for a television movie. By then, those who knew Bob expected autobiography only faintly disguised as fiction, and they were not wrong to do so. The story concerns a successful lawyer named Jack whose wife suddenly asks for a divorce. He is surprised and then hurt, although he has already begun an affair with a friend's wife. Jack moves to Cambridge, Massachusetts, where he meets a young divorcée. Stuck in his male menopause, he ultimately finds comfort only with his Irish setter: his wife will not take him back, as she has had enough of marriage.

The book caused no great excitement in bookshops, nor did it ring up impressive sales. But Bob now had a contract to edit a four-volume set of literature textbooks for students, which brought him a consistently high income for the rest of his life.

"I tried for two years to get Teresa to reconsider the idea of a divorce," Bob wrote to Eva Marie Saint four days after signing the decree. "But she just won't. The last book had a lot to do with it, but that's a complicated story."

So was his intimate life. "Bob was furious that Teresa would not re-marry him after their divorce," recalled Christine Miller. "He went around saying, 'If Teresa doesn't marry me again, I'll leave all my money to the Dramatists Guild!'" That threat was never realized.

He may indeed have been lonely and forlorn (words he frequently employed in letters to lawyers, accountants, agents and friends), but Bob found his emotional compensations. The ink on the divorce decree had scarcely dried when—as life imitated *Getting Up and Going Home* and Bob reflected the character Jack—he began an affair with Hope Lange. This attractive, busy actress, sixteen years younger than Bob, had gone from her marriage to actor Don Murray to a romance with Glenn Ford before she wed and divorced director Alan J. Pakula. She was subsequently in-volved with Frank Sinatra and then with the author John Cheever (an unlikely mate on several counts).

Hope's favor then fell on Bob, and they became, in the language of the day, "an item." *New York* magazine wrongly published news of their marriage—"they finally got around to it"—but that was merely a way of avoiding litigation. On her side, Teresa was now beyond disquiet over such antics.

❦

CHAPTER FOURTEEN

1978–1984

"THEIR DIVORCE TOOK A STRANGE TURN," TERRY RECALLED. "IN FACT, it didn't seem to have 'taken' at all. They had two residences but seemed to spend a great deal of time together in one or another location, doing pretty much what they had been doing before the divorce." The apprehension of those like myself, who feared losing contact with either Teresa or Bob, was entirely groundless. If we could not reach Teresa after a few days, we rang Bob's number at Sutton Place South, and there she was; if we wanted to speak with Bob, we had only to find Teresa. In some ways, the arrangement apparently suited them both.

From 1978, she moved frequently: to a condominium in Branford, Connecticut; to an apartment in Manhattan Plaza; to a sublet on Mitchell Place; to a flat on the West Side—it was often difficult for her friends to keep up, but we helped to load a truck when she relocated from one residence to another.

Bob continued to make financial contributions for Teresa's livelihood, which allowed her to live more comfortably than if she were entirely self-supporting. And if she was in distress—as, for example, during a hospital stay in California, when she went down with pneumonia—Bob at once went to her side. Respiratory problems troubled her for the rest of her life, as did occasional insomnia, a case of late-onset vitiligo, and problems with her toes and feet that eventually required surgery. "After years of wearing high heels onstage and in movies, she was in trouble, and high arches put a lot of pressure on her feet," recalled Mary-Kelly.

I knew that I could not invite Teresa for dinner or any social event without including Bob, or Bob without Teresa. But the atmosphere was not invariably smooth when they were together. Phyllis was always the unseen guest and the standard for everything good, and Teresa fared poorly by comparison. One winter evening in 1981, I invited them to my apartment. "Teresa," said Bob, "why can't you be neat and organized like Donald?" This remark was difficult to counter, but when Bob rang me the following day, I told him that he really should not say such things. He laughed.

In time, Bob lost a number of friends and companions who would not sustain this sort of denunciation: the Kazans withdrew, as did the Widmarks, the Maldens, the Gurneys and others, all of whom tried to see Teresa on her own. "It was just too embarrassing when Bob and Teresa were together," as Chris Miller recalled. "We all hurt for her." As for Bob, he usually insisted that he was the one who suffered. "In a way, it was the perfect arrangement for him," said Mary-Kelly. "It served his sense of melancholy and his lifelong sense of being rejected."

In October 1978, Teresa was in Los Angeles, filming a role in a television series. She took a fall at Paramount Studios and broke her wrist but gamely finished the assignment and returned to New York, where she recuperated at Bob's apartment with the help of a part-time assistant. On November 11, I received a letter of thanks for remembering her birthday: "My broken wrist makes everything, including writing, difficult for me. A friend is typing this, so you'll receive my thanks in neat, cold type rather than in my old scrawl."[1] (Her handwriting, on the contrary, was always easy to read.)

On March 7, 1979, the American Film Institute honored Alfred Hitchcock with its Lifetime Achievement Award at a gala dinner in Beverly Hills. By that time, I had come to know Hitch quite well—most notably during July 1975, when he invited me to watch the filming of *Family Plot* (as it turned out, his last picture). My taped interviews with Hitch were included in *The Art of Alfred Hitchcock* and added greatly to its success.

The producers of the AFI tribute invited me to make some contributions to the show, to prepare program notes and to meet in advance with Ingrid Bergman, John Houseman and François Truffaut, the hosts of the evening. I escorted Teresa, who gave a brief salute to Hitch, and at the conclusion of the evening (filmed for nationwide broadcast on March

1. Teresa's many letters to me included generous comments when my books were published. She never failed to offer support—as did Bob, who interrupted his work in Connecticut to attend the launch party for my second and third books in October 1978, when Teresa was at Paramount.

12), she and I joined Ingrid for a nightcap; despite grave illness, Ingrid had traveled from her home in London for the event.

That same season, Bob asked me to read the first draft of his new play, *Free and Clear*. I did not report back to him that I wished that the dialogue had not been quite so verbose and repetitive; I simply said, "Well, Bob, you've done it again!" and kept my counsel. Several years passed before *Free and Clear* was produced. "The literary community simply will not accept me," he wrote back. "I think that my subject matter, relationships and sex, threatens too many of the brethren. So I feel as fidgety as a pregnant woman."

He continued to be a faithful friend to those he trusted. In late April 1980, Ingrid was in New York when Alfred Hitchcock died in California. Bob rang me to report that Ingrid had been invited to the funeral—but that she did not want to attend: she felt that the appearance of stars would adversely affect the dignity of a memorial service. "She's very upset," Bob told me, "because she doesn't know if she should go to the funeral or not. But she doesn't want to be selfish about it. Ingrid likes you—why don't you call her?" She was staying in Manhattan with her old friend Irene Selznick. I rang her, and we had a long phone chat.

"It will be such a circus if some of us go to the funeral," Ingrid said. "I was very fond of Hitch, but I think the funeral should not be turned into another show. What do you think?" I told her that I thought she was quite right and added that I knew she was busy in New York with plans for the imminent publication of her autobiography, and I also knew that she was unwell with the cancer that eventually killed her—why place another burden on herself? She remained in New York and wrote me a very kind note the following day.

Bob and Ingrid and I were reunited later that year, in October, when he invited me to accompany him to the reception for Ingrid at the Museum of Modern Art, which was celebrating the publication of her book. We three sat in the last row of the museum's theatre for the screening of *Notorious*, certainly one of Hitchcock's masterworks and hers. At its conclusion, Ingrid turned to me: "It's always fun to see it, but do you think the movie will survive?" I replied that it had already survived after more than thirty years and was likely to be popular forever. She then went to make some comments to the audience, and Bob leaned over to ask me, "Have you ever seen a worse movie in your life? Who wrote that trash?" I was too astonished to reply that the screenplay was written by the great Ben Hecht.

The year 1979 was one of Teresa's busiest. In February and August, she appeared onstage as an unhappy mother dying of cancer, in Jonathan Bolt's play *Threads*. She then hurried to California to film *The Golden Honeymoon* for Public Broadcasting, in which she played the long-suffering wife of a cantankerous husband. During the summer she rang me from Mackinac Island, northern Michigan, where she was battling mosquitoes and tourists while appearing in the romantic fantasy *Somewhere In Time*, with Christopher Reeve. To shorten the running time, Teresa's supporting role was eventually cut so drastically that she scarcely appears in the picture. Privately, she expressed her disappointment, for the character she played was central to the story.

"I had been terribly spoiled by the theatre," Teresa told journalist Rex Reed. "In movies, I missed the theatre's rehearsal periods, the preparation time—which very few directors could afford. I think I've found my niche now, in the theatre, with artists I respect and admire. And I don't want to be remembered because I was pretty or sweet or wore nice hats. I just want to be recognized for the quality of my work."

Returning to New York, she was once again eager to meet students in my annual seminar on Hitchcock at the New School: "Of course I would be delighted to talk to your class," she wrote on October 5; in fact, she completely rearranged her schedule for that week to come to Greenwich Village. Her remarks on *Shadow of a Doubt* were as usual worth noting— as the New York press did that season when they reported her appearance at the seminar.

Teresa's most important and rewarding experience that year was in a revival of Paul Osborn's 1939 play *Morning's at Seven*. Vivian Matalon, an internationally respected director with major theatre credits in England and America, had been appointed artistic director of the Academy Festival Theater in Lake Forest, Illinois. Aware that Osborn's play had a few respectful but limited revivals, Vivian reread the play, reimagined its possibilities and decided to stage it that year at Lake Forest.

"I didn't audition Teresa for the role [of Cora]," he recalled. "I had lunch with her and asked what part she wanted to play. Every actress who has ever read that play always wants to play Arry. I said that I didn't think that was such a good idea for her. 'What do *you* think?' she asked. 'Cora,' I said. 'OK,' she said. And that was that."

Among Vivian's signal contributions to the play was the alteration of the time—from 1938, as in the original production, to 1922. "I told Osborn that 1922 was the time of America's last innocence, before the Harding scandals broke. Osborn had set it in 1938, when Europe was in flames—and here were these characters, not reacting to anything but their own petty concerns. But setting it in 1922 made sense. When audiences arrived, they were watching their grandparents." The playwright was forever grateful for this change and later wrote to Vivian, "I never will see the play so brilliantly acted and directed again."

A trio of perceptive New York producers saw the play at Lake Forest and immediately decided to bring it to Broadway, where *Morning's at Seven* opened to spectacular notices at the Lyceum Theater on April 10, 1980, and ran for 564 performances, until August 16, 1981 (which explains her absence from the tribute to Ingrid in October 1980).[2] Teresa had not forgotten that the first Broadway play she saw had been performed at the Lyceum, when, at the age of fourteen in 1932, she had a ticket to Cornelia Otis Skinner's one-woman performance.

Morning's at Seven concerns four Midwestern sisters (played by Teresa, Elizabeth Wilson, Maureen O'Sullivan and Nancy Marchand) and three of their husbands (Gary Merrill, Maurice Copeland and Richard Hamilton).[3] Advertised as a comedy, the play is certainly not a farce, much less a satire on good country folk. With unerring wit and insight, it presents deeply unsatisfied lives so drenched in tedium and monotony that they tend to regard as earthshaking what is essentially ordinary.

The play has rich humor and a kind of grave wisdom in every scene. Teresa had a singular moment when, after a character lists everything in Cora's life that has made for happiness, she replies: "That's a lot." Pause. "If that's all you can get." At the several performances I attended, the audience laughed knowingly at first, but then I heard something like a collective sigh of recognition.

The play was not only one of the great successes of two Broadway seasons: it also marked the historic triumph of an unusually gifted quartet of actresses "doing the very best work of their careers," as Walter Kerr wrote in a long rave review in the *New York Times*. "These nine charmed people [the entire cast], play together, under Vivian Matalon's extraordinarily perceptive stage direction, as though they'd been happily related

2. Very soon after Teresa began her Broadway career at the Empire Theater in *Life With Father* (on November 8, 1939), the original production of *Morning's at Seven* opened at the Longacre. It lasted for only forty-four performances.

3. The first word in the title is not a plural: "Morning's at seven" is a contraction of "Morning is at seven," that is, "at seven o'clock." The line is from Robert Browning's play *Pippa Passes*: "The year's at the spring/And day's at the morn/Morning's at seven/The hillside's dew-pearled/The lark's on the wing/The snail's on the thorn/God's in His heaven—/All's right with the world!"

colleagues for years and years. If you want to show people what a repertory company should look like, the Lyceum would be the place to take
them."

The director and critic Harold Clurman, not given to facile praise, focused on the play's human values. "These characters have a fundamental
innocence in spite of all the frustrations, aberrations and imbecilities—
the tokens of our common humanity. With all their upsets and eccentric-
ities, [Osborn's] characters remain both funny and real: we are always
conscious of what makes them our kin. The play is delightful, one of the
best American comedies."

When the time came for theatre awards, Vivian Matalon took home a
Tony and a Drama Desk Award for his direction, and the actors received
several honors, mostly as an ensemble.

"I can't recall one moment of conflict with that cast," said Vivian. "The
sisters in the play became sisters in life. As for Teresa, she had a wonderful stillness about her, and very occasionally, there would also be a
certain obstinacy during rehearsals. But when she *was* obstinate, I always
listened to her, because she always had a significant reason. So I always
took notice of what she had to say." He also recalled that unlike many
others in and out of the theatre and film world, "the list of wonderful
performers and directors she worked with, and the wonderful characters she played, rarely came up in conversation with her. And I never
heard her gossip or drop a name. That aspect of so-called 'show business'
seemed to hold no interest for her."

When I went backstage after the third performance, Teresa was radiant—and when I revisited the play months later and then a third time
toward the closing date, her attitude was the same: "It's a *joy!*" she told
a reporter from California. "I am *always* looking forward to coming to
work. The parts are so beautifully written that everybody has a major
scene."

To no one's surprise, *Morning's at Seven* transferred to Los Angeles,
where the production at the Ahmanson was sold out and recorded on
film. The company then moved to a number of American cities before it
opened in England. Even as some of her co-stars gradually left the production and were replaced, Teresa remained.

∽

On April 5, 1981, Bob was formally inducted into the Theater Hall
of Fame and received a scroll of honor during ceremonies at the Uris

(later the Gershwin) Theatre.[4] Teresa's play was not performed on Sundays, and so she and Bob invited me to attend the event. Chatting with friends at a party later that evening, Bob was eloquent in his praise of her achievements in *Long Day's Journey into Night*, *Death of a Salesman* and *Morning's at Seven*.

Soon after, he and Teresa arranged for me to be included at another party, this time at the home of Lucille Lortel, one of the great patrons of the American theatre and the producer of over 500 plays. She lived in an apartment that occupied an entire floor at the Sherry-Netherland Hotel, where her parties easily accommodated a hundred or more guests. Two memories survive from that evening.

First, I spent almost the entire time with the great Stella Adler, the acclaimed drama teacher who insisted that I accompany her from the buffet table and back to her place on a sofa. There, she regaled me for several hours with long, fascinating tales of her work with Stanislavski, Strasberg, Clurman, Meisner and Kazan—and her years as the acting coach of Marlon Brando, Judy Garland, Elizabeth Taylor, Lena Horne, Robert De Niro, Elaine Stritch and Warren Beatty, among others who owed her a great debt. Stella was no name-dropper: she simply described how some of her most famous students developed (or abandoned) their talents. Each time I tried to free her from my obviously awe-stricken company, she pulled me back into the capacious light she shone as a legendary teacher.

That evening, Stella clarified for me the differences between her approach and that, for example, of Lee Strasberg, and I was engrossed by her eyewitness account of working with Stanislavski in Paris. Thanks to Stella, I left the party enriched by a new friendship and a clearer idea about the classic theories of acting.

The second indelible recollection of Lucille's party was the ride at the end of the evening. Among the guests was the caricaturist Al Hirschfeld, a witty raconteur and a brilliant artist, who offered to deliver me, Bob and Teresa back home. His wife, the actress Dolly Haas (another Hitchcock alumna, for her role in *I Confess*), sat up front with Al, then well into his eighties, while we three in the back seat endured a journey from which our survival was increasingly in grave doubt. Ignoring his daredevil driving, Dolly encouraged Al's stream-of-consciousness banter while he blithely ignored traffic signals and the posted speed limits.

4. The cover of the playbill for that memorable evening is curious for its variant orthography: the Theater Hall of Fame was permanently located at the Uris Theatre; certain legal formalities evidently prevailed.

Dolly was unfazed, doubtless from years of experience with her husband at the wheel, while the anxious murmurs of the rear-seat passengers went unattended. First, Al and Dolly deposited my two friends at 14 Sutton Place South, where Teresa winked at me and gaily cried, "Get home safely!" From there I was driven at record speed to my apartment in Greenwich Village, where on arrival I offered my thanks to the Hirschfelds—and silently to Providence, for granting me a reprieve from imminent disaster. One does not forget evenings marked by such uncommon and unforgettable characters as Stella Adler and Al Hirschfeld.

But the lively events during the spring of 1981 were clouded by the sudden illness of Audrey Wood, Bob's agent since the time of *Tea and Sympathy*. On April 28, Bob's birthday, he invited me to join him for dinner with Teresa and Audrey, who also represented William Inge, Arthur Kopit and, for almost his entire career, Tennessee Williams. At seventy-six, Audrey was a petite woman with a fund of anecdotes, a remarkable memory for detail, keen intelligence, sly humor and considerable charm. She was also what is called a legend in the theatre, but there was not an atom of attitude about her. Like Bob and Teresa, I regarded Audrey as a lovable soul.

Bob and I escorted Audrey back to her Manhattan residence at the Royalton Hotel. At the entrance, she waved and promised to telephone us soon for a reunion. Two days later, in the same spot, Audrey Wood collapsed with a massive stroke. She remained in a coma for almost five years, until her death in December 1985.

I was forever grateful to Bob for introducing me to this extraordinary lady—a kindness he repeated over many years when he insisted that I meet people he considered important to him and might, he hoped, be interesting for me to meet. He began this generous tradition with Ingrid in 1975; it continued as long as his social life endured, and Teresa joined him in keeping the habit alive. I can think of no surer or even rarer sign of affection than to acquaint friends with one another and then to watch contentedly as they, too, become friends.

∽

In 1982, Terry Busch married Francesca Jegge in San Mateo, California. Niven Busch and his fifth wife, Suzanne Te Roller de Sanz, were there, and Teresa, too. "As I remember, everyone was polite, smiling and civil—no evidence of past hard feelings," said Terry.

"Teresa loved both Francesca and Katie [their daughter, born in 1987]," Terry continued, "and she was a most attentive grandmother, doing whatever she could to be a part of Katie's life despite the many miles of separation." Terry also recalled that during the 1980s, Bob often told him how much he wanted to remarry Teresa and how he tried to persuade her to do so—"but he made no headway. She was fine with things as they stood. She enjoyed the degree of independence she had. And for his part, though he pressed the idea of remarriage and clearly was devoted to her, somehow he could not keep himself from continuing those old habits that drove Mom away: the mocking jokes and the stories of Phyllis."

Mary-Kelly remembered another issue.

> Mom felt intimidated by people who hawked their advanced education, since she had so little formal schooling herself. Bob's talk about "Harvard this" and "Harvard that" made her uneasy. Deep within him, there was a feeling of insecurity despite his big ego, and he hoped to balance this by associating with people whose backgrounds and achievements he considered worthy of recognition. Status was always a consideration for Bob. He was impressed by status in ways my father and mother were not. Bob looked first at a person's credentials, and then he often felt like an outsider. I'm sure this contributed to his kindness and his range of friends. Mom thought that celebrity got in the way. She believed that for actors, publicity should not be about glamour or looks or wardrobe, but about the quality of one's work.

Teresa also resented the finery worn by actresses on the so-called red carpet. "People think the actors can afford these expensive gowns, but they cannot. The clothes are loaned out to them for advertising! Instead, the focus should be on the work."

On August 29, 1982, Ingrid Bergman died at home in London, on her sixty-seventh birthday: the news was broadcast very early the next morning in New York. I could not reach Teresa, who was traveling from one assignment to another, but Bob was at home. When I phoned, he had just heard the news and could not speak for his sobbing. Ingrid had transformed their brief affair of long ago into an enduring, rich and loyal friendship.

⁓

In November, Fred Zinnemann came to New York for the premiere of his most recent (and, as it happened, his last) picture—*Five Days One Summer*.

A press screening was arranged at the Directors Guild, and Teresa invited me to join her. Fred was obviously delighted to see her, and we three had time to chat about *The Men* and *The Nun's Story*.

That Christmas, Teresa appeared on (of all things) an episode of the long-running series *The Love Boat*, which aimed to be about the comic and romantic antics of passengers on a luxury liner. As an Irish nun named Sister Regina, accompanying a dozen young orphans to a school in Mexico, Teresa affected a flawless accent and was forced to wear the antique garb then mostly abandoned by Catholic sisters. But according to the creed of Hollywood, a nun is never a nun unless she dresses in an ancient habit and veil.

A few days after the broadcast on December 18, I fell ill with a bout of bronchial pneumonia. Teresa heard of this from Bob when she returned from California, and one rainy afternoon my doorbell rang. I shuffled to the door in a heavy robe, clutching a box of tissues, looking and sounding like something awful.

There was Teresa, drenched in an old mackintosh, with a floppy rain hat providing not much protection; she was carrying two shopping bags. "Oh, sir," she said in a thick Irish brogue, "I hear that there's a gentleman here who has gone down sick." With that, she took over my small kitchen, where she proceeded to prepare enough homemade soups for a week and, now in her own voice, to detail the fine points of what I should do for a quick recovery. "Start with this," she said, handing me a bottle of something or other. "It's homeopathic," which was one of her pet concerns at the time. "You'll feel better very quickly." In fact, I was soon up and about. "Sister Regina," minus the black attire, had come to my rescue.

∽

The next two years, 1983 and 1984, were full of travel and activities for me, as they were for Teresa and Bob, but we made certain that our paths often crossed. I dined with Teresa on February 9—just the two of us, for she wanted to talk about matters concerning Bob, while I was unhappy in a hopeless facsimile of a romance, from which she gave me much of the courage to extricate myself.

For several months that spring of 1983, I was sent out to promote the publication of my new book, *The Dark Side of Genius: The Life of Alfred Hitchcock*. The tour took me all over the United States, and then to Canada, England, Scotland and Ireland. By happy coincidence, I was assigned a week of media appearances and interviews in Southern California when Teresa was performing in Arthur Kopit's play *Wings* in San Diego. This exquisitely moving and difficult drama, staged at the Old Globe in March and April, takes place in the mind of a woman who has suffered a disabling stroke. For her Herculean efforts, Teresa was paid only $425 a week, the usual rate at the Globe, even for major visiting stars.

After the performance I attended on March 24, Teresa joined me for supper, and we drove slowly out of the theatre's parking lot in my rented sedan. But when I looked into my rearview mirror, I saw a flurry of papers scattering behind us, along with a notebook and purse that had fallen onto the road. Teresa had deposited all this and more on top of the car while putting other things in the back seat. When I saw our blunder, I drove back and to our mutual amazement, we were able to recover everything. The sight of us, rushing to pick up various scattered paraphernalia, must have amused passersby. The rest of the day and evening passed without incident, and we toasted our good luck in the dining room of her hotel, the Park Manor Suites.

While she was in California, Teresa appeared in a teleplay with Mickey Rooney called *Bill on His Own*, in which she played a sympathetic teacher to his role as a man mentally challenged. This time, her compensation was more deserving: $6,250 for three weeks of work.

She returned home in time for the six-week run of Bob's play *Free and Clear*, which was finally ready for production at the Long Wharf under Arvin Brown's direction. She, Bob and I were in the audience on April 15; later, Teresa and I agreed that we were not surprised that *Free and Clear* was but the latest installment in the author's autobiographical plays. This one is set on the porch of a family's home in Westchester County on a summer day in 1940 and features two sons—a lawyer and a writer who is ten years younger than his fiancée—who return for their mother's birthday and confront their father on several accounts. If the characters had been given the surname Anderson, it would have been a documentary drama. "Ponderous and irredeemable" were two of the gentler adjectives used by critics.

"One of the sad things about *Free and Clear* was the inevitable comparison people made to O'Neill's *Long Day's Journey into Night*," Arvin said. "But there was very little in common apart from the family situation, and because it was so unfavorably and unjustly compared to O'Neill, Bob suffered for it." Arvin made an important point, but it must also be admitted that Bob's play suffered from a surfeit of prolixity and a lack of dramatic power.

It was evident to me and to Teresa that Bob would benefit from friendly distractions, and so we spent the weekends of July 30 and August 20
together—I in the guestroom of Teresa's Connecticut condominium, and
Bob arriving each day from Bridgewater. Except for his rueful complaints
of professional rejection, he was in good spirits, and we took pleasant
drives through the local countryside. But Teresa needed some comfort,
too: on July 28, she received a call from Martin Manulis; his wife, her
close friend Katie, had died that morning after a long illness. That weekend, Teresa reminisced about her forty-five-year friendship with Katherine Bard Manulis, a mutual devotion that began during *Life With Father*.

In September, Teresa and I were committed to supporting the American
Cinema Awards at the Beverly Hilton Hotel, Beverly Hills. The event, on
September 10, honored Joseph Cotten; Joel McCrea and his wife, Frances Dee; Janet Gaynor; and Ruby Keeler. For two reasons, Teresa and I
placed the evening under the bell jar of memory.

First, we were seated at dinner with her old friend Joe Cotten and his
wife, the actress Patricia Medina. Joe had undergone surgery for throat
cancer and was forced to rely on a hand-held voice-enhancing device,
but he and Teresa held forth on Hitchcock and other directors with great
wit and style. Also at the table were Alida Valli (the star of Hitchcock's
The Paradine Case and Carol Reed's *The Third Man*); the great English actress Dame Wendy Hiller; and Dorothy and Robert Mitchum.

The second cause for recalling the evening occurred toward the end
of dinner, when Mitchum had consumed his usual generous quota of
gin martinis ("straight up, very cold, very dry and no vegetation" was his
prescription). Wendy Hiller was seated next to Mitchum when the conversation briefly turned to the name of an actress they both knew. "I tell
you," he said in his resonant bass-baritone for the entire table to hear,
"that woman was a *real cunt*." No one laughed, everyone was stone silent
and uncomfortable, most of all for Dame Wendy, who at once proved her
gentility about how to defuse awkwardness: "Oh," she said calmly and
with great charm, "a difficult woman, then, was she?"

Christmas that year was a time of mixed emotions. Teresa wrote a
message on her card to me, as she was thinking of Katie, Ingrid and others: "Dear, dear friend," she began, "We must take time to spend at least
an afternoon together during the holidays—a Village walk, maybe—a
tea or something. The days and years go so fast and our talk is always of

tomorrow—and now so many friends have lost their tomorrows. I'll call you soon.—Love from Teresa."

Meanwhile, after she and I dined with Bob, he wrote to his brother on December 28: "Teresa came into town yesterday. She is so completely disorganized with no ability to cut down on the junk she accumulates. It's really sad. It amounts to a sickness, accumulating and not letting anything get thrown away."

∽

New York was officially a week into springtime when a nor'easter arrived on March 28. Two inches of snow were measured in Central Park by late afternoon, but Bob was not to be deterred from attending a revival of his play *Silent Night, Lonely Night* at a small theatre in the East Village. He invited me to be his guest. Chilled but cheerful, we arrived a quarter-hour late, and the house manager finally sent a message backstage to raise the curtain.

The set, a room in a country inn, was modest but had the proper warm ambience. The actors began to speak, and everything seemed agreeable—until about twenty minutes later, when Bob said to me in a low voice: "They've cut pages of dialogue!" Before the end of the first act, he added: "The play has been cut so much that it's unrecognizable." I had neither seen nor read the work, but by this time not much onstage seemed to make much sense. "Come on, we're going backstage," he said, and we made our way down the aisle.

"Listen, folks," Bob said to the assembled cast. "This is not my play you are performing tonight. You have cut so much and revised so much that I can scarcely recognize my own play."

Someone representing the cast spoke up: "We thought it would improve the play—would give it more sense if—"

Those were not the right words to address to any playwright. But Bob did not lose his temper. He simply said with steely insistence: "You know, the Dramatists Guild and Equity would permit me to close down this play tonight—*tonight*, right now. I won't do that. But if the play is not presented as I wrote it—or if you do not submit your ideas for a revision to my agent by tomorrow afternoon, a closing notice will be posted."

We left the theatre at once and repaired to a cozy bar nearby for restorative drinks. Next evening, he invited me to dinner at his apartment: I think he wanted some support as he described the incident to Teresa. She and I fully agreed not only with Bob's principle but also with his gentlemanly way of dealing with the presumptuous theatre group. The revival did not survive the wretched weather or the failure of the company to "improve the play."

⌖

Teresa, meanwhile, was bustling about, preparing to leave for England, for the tour of Vivian Matalon's production of *Morning's at Seven*. "I was told by British Equity," he recalled, "that I could bring one person from the Broadway production"—the rest of the cast would have to be composed of actors from the United Kingdom, according to the agreements between British and American Actors' Equity Associations. "That was an easy choice for me, and without any hesitation, I selected Teresa because I always thought that her Cora was the rock on which the entire play rested. There were several splendid performances in our British cast, but somehow the quiet element Teresa brought to Cora was the defining style that informed the play. Hers was the least flashy part, but Teresa made her the glue that held the play together. To me she was irreplaceable."

Vivian spoke of Teresa's inability to play the prima donna or the star: "She had a kind of ferocious modesty—and such delicacy and sensitivity. I also felt that there was a subtle, unobtrusive sexuality within that she never exploited in her work or in her life."

By early April, Teresa was in London, installed in a comfortable flat in Hallam Street, Marylebone; Vivian was living in the same building. "As usual, she was sometimes quite scatterbrained," Vivian recalled. "I devoted about a half-hour instructing her how to cross the street in London—to look one way, then the other and back again and to be sure she knew about English traffic regulations. But I was certain she was going to be knocked down by a car."

Rehearsals were held in Watford at the Palace Theatre, about seventeen miles northwest of central London. "I had a car," Vivian said,

and Teresa and I rode out to Watford every morning. One day she told me about her childhood, and I was absolutely shocked to hear what her mother did with men she invited into the same bed with her own little daughter. That someone who had known that kind of horror as a child could have grown up to be such a sweet, loving personality and such a great talent was stunning to me. Teresa said she had tried to escape it when it happened, but she could not—and obviously the memory of it was still clear and painful so many years later.

During another journey, Teresa confided that she loved and admired Bob, but that he could drive her quite mad. Vivian sympathized: "I directed *I Never Sang for My Father* in London, and Bob came over for that. He was very difficult about everything, and he drove me to distraction."

"The management of the play could not be praised for honesty," Vivian continued.

> The salaries of the actors were to have been according to the favored-nations structure [each was guaranteed the highest payment offered to any other] but things did not turn out that way. Maggie Tyzack, for example, was paid more than Teresa. Then, when we were out of town, performing first in Watford and then in Bath, the management offered to pay for Teresa's accommodations because she was from abroad. But when she learned that the British actors had to pay their own travel expenses, she refused to take the money for her hotels. I told her that wasn't necessary, but she insisted that she would not be treated any differently from the rest of the company—when in fact she was being treated much worse. She refunded the money to the management—and the management took it.

❧

As it happened, that season I had research to do in London for a new book, and I arranged my schedule to coincide with Teresa's time there. "Rehearsals are underway," she wrote to me on Sunday, April 15, "and they are going great, though all the actors are already exhausted by the traveling—for some, it's an hour and a half trip before and after rather strenuous rehearsals. But they are marvelous and I *really* look forward to each day—though I must say I'm totally enjoying a *quiet* day alone today, doing laundry, writing letters, reading the papers, etc. But I do love London so much—I could live here for a year. Can't wait to see you!—Love, Teresa."

The British premiere of *Morning's at Seven* was given at the Palace Theatre in Watford on May 1. I arrived on May 9 and invited Teresa to luncheon on Sunday, May 13—Mother's Day. We then went out to the Royal Gardens at Kew, where there is a magnificent herbarium along with the world's largest collection of living plants.

After engagements in Watford and at the Theatre Royal in Bath, *Morning's at Seven* opened to very favorable notices on June 19 at the

Westminster Theatre, London. Bob reported Teresa's comings and goings to his brother: "Talked with Teresa in London today. She is still having a ball. Playing to appreciative, sold-out houses. She has found old friends and new friends, and I have rarely heard her happier." The last performance was given on August 11, and at the end of the month Teresa was back home in New York.

CHAPTER FIFTEEN

1985–1990

IN THE 1980S, THE PRESTIGIOUS MAYO CLINIC, ONE OF THE FINEST health care centers and teaching hospitals in America, began a series of presentations nationwide. Called "Insight," the aim was to study human behavior through the art of the theatre—not to give answers, but to understand more deeply some of the problems that come to every physician's practice. "Physicians don't need any more facts," said Mary Adams Martin, director of the series and aftercare director in Mayo's chemical dependency treatment program, "and the time they can spend on human problems, their own and others, is very limited. The theatre can move into that gap." The structure of the Insight series was to offer dramatic readings followed by discussions with actors and doctors.

Jason Robards was the first actor to appear in a Mayo program: in 1980, he read a long monologue from O'Neill's *The Iceman Cometh*. "We took it all over the country for doctors," Robards recalled, "and we discussed denial and enablement in drinking. I never thought of [the play] as a teaching tool, but it is, and through reaching doctors, you reach hundreds and thousands of people."

In 1985, Teresa was invited to join Jason, his son Sam Robards and the actress and writer Margaret Hunt in specific scenes dealing with narcotic addition and the family's reactions in *Long Day's Journey Into Night*.[1] The event was held before 1600 staff physicians, residents and personnel on April 13, 1985, at the annual assembly of the American Academy of Family Physicians, sponsored by the Mayo Clinic and Foundation; it was

---

1. Jason Robards had appeared as the son Jamie in the 1956 Broadway premiere of the play starring Fredric March; now, he played James Sr., and Sam Robards assumed the younger role.

repeated on September 29, 1986, with Dan O'Herlihy and Francis Guinan replacing Jason and Sam Robards.

The players received only a small monetary honorarium, but most of them also accepted the offer of a free weekend for a complete physical examination and workup at the Mayo Clinic in Rochester, Minnesota. Many who attended the dramatic readings and discussions clearly recalled Teresa's speech from the play, beginning: "I hate doctors! They'll do anything—anything—to keep you coming to them. They'll sell their souls! What's worse, they'll sell yours!" A ripple of laughter spread through the audience at that moment, but afterwards there was a serious discussion of the uncomfortable, all-too-frequent reality beneath the character's outburst.

Teresa and Margaret became good friends during the tours and remained so forever after. "For a person who had such memorable success—and had it when she was so young—she was stunningly unassuming," recalled Margaret, who had the role of the maid Cathleen in the readings from *Long Day's Journey*.[2] "Teresa always had a wonderfully benign spirit, and she could speak with anyone in the course of an ordinary exchange—on a bus, in a bank, anywhere. She was interested in people and open to the possibility of learning from them. I felt that she was always living wonderfully in the moment."

As did others of Teresa's friends, Margaret saw how droll Teresa could be, and how sharp was her gift for mimicry. Decades after she won her Oscar for *Mrs. Miniver*, Teresa could recall the complexities of a scene that had caused the cast some anxiety. Richard Ney, age twenty-five at the time, made his movie debut in that picture, but he did not attend to suggestions from either William Wyler or from the veteran, highly respected player Dame May Whitty. Three times one afternoon, she quietly offered Richard a necessary correction to his manner of speaking a certain line. "But I prefer it *my* way," he said to the entire assembled company. With that, the formidable Dame May announced her verdict: "Young man, you don't *have* a way." Teresa rendered the entire episode with every actor's speech and manner, *à la* Cornelia Otis Skinner.

❧

That summer of 1985, the Chautauqua Conservatory Theater Company (near Jamestown, New York) had scheduled a production of Tennessee

---

2. Among other actors who participated in various Insight events: Helen Hayes, who read scenes from *Victoria Regina* for a program on aging; and Kathy Bates and Anne Pitoniak, in scenes from *'night, Mother*, for a discussion of suicide.

Williams's *The Glass Menagerie*. Tom Hulce, Melissa Gilbert and Mark Arnott were in the cast assembled by director Michael Kahn. He invited Teresa to play Amanda Wingfield, whose antecedent was the playwright's mother, Edwina Williams.

"I didn't want to take on such an exquisite role that had already been played by some of the greatest actresses in the theatre without lots and lots of preparation. I thought I needed many months before I dared step onstage in that part. Of course that wasn't possible, but Michael Kahn has a way of reassuring actors and enabling them to give their best. It was a great joy to work with him."

Teresa wanted to be certain that Michael believed she was right for the role, so she flew up to Chautauqua from New York and asked if they might read the play aloud together. "No one had ever done that before," he recalled, "and I thought it was so classy of her. We read, and she was perfect. I told her that I'd be thrilled to have her in the cast. Teresa was a movie star, but she never acted like one. Our cast loved her and took care of her—in a way, they regarded her as the cast mother. I understood why Kazan had chosen her for *The Dark at the Top of the Stairs*—she was an actress of great depth and great talent."

Like the other players, Teresa received a total of $500 for her performances at Chautauqua in *The Glass Menagerie*, which was presented in Norton Hall from August 16 to 19.

I traveled from Manhattan to see the show, and I admired how Teresa focused in one key moment the role of Amanda in all its pathos. At the end of Scene Five, the mother summons her shy, lame daughter to the doorway: "Laura, come here and make a wish. See, there's a little silver slipper of a moon. Look over your left shoulder, Laura, and make a wish on the moon!"

Laura: "What shall I wish *for*, Mother?

Amanda ["her voice trembling," according to the playwright's stage directions, "and her eyes suddenly filling with tears"]: "Oh, Laura—wish for happiness—and good fortune—and just a little bit of luck."

And with that, the soft lights fade on the scene.[3] The auditorium, filled to capacity, kept silent as everyone felt the poignancy of that single, simple moment. Tennessee Williams and his play had been well served.

---

3. Like all playwrights, Williams frequently revised his plays for publication and for revivals. Amanda's last words in this scene vary in published books, on recordings and in performance history, according to the playwright's caprices. For this 1985 production, Michael and Teresa wisely used the version I cite here.

Bob, who had just been honored at the William Inge Theatre Festival in Kansas, arrived in time for the last performance. As we awaited Teresa's emergence from her dressing room, Bob turned to me: "Teresa has now played the three great roles for women in the American theatre— Mary Tyrone, Linda Loman and Amanda Wingfield." He paused, and his voice broke: "And she has played them to perfection."

⨏

During the summer of 1986, a consortium of producers was casting for a movie based on a play called *The Whales of August*. Lillian Gish, Bette Davis, Vincent Price and Ann Sothern were on board when Davis's health, already severely compromised by cancer surgery and strokes, declined to the point that her participation was in doubt. A few senior actresses were summoned to read the role at the film's setting, on the coast of Maine. Teresa was keen to play a role very different from anything she had ever undertaken: the blind, frail, cantankerous, ill-tempered sister of the character played by her old friend Lillian Gish.

But Teresa was sensitive to the reaction of Bette Davis, who had always remained very dear to her since *The Little Foxes*. Accordingly, she would not allow her agents to submit her name for the role until she was assured of Bette's blessing, which was immediately forthcoming. And then a strange thing happened. The producers (but not the director, Lindsay Anderson) informed Teresa's agents that she would never be accepted by the moviegoing audience as such a deeply unpleasant character. With that, Davis rebounded, arrived at the filming location and, with a sudden display of titanic energy, dispatched her role in *The Whales of August*, her final motion picture.

A similar example of mogul myopia occurred a few years later, when a second remake of the classic romance *Love Affair* was prepared for Warren Beatty and Annette Bening. Teresa was considered for the small but important role of the grandmother, once played with hilarious awfulness by Maria Ouspenskaya (in the 1939 version) and then with warmth and dignity by the great Cathleen Nesbitt (in 1957).

At a meeting with one of the movie's representatives, a young man asked Teresa, "Have you ever done this kind of role before? What have you done that I might know?" Instead of leaving the room at once, she answered his questions. Bob, for one, was furious when he heard of this insulting ignorance, which did not faze Teresa.

To add to the ill treatment, Teresa was then asked to read aloud some pages of the screenplay—effectively to audition for the part, a test to which no one else of her status would have submitted. She replied that perhaps she was not right for the role after all, and she recommended Wendy Hiller or Sylvia Sidney. Katharine Hepburn was eventually engaged for the part; she fared badly both during production and in the eventual reviews.

∽

With major plays by O'Neill, Miller, Inge, Williams, Kopit, Ibsen and Coward now on her long list of theatrical accomplishments, Teresa did not hesitate to take on Chekhov. A nonprofit foundation invited her and three colleagues (Robert Lansing, Marsha Mason and James Naughton) to appear in staged readings at the Promenade Theatre (an Off-Broadway venue on Manhattan's Upper West Side) on October 27, 1986—Teresa's sixty-eighth birthday—and she accepted at once. The evening was billed as *Vaudeville by Chekhov*, who had composed parodies on the burlesques and revues popular on the Russian stage. Several of Teresa's friends attended; the consensus was that the actors were superior to the extracts.

During July 1987, Teresa was briefly in a Dallas studio and then for a longer time in the surrounding counties of rural Texas, appearing in an adaptation of a Katherine Anne Porter story, "The Fig Tree." For this, she endured record summer heat while wearing heavy period costumes. "There aren't many good roles for people my age. There aren't many good roles—period!" The part looked good on paper: an apparently obdurate, demanding grandmother who melts into graciousness over the plight of her lonely granddaughter, a child obsessed with death and dead animals after her mother died. Unfortunately, the finished television movie was an exercise in tedium, relieved only by the comic antics of Doris Roberts and Teresa's fresh take on a cliché that had lost its charm.

Both actresses were required to ride horses, and both were at first terrified. Doris completed her scene swiftly, astride a very gentle old mare. Teresa was less fortunate. She had not ridden since *California Conquest* thirty-five years earlier; more to the point, she was for some odd reason given Clint Eastwood's well-trained but wild horse once used in the movie *Bronco Billy*. "He's a horse that can act," said director Calvin Skaggs with apparent seriousness. "So Teresa gritted her teeth, mounted him, and rode away. A few times, the horse took off with her on him and shook her up a bit, but we didn't keep those scenes in the movie."

"Actually, it was the sweetest horse I've ever seen," Teresa recalled. "But I worried so much when I saw him. He looked pretty big—he *was* pretty big. The wrangler brought him over ahead of time, and I got to stroke him. After all, I didn't want to play a love scene with a horse I never met." For all the risk and the discomforts of the production, Teresa was paid $856 a week for four weeks: this was a production for Public Broadcasting.

∾

"Both Mom and Bob lived conservatively," said Mary-Kelly. "Each of them may have earned a great deal one year out of four or five years"— Bob much more frequently than Teresa—"but they felt that they had to save for the times when lucrative work was not forthcoming. The important lesson I learned about money from my mother was that having it or not having it did not make a person better or worse than someone else. 'People should be judged by their characters and their actions,' she often said, 'and not by their bank accounts.' And that's the way she lived."

At the end of the year, both Bob and Teresa were hard at work—he with a successful revival of *I Never Sang for My Father*, she with her first venture into Shakespeare. The timing of their activities prevented them from attending one another's success.

Father had first been revived at the Berkshire Festival in the spring before moving to the Kennedy Center in Washington and then playing across the country. Bob had a superb director, Josephine Abady, and a first-rate cast: Dorothy McGuire played the mother, Harold Gould the father and Daniel J. Travanti the Robert Anderson *alter ego*. Margo Skinner assumed the role created by Teresa in the 1968 production. Martin Manulis, as ever a good friend and major support to Bob, was now the artistic director of the Center Theatre Group at the Ahmanson in Los Angeles, where the play had an eight-week run from December 1987 through January 1988.

Bob invited two friends to join him for the first night in Los Angeles—Gilbert Cates (producer of the original Broadway production) and me (I had moved to Southern California a year earlier). This was a performance that moved the playwright to tears. We sat and watched his family story transmuted into drama, and then we visited the cast after the final curtain. Wistful, sometimes melancholy, occasionally mystical and always elusive, Dorothy seemed singularly happy as she repeated with the utmost sincerity, "Oh, Bob, your play is so beautiful . . . This is a lovely, lovely play, Bob . . . How lucky we actors are to be in it . . . This lovely play is so good for us all . . ."

Dorothy was as always eminently sincere, but her reaction was very unlike Gould's or Travanti's: they slapped Bob genially on his back or pumped his hand while saying, "Thanks for a good play, Bob" or, "It's great to have a good part to play." Later that evening, at our post-theatre supper, Bob complained about Dorothy's effusive remarks, but I think he preferred her hyperbolic compliments to old-boy gruffness.

Father was well received by the public and the press, and Bob gave a lengthy interview to the *Los Angeles Times*. Asked about his current work, he replied, "I do have a new play—it's called *The Kissing Was Always the Best—Scenes from a Divorce*. It's about what happens to a man during the process of his divorce. It's very funny, very sexy, very sad." Like all his plays, it was also very unashamedly autobiographical.

✐

Four days after *Father* began its Los Angeles engagement, Teresa performed in a play by Shakespeare for the first time in her career.

Following Michael Kahn's five years as head of the Chautauqua Conservatory Theatre—where he also created a successful training company for actors—he was appointed artistic director of the Shakespeare Theatre at the Folger, in the nation's capital. During the planning of his first season there, Michael decided to stage *All's Well That Ends Well*. "I immediately thought of Teresa for the role of the Countess of Rousillon"—one of Shakespeare's most complex female roles and (according to George Bernard Shaw) the most beautiful part ever written for an elderly woman.

As Teresa was completing "The Fig Tree" that summer, Michael made his offer, and the idea captivated her. "I thought, well, it's a little late in life [to undertake Shakespeare for the first time], but I've got to take the leap." At the age of sixty-nine, she had never appeared onstage in a professional poetry recitation, much less in Shakespearean drama. "It's a little intimidating, but I decided I had to try it." Her instincts served her well.

Before rehearsals began, Teresa worked with the Folger's voice and acting coach and read widely about *All's Well That Ends Well*. She then traveled to Los Angeles for a brief visit with Bea and Winston Miller and for a meeting with a movie producer. I was living in Pacific Palisades, and when her social and business appointments were finished, she stayed for a few days in my little guest room, memorizing the role of the countess. Before she left Los Angeles, Teresa arranged a first-night ticket for me at the Folger, and soon I followed her to Washington.

"It's a great wonder to me that Shakespeare knew so much," Teresa said. "He knows a mother's feelings. He's inside everybody's mind and heart more than any other playwright, and there's more revealed in his verse than any modern, stream-of-consciousness writer can convey psychologically. And it's the discovery of this by *doing* the play that is so very exciting."

The Washington premiere occurred on December 8, and performances continued for two months, through January 31, 1988. "Teresa had worked really hard with our voice coach," Michael recalled. "Of course she clearly understood the relationship of the countess to the other characters, but she was a bit nervous about the verse."

In fact, I detected a slight hesitation as she began to speak on opening night, but soon she found her way and evoked the strength and richness of the character, speaking the verse naturally and illuminating the woman's inner life. This diminutive actress, whose wig and costume at first made her appear even shorter, seemed to grow taller and more imposing in each scene for each of the three nights I was in the audience. "Yes, she got better and better as the performances continued," agreed Michael, "and once again, as in *The Glass Menagerie*, everyone in our cast loved working with her."

∽

In the late winter of 1988, the producers of a forthcoming Diane Keaton movie called *The Good Mother* asked Teresa to audition for an important supporting role. "The very fact of auditioning her at all seemed to me to be an affront to her," said Vivian Matalon with justifiable anger. But what followed was even more disturbing.

When Teresa arrived at the production offices to meet with Keaton, the place was busy and overcrowded; the director was Leonard Nimoy, best known as a space alien in the *Star Trek* television series. "Diane was so kind to me," Teresa later told a few friends (Vivian Matalon and Margaret Hunt among them). "And she was so sweet when she asked me to read the audition lines in a closet, where it was quieter—and she actually read *with* me."

Her friends were outraged: "In a closet? Why do you let people treat you like that?" Vivian asked.

"No, no—they were really busy," Teresa replied. "They couldn't have been nicer." She won the role without difficulty.

After the indecorous treatment Teresa received prior to her possible employment in *The Whales of August* and her actual engagement in *The Good Mother*, there was a third incident during the summer of 1989. She was asked to read not once or twice but five times for the role of the Irish mother in the movie *Awakenings*, starring Robin Williams and Robert De

Niro. "They told me to keep working on my Bronx accent," Teresa said after her third reading without identifying those who gave her that advice. "That was all they said. I told them I didn't *have* a Bronx accent. This went on right up to the makeup test. Then suddenly they decided to give the part to my good friend Ruth Nelson, who should have been offered it in the first place. She was absolutely marvelous in that picture."

After the fact, some of her friends could see her frank relief in the outcome. But to their shame, the producer's assistants did not take five minutes to ask about (much less to research) Teresa's half-century of achievements. "Those boys didn't seem old enough to shave" was Bob's tart comment.

సొ

The Good Mother was a strong, controversial film about the sexual awakening of a divorced and formerly frigid woman named Anna (Keaton) who meets Leo, a free-spirited artist (Liam Neeson). But this new man in her life makes a terrible mistake when he interprets frankly inappropriate behavior as merely up-to-date candor about sex. He once allowed Anna's six-year-old daughter to touch his genitals, and one night the child crawled into bed with her mother and her lover while they were in the throes of lovemaking. Throughout the story, Anna's grandmother (Teresa) provides the encouragement and strength Anna needs to bear the courtroom ordeal.

The movie does not blithely dismiss or condone the man's conduct with the child as harmlessly neutral. The result is that the romance is derailed; the child's custody is granted to the ex-husband; and everyone's life is adversely affected.

Teresa's role was absolutely central to the story; her performance was meticulously composed of small, illuminating gestures; of subtle and understated glances; and of the gentlest change of expression. Like her achievement in *Shadow of a Doubt* almost a half-century earlier, she offered a virtual textbook on film acting—but now she was playing a woman informed by suffering, not a girl enduring a dreadful moral education. As the leading lady's grandmother, Teresa dispensed common sense and quiet generosity. She also revealed the grandmother's painful past that brought her to a remarkable maturity.

It is certainly reasonable to assert that Teresa Wright never had a false moment in her art, never spoke or moved ineffectively in a role—just as it is justifiable to claim that she was a truly great actress, not merely a reliable and credible supporting player.

Notwithstanding any challenge to that assessment—and such a challenge was never made by any of her directors—no one can reasonably deny that her performance in *The Good Mother* must be rated on the highest level, an achievement of the kind for which men like Spencer Tracy and Fredric March were always commended. Teresa did not imitate life; she presented it with uncommon and powerful veracity.

From April through June 1988, principal photography of *The Good Mother* was completed in Toronto and at the Canadian lake districts. Teresa then proceeded to Hollywood, where Angela Lansbury had invited her to guest-star in an episode of the popular television series *Murder, She Wrote*. In "Mr. Penroy's Vacation," Teresa and Joan Leslie portrayed spinster sisters in a caper that had moments of high comedy. The episode is a neat twist on *Arsenic and Old Lace*. Once again, the program demonstrated Teresa's keen gift for humor and for the unexpected, startling small gesture or glance that lifted a scene from merely amusing to downright hilarious.

As if the triad of Shakespeare (in Washington), an earnest feature-film drama (in Canada) and a television episode (in Hollywood) was not sufficient for the year, Teresa continued her arduous schedule and added another remarkable credit, earned, as it happened, in Australia. She arrived in Sydney at the end of the year, just as high summer began there, and she remained for a month.

The project, "The Elders," was the eighth and final episode in *Dolphin Cove*, a short-lived television series whose title indicates the real stars. Teresa had the challenging role of an anxious grandmother visiting her unhappy grandchildren: a rebellious teenage boy and a younger girl, mute since her mother's death. All too predictably, those smiling, helpful dolphins pop right out of their cove like aquatic fairy godmothers, to help the benighted family. Teresa found the truth beneath the treacle—and for her achievement as a wise elder, she received her third Emmy nomination as "outstanding guest actress in a drama series" after the episode was broadcast on March 11, 1989.[4]

Soon after her return to New York, Teresa received news of Tom Coley's sudden death from a heart attack. They had remained close friends, never out of touch over the half-century since *Our Town*. Teresa traveled

---

4. In "The Elders," eleven-year-old Karron Graves had the role of the disturbed granddaughter, mysteriously mute since her mother's death. Karron had once before—in "The Fig Tree"—played Teresa's granddaughter, obsessed by her mother's death. Casting agents were evidently on special alert for a child good at affecting the neurotic extremes of bereavement.

at once to be with Bill Roerick, with whom Tom had shared his life for fifty-one years. Then, in November 1995, Bill was killed in an automobile crash; he and Tom are buried side by side in the Tyringham Cemetery in Berkshire County, Massachusetts.

∽

Now over seventy, Teresa did not diminish her activities—to the contrary, she accelerated them. In 1990, the Berkshire Theatre Festival offered her one of the most arduous roles in contemporary drama. *The Road to Mecca* concerns "a frail, bird-like little woman in her late sixties," wrote the playwright Athol Fugard in the published text.

"I suppose I'm at an age when other people are retiring," Teresa told a journalist. "But I simply don't want to. There are times during a strenuous rehearsal period when my arthritis hurts badly, and sometimes I gasp for breath, but I love the stage and I want to stay on it as long as I can."

The Road to Mecca, set in a small South African village, runs over two hours. Teresa's character, the artist and sculptor "Miss Helen," is onstage for the duration, speaking rapid-fire dialogue—and one monologue that lasts four pages. With her the entire time is her young friend and visitor, the social worker Elsa, a role played by the estimable Maryann Plunkett.

"Miss Helen has had visions," Teresa said, "and she has expressed them in sculptures which would be labeled far-out modern art. The sculptures are all over her property, and along with her reclusive lifestyle, have become repellent to the people of the town. Elsa wants Miss Helen to have the freedom to live however she wishes. But the town's minister [played by George Grizzard] arrives to see that Helen is quietly put away in a home, an asylum."

The Road to Mecca throws an angry, impassioned light on several kinds of intolerance, but as Teresa always said, "The main issue in this play, it seems to me, is the matter of trust between the two women—the younger one, who wants her friend to have the creative freedom she deserves, and the older one, who builds a bridge of faith. After all, creativity is a form of authentic spirituality."

The play opened on August 1 and, to keep the festival's summer schedule intact, closed on August 11. Perhaps never in her career had Teresa expended equivalent energy, during rehearsals and over the course of eleven performance days, on behalf of so serious a play. "We offered *The Glass Menagerie* only for a long weekend," she said, "but somehow *The Road to Mecca* was far more taxing."

"Teresa was the soul of goodness," recalled Maryann Plunkett years later. "I don't mean the kind of goodness that is weak and passive, but the kind that comes from a fierce life force. I can't imagine anyone not learning from her, in or out of the theatre. She was devoted to the theatre and equally devoted to her friends. Teresa had such joy in life, she was so alive and present in every moment—and she made us laugh, even when she was preparing for an operation on her foot. She was always happy to be part of anything connected to the festival, to the theatre, and to our play."

With Maryann, Teresa added to the list of colleagues who became friends—an affection extended to Maryann's husband, the actor Jay O. Sanders, and eventually to their son Jamie, born in 1994. Long after *The Road to Mecca* was in their respective theatrical histories, Maryann and her family remained very close to Teresa.

"She astonished me," Maryann added. "She was so tiny onstage, but looking into her wonderful blue eyes at the very end of the play, when Elsa says to Helen, 'Open your arms and catch me—I'm going to jump' . . . this moment revealed that it was a story about faith and trust, and everything came together at that moment."

Bob was certainly as moved by Teresa's achievement as anyone. "I told many people about her magnificent performance in *The Road to Mecca*," he wrote in a 1990 journal. As Pete Gurney recalled, "Bob was wonderfully supportive and proud of Teresa when she did the Fugard play. When she revealed her art, she had no better or more vocal fan than Bob."

He also did so publicly, at a birthday party for Teresa in October, but he had the same complaints about her offstage life: "She makes fun of herself as a pack rat and a bag lady, living in chaos, not being able to find anything—and she doesn't seem to realize that it's fatal to our getting together. Her chaos is a sickness, like alcohol or drugs."

◊

CHAPTER SIXTEEN

1991–2005

TERESA'S SCHEDULE OF ACHIEVEMENTS CONTINUED WITH REMARKABLE energy in 1991. She appeared that winter in several episodes of a part-fiction, part-documentary series called *A Century of Women*, in which she played a representative type of ordinary but sterling character. During her time in Los Angeles, she invited me to join her on several evenings for dinners with some of her oldest and closest friends—and so she made possible my lasting friendships with Dorothy McGuire, Jane Wyatt, and Mona and Karl Malden, among others. It was typical of Teresa to introduce people she knew would find good reasons to form enduring attachments.

She then returned east for a major television drama. She agreed to this role, in a Public Broadcasting production called *Lethal Innocence*, because of its subject and treatment, which were based on fact: an entire New England town had adopted a family of Cambodian refugees. In the film, American officials are unsympathetically portrayed for their mishandling of both the war and its aftermath.

"I thought it was brave to present that view, to come right out and say it," said Teresa, who played the one character able to reach out and help a Cambodian boy psychologically scarred by his experiences. "Teresa Wright nearly steals the film," according to the *New York Times* critic.

She made one request of the producers, to which they gladly consented. Teresa wanted to complete her part in time for Mary-Kelly's marriage (her first had ended in divorce) to Daniel Picchioni, a school counselor, on May 25. "He's such a fine man," Teresa told me. "He's intelligent, he's sensitive—he's everything one could hope for in a son-in-law."

Like Terry, Mary-Kelly and Dan had visited Niven in California, but he was too frail to attend her wedding. He had been an important writer in his time, a gifted editor, an enthusiastic rancher and always a devoted father. In the course of his long and vivid life, Niven had five wives and seven children: Peter Briton was his son by the first wife, Sonia Frey; his second son, Briton Cooper, was his son by Phyllis Cooper; Teresa gave him Niven Terence and Mary-Kelly; his fourth wife, Carmencita Baker, bore him Joseph and the twins Nicholas and Eliza; and his fifth wife, Suzanne Te Roller de Sanz, brought into their combined household her three children, Miguel, Juanita and Mark. Mary-Kelly's visit was timely, for Niven Busch died of heart failure at his San Francisco home on August 25, 1991, at the age of eighty-eight.

∽

That September, Teresa was invited to join a television seminar, one of the American Theatre Wing's "Performance" series. On the panel, moderated by the producer Jean Dalrymple and the critic Brendan Gill, were the actors Roy Dotrice, Stephanie Zimbalist, Timothy Hutton, Mary Louise Parker and Hinton Battle. Filmed for New York public television, the program was oddly disappointing. Teresa had more experience onstage and in films than all the others combined, but as usual she never turned the spotlight on herself, nor did she interrupt others to make a point. In addition, her younger colleagues did not seem remotely interested in putting any question to her about her historic career and credits. The result was that she faded into the background—a loss for the audience that day and for viewers of the recorded program ever since.

She did, however, manage to interject two points during the closing moments. When a member of the audience asked her how hopeful young actors can find an agent or a job, Teresa replied: "First, get together with your friends, do readings with them—at least you'll be doing something. And find a place to gather. Manhattan Plaza [the vast apartment complex open to people in the arts] has a fine, free space. You just have to sign up for it, so go ahead!"

Another student asked how she knew when a role was right for her. "You have to feel an inner sympathy with a character," she replied. "Sometimes I don't, and then I know I would be false in that role—and I say so, and I turn it down."

She was always eager to counsel young actors: "Have a good education," she had said at the time of *Morning's at Seven*. "An apprenticeship with a good resident company is invaluable—at a place like the Cleveland Playhouse or the Guthrie Theatre in Minneapolis, where you can learn everything there is to know technically, and also where you can realize what you have to do when it comes to a paying audience. I think that an isolated classroom—unless you can apply what you learn right away—is too insulated, too protective. It's not the way life is."

Teresa was soon invited to appear in a Broadway production of another Paul Osborn revival—*On Borrowed Time*, with George C. Scott again as director and co-star. This was a comic moral fantasy about an old man (Scott) who chases personified Death (Nathan Lane) up a tree so that he can spend more time with his grandson and his wife, a wise granny played by Teresa with gritty charm. The play ran at the Circle in the Square from October 9, 1991, to January 5, 1992. "It's a comedy," Teresa said at the time, "and there's nothing like hearing an audience laugh. Oh, it's nice to be able to make people cry, but it's nicer to make them laugh."

The winter was harsh in New York, and at the age of seventy-three, Teresa only just withstood a flare-up of a recurring respiratory infection. "I feel my age, and I shouldn't allow myself to get tired or stressful—lots of luck in this business. Especially in the winter, I'm terrified of getting sick and not being able to perform. Maybe I'll just become a summertime actress." That season, she arrived at the theatre two hours before curtain time: "not to get myself into the role—I know the person—but I want to have enough energy to play her." Some critics were lukewarm to the play, but none was to Teresa, who was singled out among the "solid supporting players as a beautiful, no-nonsense granny."

On Borrowed Time was a happy experience—Scott rarely misbehaved—but the extended run during so much inclement weather left her exhausted. After the final performance, she wisely took some time for herself, interrupted only by a six-day run in Gurney's play *Love Letters* at the Martha's Vineyard Playhouse in July 1993.

In honor of Teresa's seventy-fifth birthday that October, Bob arranged a celebration at the Westbury Hotel in New York. I was grateful to be on the guest list that included Mary-Kelly and Dan; Frances and Elia Kazan; Arvin Brown and his wife, Joyce Ebert; Maryann Plunkett and Jay O. Sanders; Margaret Hunt; Pete and Molly Gurney; Bill Roerick; George Grizzard; Chris Miller; and Betty Smith.

Among the memories of that evening was a conversation I had with Elia Kazan, whom I had known for a decade, since our interviews for my biography of Tennessee Williams. Somehow Brando's name came up, and Kazan's tone became sad and angry: "It's difficult for me even to say his name. Marlon was the biggest disappointment of my life—because of his contempt for whatever related to the theater and to his talent. He could have become one of our finest stage actors, but he did nothing but movies after [the Broadway production of] *Streetcar*. After we made the film version, I thought, well, there's much more for him to do onstage, so much greatness ahead, waiting for him. But no: he turned his back on the theatre forever."

Later, I was again in New York and spent most of my free time with Teresa and Bob, at their respective apartments or, usually, together at Sutton Place. One evening, after several visits as their guest, I invited them to a little restaurant I knew could provide a quiet table. "It was good to be in your calming presence," Bob wrote next day, "and Teresa was so happy to see you as always. She was sent a script the next day and met with the producer at the Four Seasons. At the moment, she is *very* tired and low with a cough, so she wonders if she should take this small part in a Francis Ford Coppola picture." Four days later, another letter followed: "I know you're as happy as I am with Teresa's news: she will do the Coppola movie!"

And so she did. In October, she traveled to Memphis for location shooting on *The Rainmaker*, in which she had the role of the widow Birdsong, known affectionately as Miss Birdie. In the editing room, much of her performance was cut for reasons of the film's final running time. But what remains is a deliciously comic and subtly poignant portrait of an occasionally misguided old lady whose kindness and generosity are important for the leading characters played by Matt Damon and Claire Danes.

"Teresa is weary in Memphis," Bob wrote on November 5, "but she's glad to be back among the 'gang.'"

"I saw Matt Damon in *Good Will Hunting*," Teresa said. "And I must say there are some scenes where the acting is just marvelous. Matt was a rock to work with—so sure, so present for you all the time. For a young man, that's really quite unusual."

When she telephoned me from Memphis, she sounded delighted to be working with Coppola and with a gifted young company: "Francis creates a family here in Memphis, just as he did when he invited us all to his place in Napa Valley for script readings and rehearsals before we came here. He makes us all feel like welcome collaborators. It was the same when we got to Memphis—he likes to have lots of rehearsals, which I appreciate. It's the first time that has happened to me since my days with

Wyler and Hitchcock. And Matt Damon and Claire Danes give me hope for the future of movie acting. They are really talented young people, and they have been just lovely to me. I think they will be around for a long time."

The veteran film critic Bob Thomas hoped the same for Teresa and noted: "The flawless beauty of her years as a leading lady still lingers in her face as an eccentric, warmhearted oldster." Her performance in *The Rainmaker* brought a bundle of offers for her to play nice old fussbudgets in TV dramas, characters usually in various stages of dementia and confined to hospitals. She politely rejected every such offer: "There's no depth in those roles. It's really not very rewarding. Nothing could match the character Francis created for me in *The Rainmaker*." Miss Birdie was Teresa Wright's twenty-seventh movie role. It also marked her last appearance in a feature film.

But she still accepted good parts on television. Her good friend and stage director Arvin Brown invited her to appear in an episode of the popular series *Picket Fences*. "She played in a segment called 'My Romance,'" Arvin recalled, "as a woman who had years earlier been in love with the character played by Ray Walston. In fact, Ray told me that for most of his life he had a massive crush on Teresa, so doing the show with her meant very much to him."

∽

For the year 1997, the Academy Awards were presented on March 23, 1998. To celebrate the seventieth year of the Oscars, the producers of the show arranged an impressive lineup of seventy previous winners, seated alphabetically onstage from Anne Bancroft to Teresa Wright.[1]

That July 4 marked the fifty-ninth anniversary of Lou Gehrig Appreciation Day—the date of his historic farewell address, when fatal illness forced him to retire forever from baseball. The New York Yankees always retained a special fondness for *The Pride of the Yankees*, and so Rick Cerrone, the publicist for the team, invited Teresa to throw out the first ball on the annual memorial of Gehrig's speech. "But I could never throw a ball at the age of eight, and I can't do it at 80," she replied. Cerrone politely pressed his case: she didn't have to be an expert . . . it would be great fun for her . . . they really wanted to honor her as much as they wanted to remember Gehrig . . .

1. A two-page photo spread of that group is included at the beginning of Robert Osborne's invaluable book on the history of the Academy Awards; see the Bibliography.

At last she accepted, and after some practice throwing baseballs back and forth with her grandson Jonah, Teresa went to Yankee Stadium. Wearing a Yankees jacket and cap, she was introduced to first baseman Tino Martinez, who presented her with a bouquet of roses. Then she had her photo taken with team manager Joe Torre before being escorted onto the field, where she threw the ceremonial first pitch.

From that day, Teresa became an ardent Yankee fan. "The whole thing is pure theatre to me. I love every minute of it, and I get great pleasure watching talented players like Derek Jeter and Bernie Williams. You know they love to play, and I admire their spirit above all."

In the years to come, the first page she turned to in the morning papers was news of the Yankees. She watched every game she could, often late into the night. "It was as if she was possessed," said Mary-Kelly. "She couldn't get enough of her Yankees—it was really very darling to see." As Teresa told sports commentator Keith Olbermann, "On that day, July 4, 1998, I saw my first baseball game ever, and I've been just a great, mad fan ever since. I started watching and reading, and the more I watched and the more I read, the more fascinated I was by it."

Teresa's family arranged for her to see the first game of the American League Championship against Cleveland in October. She threw no pitches but she proudly wore her Yankees cap. This, she said, was the perfect way to celebrate her eightieth birthday.

Her connection to the Yankees continued. On February 6, 2000, she was seated at dinner next to Yankee shortstop Derek Jeter when he received an award from the Baseball Writers Association of America. When a reporter asked her that evening why she was such an enthusiastic fan of the team, Teresa replied, "You see the skill, the professionalism—and when they win, you see the smile reflected all over Joe Torre's face and you live it all over again." And on April 29, she attended a special screening of *The Pride of the Yankees* at the Baseball Hall of Fame in Cooperstown, New York, where she greeted the public and made brief but moving remarks about the production of the picture.

As Margaret Hunt recalled, "She just adored the Yankees and followed them religiously. Once when she telephoned me and I asked, 'How are you?' she replied, 'Not so good—didn't you see what happened to the Yankees last night?'"

☙

The centenary of Alfred Hitchcock's birth in 1999 was marked by film festivals worldwide and by tributes to the director. For two days—October

20 and 21, 1999—an event at Hofstra University on Long Island gathered together many students and critics to honor Hitchcock by celebrating the achievements of two of his leading ladies: Teresa Wright, for her performance in *Shadow of a Doubt*, and Tippi Hedren, for *The Birds* and *Marnie*. They were awarded the university's Presidential Medal and spoke about their work for Hitchcock. Professor Ruth Prigozy of Hofstra invited me to help organize the symposium and to join a panel.

Accompanied by Bob, Teresa seemed to everyone in fine form during those two days, but in fact she had unremittingly severe foot pain after a previous unsuccessful operation. In December, she submitted to surgery once again, and after weeks of convalescence at Bob's apartment, she had graduated from a wheelchair to a walker to a cane—hence she was able to attend her induction into the Theatre Hall of Fame on January 31, 2000.

That year, I thought that during conversations Bob was more repetitive than usual; that he sometimes confused the names of people he knew very well; and that his gait was unsteady. Teresa said that she, too, was concerned, and she recommended a complete physical workup. Because Bob was sleeping very little, she also advised him to consult a sleep disturbance clinic.

∽

Just as Hofstra University had honored Teresa in October 1999, so they chose to celebrate Bob's career the following year. On October 26 and 27, 2000, "A Robert Anderson Retrospective" featured panel discussions, lectures, screenings and performances of Bob's plays, and scholars spoke of important themes in his work. I was invited to deliver the keynote address, and his eminent colleagues Edward Albee, A.R. Gurney and Donald Margulies addressed Bob's achievements.

During a panel discussion called "Acting in a Robert Anderson Play," four veterans spoke wittily and compellingly about their experiences: John Kerr, George Grizzard, Eileen Heckart and Teresa. But something odd happened. As Teresa was giving her laudatory remarks about Bob's plays and screenplays, extolling his discipline and courage, suddenly she paused: there was a sob in her throat, and she had to compose herself before continuing. This was extraordinarily unusual, for Teresa always had great control over her emotions in public, nor was she ever given to easy tears. That day, I was not alone in wondering what was the trouble, but the matter was not clarified until a year later. Teresa was the first to suspect that Bob was showing the irrefutable signs of Alzheimer's Disease.

He was still well enough to attend important functions. A month after the celebration at Hofstra, on November 21, the Academy of Motion Picture Arts and Sciences, in cooperation with the Film Society of Lincoln Center and the Academy Foundation, honored Teresa at a gala tribute in New York, held at the Walter Reade Theater. Robert Osborne was the host for the evening that included ten film clips and remarks by colleagues and friends; at Teresa's insistence, the program listed Harold Russell and myself as Special Guests; unfortunately, Russell could not attend due to illness.

∽

As Pete Gurney said, "Bob's obsession with Phyllis began to dwindle when he became ill, and Teresa became much more the object of his conversation and his concern."

Terry noticed the changes in Bob, too. At Jonah Smith's wedding in 2002, Terry made a point of spending prolonged time with Bob while others were politely ignoring him. "We had a couple of long, nice talks that day. My Mom found me, hugged me and gave me a look of pure love, saying, 'Thank you for spending time with Bob. It means so much to him—and to me.'" For Terry, it was a simple matter: he loved Bob dearly, as did Mary-Kelly.

As everyone knew, Teresa could do nothing except be present with Bob, keep him company, hold his hand, read to him—but that was very much indeed, and she never ceased to visit him and to be attentive to his needs. As for the eventual tasks of engaging caregivers and seeing to countless legal and medical details, Mary-Kelly was (in the words of Chris Miller) "a living saint—she was *the* person without whom the situation would have become sheer chaos."

Later, Bob was unable to read a novel or story because he could not recall what he had read at the beginning. "He fought the initial diagnosis of his illness," recalled Pete Gurney. "Teresa escorted him to meet a group of people in the early stages of Alzheimer's, at a clinic where they could discuss such things as failing memory. But when someone said, 'Well, we're all at some stage of this disease,' Bob was outraged. He fought it with all his might, even as he became more and more vague."

The inexorable course of the disease eventually required round-the-clock care, and for this Mary-Kelly engaged a team of nurses whom I and others remember as shining, heroic lights.

When I was in New York in 2003, I paid a visit to Bob, who could no longer write letters or cards. But on a fine autumn afternoon, one of the

nurses bundled him into a wheelchair and together the three of us made
our way the short distance to a small café on First Avenue. Bob was still
able to speak on that occasion, and he seemed in good humor. But there
were lapses, and at times he gazed into space and could not respond to
a question or statement. As we sipped tea, I once again detailed for Bob
my lifelong admiration for his screenplay of *The Nun's Story*. "Bob, you
certainly gave Hepburn the role of her lifetime."

There was a pause, and then he replied sadly:

"Did I ever work with Katharine Hepburn? I don't remember that."

Teresa was, as Mary-Kelly said, "a bit of a gypsy" as she moved from
place to place over the years. For a time she was in Norwalk; then she
was on a high floor on West Forty-eighth Street; then her address was on
West Sixtieth; then she moved to Mitchell Place; then to West End Avenue; and then she was back in Connecticut. "She had a talent for making each place inviting and cheerful," Mary-Kelly added. She and Dan
were able to prepare Teresa's condominium in Connecticut, for sale—a
daunting task, since Teresa saved just about every piece of paper she had
accumulated over many decades. The sale was closed in October 2004.

The chores relative to both Teresa and Bob fell to Mary-Kelly, tasks
she never regarded as burdens but assumed with undiluted love: the
details relating to Teresa's various relocations, the sorting of possessions
and archives, the management of her declining health and her need of
medical care. Mary-Kelly had become so indispensable and so quiet and
unassuming a helper and protector that Teresa said Mary-Kelly was like
a mother to her, and often called her "Mom," partly in jest and yet in a
sense with absolute accuracy.

The touching irony was that if Teresa had an early mother figure in
her life, it was her grandmother, Mary Kelly, for whom Teresa named
her own daughter. In her last years, then, Teresa had finally found the
kind of nurturing devotion that she always longed for—and which, by a
certain wonderful force of nature, she had given to her daughter.

The previous December, Teresa signed a one-year lease on an apartment
on East Seventy-first Street—to be close to Bob on Sutton Place South,
and to her own Manhattan doctor. In July 2004, I was visiting New York
from my home in Denmark, where I had relocated when I married a
Dane, Ole Flemming Larsen. When he and I came to Manhattan, our

first stop was Teresa's apartment, where she had invited us for tea. I accepted on the condition that she go to no trouble or bother, as I knew she was still suffering pain in her feet. I insisted that we were just coming to visit her and we wanted only her presence.

We arrived at her one-bedroom apartment on the twentieth floor, which commanded a wide view over the city. I immediately thought that Teresa looked smaller, frailer than I had ever seen her. But she was in good spirits, embracing us and showing us into her sparsely furnished living room, where she at once brought out a variety of cheeses and breads and a bottle of wine—"just a few things I picked up this morning," she said. We sat for several hours, filling in the recent gaps in our lives and reminiscing about happy times past. Ole took a photo of Teresa and me that appears in this book.

Margaret Hunt frequently met Teresa for lunch or dinner or a play, and in November they attended Michael Kahn's production of *Five by Tenn*, an evening of one-act plays by Tennessee Williams. "After the performance," Margaret recalled, "she went backstage to thank every actor in the cast. You may imagine how delighted and grateful they were for her visit."

Teresa was also in regular contact with Maryann Plunkett. "It was amazing how Teresa made us laugh. I was so grateful to have her in my life, and one day in late winter I called her. I had just seen *Shadow of a Doubt* again, on television, and I had to tell her how much I enjoyed it, most of all because of her performance. As usual, she was just wonderful to chat with—you would never have known she was ill."

By the end of 2004, Teresa decided, quite on her own, that it would be prudent to move into an assisted living senior residence near Mary-Kelly and Dan in Connecticut. She chose a place that was also not far from the New Haven railway station, so that she could travel to visit Bob on her own. From her one-bedroom apartment at the residence, she had an expansive view south, toward Long Island Sound. She was settled in before Christmas 2004.

The location was fine and the services good, "but this wasn't a happy move," as Mary-Kelly said. Teresa was having more serious health problems and required visits to her doctor twice a week. At the age of eighty-six, her heart was failing.

One day she was trying to deal with an insurance company on the telephone, and she was frustrated that the representative could not understand her address correctly. After several more attempts, Teresa said, "It's one of those places where old people go to die!"

In January 2005, Bob contracted pneumonia and was admitted to a New York hospital. At the same time, Dan's ninety-five-year-old mother, who lived alone, broke her elbow. On Saturday, February 26, Mary-Kelly drove Teresa to New York for a day's visit with Bob, who had returned to his apartment. "I think she felt she had lost him, because now he seemed unreachable, with no glimmer of light in his eyes." On Monday, February 28, Mary-Kelly escorted Teresa to a doctor appointment, and on Thursday, March 3, Mary-Kelly again drove to Manhattan, to take Bob to his neurologist.

Bob's decline continued slowly and inevitably over the next four years until he died at the age of ninety-one, on February 9, 2009. All during this time, Mary-Kelly supervised his caregivers, assumed innumerable duties and spent an enormous amount of time with him. "She took the most wonderful care of him," as Chris Miller said and all Bob's friends knew. "No daughter could have done more."

Bob's illness robbed him of speech and finally of comprehension and mobility. Despite his niggling peccadilloes, he was always essentially generous, kind and sympathetic, quick to respond to another's need and invariably a gentleman and a gentle man.

He loved Terry and Mary-Kelly as if they were his own children, and they returned his devotion fully and gratefully. His friends could always rely on his good will and kind-heartedness; those of us who were writers were gratified by his attentive reading of our work, his honest encouragement, his wise counsel. For all these good reasons and more, Robert Anderson remains brightly and dearly in the memories of those many lives he touched—in his art and in his life.

~

On Friday evening, March 4, 2005, I rang Teresa from Los Angeles, where I was researching material for a new book. She admitted that she was constantly tired, but her voice was warm, clear and enthusiastic. "It's been chilly here," she said, "but I think the first spring flowers are about to bloom. You must come soon and see our garden." I promised to visit a week later.

The next day, Teresa and her daughter went out to lunch and then to a movie. "We wanted to do more than just go for doctor visits," said Mary-Kelly. But Teresa was pale and weak, and the day's activities, which she so much enjoyed, left her exhausted.

At seven the next morning—Sunday, March 6—the telephone rang at the home of Mary-Kelly and Dan. A nurse at the senior residence said that she had been sitting for a while with Teresa, who feared she was having a heart attack. Teresa had deliberately waited until this time to call because she had not wanted to disturb Mary-Kelly by phoning earlier. It was agreed at once that Teresa should be transferred to Yale-New Haven Hospital, a short distance away, and that Mary-Kelly would meet her there.

When she was wheeled into the emergency area, Teresa saw her daughter and said with great tenderness, "There she is—there's my Mom!" Not long after, a doctor informed Mary-Kelly that her mother's heart was now failing rapidly. Dan arrived after finding someone to stay with his mother after her elbow-replacement surgery. Teresa took his hand and Mary-Kelly's. A few moments later, they rang Terry in Indianapolis, and he and Teresa said their goodbyes. The atmosphere in the narrow holding room was thick with pain but warm with love. The hours passed slowly that Sunday morning.

ℴℴ

Those who worked with Teresa Wright over many decades in the theatre, in movies and on television were unanimous: her kind and unassuming manner, her humor, her unwavering professionalism and great kindness were accompanied by an admirable toughness when that was required. That amalgamation of qualities may help to explain how she survived a dreadful childhood and a lonely adolescence. But nothing really explicates the emergence of her talent, for which those commonplace words "unique" and "mysterious" are pale and insufficient.

As an actress, she pushed the conventions of glamour clean off the stage and the screen, bringing a quality of naturalness, of immediacy, of—yes—*honor* to the human qualities she found in a role. From the winsome Alexandra in *The Little Foxes*, whose innocence is harshly tested; to the moral education of young Charlie in *Shadow of a Doubt*; and to the tender daffiness of Miss Birdie in *The Rainmaker*, the catalogue of her movie roles allows us access not only to a memorable array of credible characters but also to qualities we may covet for ourselves.

She appeared in only nine color films, but somehow her pellucid beauty, her flawless alabaster skin, those expressive blue-green eyes and her radiant, unaffected smile shine in every one of her black-and-white movies, too. At the beginning of her film career in 1941, William Wyler, not a man given to hyperbole, described Teresa as the most gifted and promising young actress he had ever met. In the decades that followed, she more than fulfilled that estimation.

She appeared in more than one hundred films and television dramas; she had worked with the finest and most exacting directors in Hollywood and on Broadway; and she was chosen to be Marlon Brando's leading lady in his first film. Onstage, her forty roles encompassed classic plays by Shakespeare and Ibsen, and modern works by Clifford Odets, William Inge, Arthur Miller, Eugene O'Neill, Tennessee Williams, Clifford Odets, John van Druten, Noël Coward, Arthur Kopit and Robert Anderson. She left a remarkable professional legacy—and friends past counting.

∽

Throughout that Sunday morning, March 6, 2005, Teresa was never alone but was constantly comforted by Mary-Kelly and Dan. Finally, with one long sigh, her struggle was over. But there was no end to her wide-ranging, benevolent influence, nor to the incalculable pleasure her art gives to each new generation of moviegoers. Of all this and more, as a friend once told her, there is no shadow of a doubt.

∽

NOTES

Where there is no attribution for statements made by Teresa Wright, these derive from written notes, taped interviews, the author's diary entries or her conversations with the author during the years from 1974 to 2005. All the comments attributed to her son and daughter, Niven Terence Busch and Mary-Kelly Busch, were made directly by them to the author in recorded conversations or e-mails.

For brevity's sake, details of interviews are supplied only at the first citation; unless otherwise noted, subsequent quotations from the same source derive from the identical interview.

ABBREVIATIONS

TW: Teresa Wright (birth name: Muriel Teresa Wright)

SG/AMPAS: The Samuel Goldwyn Collection in the Margaret Herrick Library at the Academy of Motion Picture Art and Sciences, Beverly Hills, CA.

CCOHC: Columbia Center for Oral History Collection at Columbia University, New York City; a citation from this long interview with TW, conducted in New York in June 1959, is followed by the page number. (Curiously, the file is misnamed as the "Theresa Wright" interview.)

NB: Niven Busch (birth name: Briton Niven Busch)

RWA: Robert Woodruff Anderson

NYT: *New York Times*

TW Papers: The collection of her papers at Harvard University/Theatre Collection: Harvard Depository identification number S2006MT-201

CHAPTER ONE: MARCH 4, 1943

On the history of the Ambassador Hotel and the Cocoanut Grove, see, e.g., Hadley Meares, "The Cocoanut Grove: The Los Angeles Inspiration for Las Vegas," a feature of KCET-TV Los Angeles (www.kcet.org/living/food/the-nosh/the-cocoanut-grove-the-ambassador-hotel.html).

The annual Oscar presentations from 1929 to 1997 are meticulously and engagingly recorded by Osborne; for the awards honoring movies of 1942, see 74–77.

wildly demonstrative: "Young Aide Leads Philharmonic, Steps In when Bruno Walter Is Ill," *NYT*, Nov. 15, 1943.

a thrillingly good performance: "A Story Old and Ever New," *NYT*, Nov. 16, 1943.

In Detroit/who had: "The American Experience: Detroit Race Riots," pbs.org.

On the House Un-American Committee's sortie against Marlowe and Euripides: Benedict Nightingale, "Mr. Euripides Goes to Washington," *NYT*, Sept. 18, 1988.

After all, the KKK: Newton, 102.

CHAPTER TWO: 1918–1935

There is a vast literature on the so-called Spanish Influenza epidemic, which did not originate in Spain but in France during World War I. In an effort to sustain morale among the troops, censors in combating countries downplayed reports of illness and death. But newspapers were not restricted in neutral Spain, where there was no censorship of news about the sudden, massive number of deaths from a strange and virulent illness among troops from every nation. This gave rise to the unfortunate impression that Spain was the source of the pandemic.

The United States Department of Health and Human Services has maintained a detailed account of the pandemic: "The Great Pandemic" (see www.flu.gov /pandemic/ history/1918/your_state/northeast/ newyork/). Among the most detailed contemporary news accounts, see "Spanish Influenza Much Like Grippe," *NYT*, Sept. 22, 1918; also, Oct. 4 and 17, 1918. A century later, the epidemic was still the subject of major essays— e.g., Carl Zimmer, "In 1918 Flu Epidemic, Timing Was a Killer," *NYT*, Apr. 30, 2014. See also the Museum of Health and Medicine in Washington, D.C. One of the most important modern contributions to the history of the epidemic has been made by Molly Billings, MD, of Stanford University: see www.stanford.edu/group /virus/uda/index.html and her appended, extensive Bibliography. See also D.J. Tice, "Flu Deaths Rivaled, Ran Alongside World War I," *Pioneer Planet*, Mar. 10, 1997.

only [!] 48,024 deaths: *NYT*, Oct. 17, 1918.

My wife: Birth Affidavit, Department of State, signed by Arthur H. Wright, June 22, 1953, in Los Angeles, CA. This sworn and signed document testifies only to the city and date of TW's birth; it was necessary when she applied for a U.S. passport that year but her birth certificate was unobtainable. TW's father was with the U.S. Army in Europe when she was born, and her mother was soon absent. Apart from the city and date of her birth—reported to her father by his mother—all other details of the child's entrance into the world were unknown during her lifetime, and so they remain a century later.

On the Wright family: some cousins of John Wright claimed that he was related to Wilbur and Orville Wright. But those brothers never married, and there is no indication of any relationship to their siblings, most of whom survived well into the twentieth century. If indeed John was kin to the famous Wright brothers, he would certainly have shared this information with, among others, his many children. In any case, Wright is the sixteenth most common name in England, and it is found in profusion in the United States.

My mother was: E.g., Shafer, 197. TW's long interview for this book was conducted in July 1999.

and she was not around: Quoted in Adam Bernstein, "Actress Teresa Wright, 86; Won Oscar in 'Mrs. Miniver,'" *Washington Post*, Mar. 9, 2005.

My grandmother wore: TW recalled the woman's dress and conduct during conversations with MKB and DS; see also Shafer, 203.

I've never talked: Objecting to some assertions in an article by journalist Rex Reed in 1975, TW drafted on yellow lined paper a long corrective reply which she never sent; this statement was written on the third page. But she kept the document among her papers, which were inherited by MKB.

The account of young Muriel's experiences when her mother brought men to bed were confided by TW to her daughter MKB and to director Vivian Matalon (to DS, Oct. 23, 2014). TW shared these memories with Matalon during the London run of *Morning's at Seven* in 1984. See Chapter 14 below.

was so miserable: RWA to Ken Holmes, Apr. 11, 1999.

I didn't have much of a home life: Shafer, 197; also, Blake Green, "A Granny Who Really Gets Around," *Newsday*, Nov. 13, 1991; and Pearl Sheffy Gefen, "Oscar-winner Wright returning to screen in Toronto," *Toronto Star*, June 18, 1988.

I was boarded out: James Reid, "Surprising, what?" *Silver Screen Magazine*, June 1942.

I didn't know anybody: Shafer, 197–98.

This girl cannot: "Teresa Wright in Reunion at Paper Mill Playhouse," *Newark Sunday News*, June 30, 1963.

there's also the important little matter: Reid, *art.cit.*; see also *Newark Sunday News*, June 30, 1963; and Shafer, 198. It was often erroneously reported that Muriel's father and uncle appeared in amateur theatricals. But that was contradicted by TW: "No one in my family, as far as I know, was ever in the theatre," CCOHC, 663.

My father always: Ibid.

CHAPTER THREE: 1935–1939 .

When I could get: Shafer, 198.

Seeing that play: Reid, *art.cit.*

For a contemporary assessment of Helen Hayes as Victoria Regina, see the cover story of *Time*, Dec. 30, 1935.

I had an opportunity: Reid, *art.cit.*, and CCOHC, 664.

I use many recordings: Evelyn Burke, "Does Your Speech Reveal You're From Squeedunk?" *Pittsburgh Press*, Jan. 31, 1927. See also Sanford Robbins, "Edith Warman Skinner: A Former Student's Recollection and Appreciation," *Voice and Speech Review* 1, no. 1 (2000): 55–60.

On the life and career of Edith Warman Skinner and her husband, Neil McFee, see the Papers of Edith Warman Skinner, 1902–1981 in the Curtis Theatre Collection (1984.01), University of Pittsburgh (PA). Also important are the Neil McFee Skinner Papers, 1929–1944: MSS. Coll. 2770, and two boxes numbered 59M127, at the New York Public Library/Archives and Manuscripts.

The speech of the character: Skinner, iii.

She seemed like: Brooks Baldwin to DS, July 19, 2013.

Muriel Wright, a youngster/Muriel Wright is: Two unsigned, undated reviews in Cape Cod newspapers; TW saved the reviews, which remain in the clipping file "Wharf Players in Provincetown," TW Papers.

You can't do: From 1975 to 1987, TW often addressed my students in film classes at the New School for Social Research, New York City. This statement about acting in repertory and stock companies is drawn from a compilation of her talks. Because she meticulously prepared notes before her visits, this is similar to CCOHC, 669, which she seems to have consulted in advance.

Regarding Martha Scott's departure from *Our Town*: TW frequently (and incorrectly) claimed that Scott left the play in late summer 1938 to go to Hollywood for the movie version of *Our Town*. But in fact Scott departed to make a screen test for *Gone With the Wind* (viz., the role of Melanie Hamilton). When Olivia de Havilland won that part, Scott remained in Hollywood, where the movie of *Our Town* was finally produced, from January to March 1940—and for which Scott ultimately earned an Oscar nomination as best actress. See also *NYT*, Aug. 23 and Sept. 3, 1938.

I was terrified: CCOHC, 667.

No curtain. No scenery: Wilder, 5 (beginning of Act I).

The excerpts from *Our Town* are spoken in the last moments of the play: Wilder, 110–13.

took occasion: E.C. Sherburne, "'Our Town' in New Hands," *Boston Post*, Apr. 25, 1939.

CHAPTER FOUR: 1939–1941

a very pretty: Osborn, *The Vinegar Tree*, 3.

I am a virgin: Ibid., 55–57.

a pretty, wide-eyed girl: Lindsay and Crouse, 28–30.

Sooner or later: Brooks Atkinson, in *NYT*, Nov. 9, 1939.

Teresa Wright plays with: Atkinson, Nov. 19, 1939 (his second essay on *Life With Father*).

I ask myself: CCOHC, 673–74; similarly to DS.

What a way: Kim Garfield, "Teresa Wright: Back on Broadway in 'Morning's,'" *Hollywood Drama-Logue*, Aug. 21–27, 1980.

I'd seen too many: Hedda Hopper, "Turn to the Wright!" *Chicago Tribune* (syndicated), June 28, 1942.

I saw you Saturday night: Kyle Crichton, "No Glamour Girl," *Collier's Weekly*, May 23, 1942.

I'll never forget it: Joe Brown, "At the Folger, The Wright Stuff," *Washington Post Weekend*, Dec. 11, 1987.

I knew she was: "The New Pictures," *Time*, Aug. 3, 1942.

Miss Wright was seated: Berg, 358.

This means that she: Memo to Abe Lastfogel, July 10, 1940, SG/AMPAS, file, *The Little Foxes*.

Do you want Teresa: Ibid., memo dated July 17, 1940.

No place in the country: Delmar, 5–6. These excerpts from her novel *About Mrs. Leslie* were captured in the 1954 movie based on it and starring Shirley Booth, have undeservedly been all but forgotten. Delmar (born Alvina Croter) wrote fine, often controversial novels and witty screenplays, usually in collaboration with her husband, Albert Zimmerman.

What do you want: Crichton, *art.cit.*, and Gladwin Hill, "New Starlet Doesn't Mind One Brickbat," *Indianapolis Sunday Star*, Sept. 21, 1941.

Go home and brush your hair: Kirtley Baskett, "That's Wright!" *Photoplay*, no. 22 (January 1943): 44f.

He was inarticulate: *Directed by William Wyler*, a documentary dir. by Aviva Slesin (exec. prod. Catherine Wyler), 1986.

Bette was very generous: Jane Sumner, "Teresa Wright is Still Aglow," *Dallas Morning News*, Aug. 4, 1987; and Malcolm L. Johnson, "Hollywood's Lady Graces State's Stages," *Hartford Courant*, Nov. 6, 1977.

One newcomer: Thomas Brady, "Peace Comes to 'The Little Foxes,'" *NYT*, June 22, 1941.

Miss Wright is a newcomer: *Daily Variety*, Aug. 12, 1941.

Put the baby on her: Johnson, *art.cit.*

one of the most remarkably: Cited in Myrna Oliver, obituary for TW, *Los Angeles Times*, Mar. 9, 2005.

CHAPTER FIVE: 1941–1942

On Molnár in America and *The King's Maid*, see the essay by Ivan Sanders in *The Yivo Encyclopedia of Jews in Eastern Europe* (www.yivoencyclopedia.org/article.aspx/ Molnar_Ferenc).

The reviewers: SG/AMPAS, file, *The Little Foxes*.

The play was not good: Karl Malden to DS, Mar. 2007.

In addition to the problems: Mona Malden to DS, July 5, 2013.

Sam Jaffe and Teresa Wright: *NYT*, Aug. 27, 1941.

I will not pose: Teresa's wishes, composed as a codicil to her contract with Goldwyn, were first published in *Collier's*, May 1942.

but he didn't talk: Alan Hunter, "Reeling in the Years," *Scotland on Sunday*, July 7, 1996.

If you handle Mr. Wyler: *Hartford Courant*, Feb. 5, 1943.

Mrs. Miniver became: Sumner, *art.cit.*

We all felt: *Coronet*, Sept. 1949.

Masterful, faultless: *Hollywood Reporter*, July 22, 1942.

It is hard to believe: *NYT*, June 5, 1942.

box-office gold: Review of "Mrs. Miniver," *Variety*, May 13, 1942.

Much of the heart: Glenn Erickson, in his website *DVD Savant* (dvdtalk.com/dvdsavant), also in his book, q.v.

absolute reliability: Sportswriter John Kieran, quoted in Cohen, 11.

When Sam first told me: Quotations from Mrs. Gehrig are excerpted from Gehrig and Durso (see Bibliography) unless otherwise noted.

Goldwyn did not like that: Unless otherwise noted, the Niven Busch quotations in this chapter are drawn from an interview conducted by David Thompson in 1983; the transcript was published in McGilligan, 86–109.

They can't do anything: Reid, *art.cit.*

a voluptuously gentle: Callow, 50–51.

I know she was: Kashatus, 108.

cemented her rise: *Time*, Aug. 3, 1942.

CHAPTER SIX: 1942–1944

This means: Reid, *art.cit.*

It was a modest: Christine Miller to DS, Jan. 28, 2015.

Glamour might jinx: Baskette, *art.cit.*

I had to understand: Blake Green, "A Granny Who Gets round," *Newsday*, Nov. 13, 1991.

The shots of Wright: Stephan Talty, "A Genius for Decency," *Film Comment*, Sept.–Oct. 1990. This appreciative essay is one of the finest tributes ever tended to Teresa (and, I think, to any actor). Carefully researched, it was gracefully and engagingly written.

You must be thinking: CCOHC, 695.

She was lovely: Letter from Jack Skirball to Samuel Goldwyn, February 24, 1943, SG/AMPAS.

I got along very well: Alfred Hitchcock to DS, July 18, 1975, at Universal Studios, during the production of his last film, *Family Plot*.

A perceptive assessment of Teresa's performance was written by Aubyn Eli: see "Performance Spotlight: Teresa Wright in Shadow of a Doubt" (May 13, 2012; this was part of *For the Love of Film: The Film Preservation Blogathon*).

quietly authoritative: Howard Barnes, review in *New York Herald-Tribune*, Dec. 13, 1942.

an actress who can do: Ibid.

one of the great new: "Teresa Wright," *Current Biography*, 1943 (857).

Hollywood's best young: *Time*, Aug. 3, 1942.

I didn't like the script: CCOHC, 684.

I was feeling very low: TW to RWA, Feb. 21, 1958.

It was an evening: Osborne, 56.

as nervous as if: Ibid.

I always wanted: NB, "Author Page" for his novel *The Actor*, n.p. (Kindle edition).

You could watch: Pearl Sheffy Gefen, "Oscar-winner Wright returns to the screen in Toronto," *Toronto Star*, June 18, 1988.

This will make it possible: NB to SG, letter dated May 13, 1946, SG/AMPAS.

She has been: Samuel Goldwyn, SG/AMPAS; a copy of the letter was sent to TW on April 27, 1944.

CHAPTER SEVEN: 1944–1948

I'm just another: Warren Phillips, "This Week's Movies," *Collier's Weekly*, Dec. 11, 1948.

solemn, humorless: Bosley Crowther, *NYT*, May 22, 1947.

A lot of the content: Glenn Erickson, notes on *The Best Years of Our Lives* for his website *DVD Savant* (Jan. 11, 2001): www.dvdtalk.com/dvdsavant/s171best.html.

I cried: Billy Wilder, in *Directed by William Wyler*, a documentary dir. by Aviva Slesin (exec. prod. Catherine Wyler), 1986.

They had to go find him: Herman, 287; also to DS.

very quiet: Rollyson, 195.

Wright brought: Talty, *art.cit.*

This new performance: James Agee, review of *The Best Years of Our Lives*, in *The Nation*, Dec. 28, 1946.

What a great actor: Garfield, *art.cit.*

The movie captured: Dick Sheppard, "Movie grande [*sic*] dames take to the boards," *Los Angeles Herald-Examiner*, Dec. 18, 1981.

For the reflections on the title *The Best Years of Our Lives*, I am grateful for suggestions by Terry Busch (July 4 and 28, 2014).

All I ever wanted: NB, in McGilligan, 96, 106–107.

Niven Busch is a Pygmalion: Virginia Sullivan Tomlinson, "Pygmalion," *New York Journal-American*, May 27, 1950.

You think you know: I heard this from TW several times and recounted it in my eulogy for her in New York, at the Lighthouse, Mar. 19, 2005.

Women are lucky: TW in New York, to RA in London, Feb. 4, 1958.

Teresa said she: Abe Lastfogel to SG, Dec. 9, 1947, Production Memoranda, SG/AMPAS;

I don't care if it doesn't: Quoted often by TW; also, Phillips, *Collier's Weekly*, *art.cit.*

I've often been cast: Rex Reed, "On Oscar night, who remembered Teresa Wright?" *New York Daily News*, Apr. 27, 1980.

and I refused: E.J. Strong, "Teresa Wright Quitting Pictures," *Los Angeles Times*, Sept. 15, 1950.

You are hereby instructed: SG to TW, SG/AMPAS, Production Memoranda file, *Enchantment*.

The statements of SG and TW are preserved in the Goldwyn Papers at AMPAS; they were also summarily reported in the *NYT*, Dec. 19, 1948.

I guess I wanted: Often—e.g., Bernstein, *art.cit*; Tom Vallance, in the London *Independent*, Apr. 1, 2005; also to DS, etc.

Goldwyn was a fair man: Often—e.g., William Russell, "A Fox No-one Could Snare," *Herald* (Glasgow), Aug. 20, 1996.

CHAPTER EIGHT: 1949–1952

a dumb murder mystery: Bernard Carragher, "An Unexpected Visit With Teresa Wright," *New Haven Register*, Aug. 10, 1975.

Marlon Brando was terribly insecure: Fred Zinnemann to DS, Oct. 1977, recounted in Spoto, *Stanley Kramer Film Maker* 61.

He was a combination: Gefen, *art.cit.* See also Garfield, *art.cit.*

All I proved: E.g., Carragher, and Rex Reed, *art.cit.*

It was disappointing: TW to *Look* magazine, July 19, 1950.

Hollywood understands only: William Russell, "A fox no-one could snare," *Herald* (Edinburgh), Aug. 20, 1996; also, Garfield, *art.cit.*

marvelous: Dave Kehr, in a new assessment of *Something To Live For, NYT*, Apr. 28, 2012.

I am approaching: Strong, *art.cit.*

We were having: McGilligan, 108.

Every now and then: TW to RA, May 30, 1957.

She was up on the ranch: McGilligan, 108.

Our ranch is really beautiful: Hedda Hopper, *Los Angeles Times*, Sept. 14, 1951; and Sept. 2, 1951.

Niven Busch invests: Sheila Graham, *Variety*, May 22, 1952.

An actress must work: Quoted in Darr Smith, in *Los Angeles Daily News*, June 18, 1951.

This was real, real action: Hedda Hopper's syndicated column (e.g., *Los Angeles Times*, Sept. 2, 1951).

I guess the lowest point: Rex Reed, *art.cit.*

I have a new viewpoint: Darr Smith, *art.cit.*

I have reached a state: Strong, *art.cit.*

Miss Wright does: *Billboard*, Mar. 22, 1952.

lifeless and unfunny: *The Playgoer*, Mar. 19, 1952.

the second one: Gefen, *art.cit.*

The main source of my happiness: TW to RA, May 30, 1957.

I hated to see the marriage: McGilligan, 108–109.

Efforts of their friends: Louella Parsons, in *Los Angeles Examiner*, Jan. 16, 1953.

I saw The Actress: Goldwyn's Christmas letter and TW's reply, SG/AMPAS.

CHAPTER NINE: 1953–1957

I'm very proud of having known: TW to RWA, Nov. 18, 1958.

confused and deeply troubled: Ibid.

I'm not quite sure: TW to RWA, May 30, 1957.

Many people think: TW to MKB.

Her performance: Quoted in Kashner and MacNair, 285.

I worked my way: Rex Reed, "Anderson: From 'Tea' to 'Water,'" *NYT*, Mar. 26, 1967.

Every play: Ibid.

That period/If I come back/tears, letters: RWA, typed pages of a journal, Oct. 26, 1990.

I think you belong: The complete story of the Anderson-Bergman affair was told to DS in preparation for the publication of *Notorious: The Life of Ingrid Bergman*, see 325–34.

She really dedicated: RWA to DS, May 13, 1996.

In 1996, RWA gave a copy of Ingrid's letter to DS.

You can't ask: TW to RWS, June 20, 1957.

CHAPTER TEN: 1957–1959

I remember the house: Mila Malden Doerner to DS, July 5, 2013.

I have noticed: Kazan, 659.

Cora tries to dictate: Dorothy Barclay, "Star Terms Role Omen To Mothers," *NYT*, Feb. 18, 1958.

As the petulant: Jay Carmody, *(Washington) Evening Star*, Dec. 20, 1957.

What I admired: Bernard F. Dick to DS, Feb. 11, 2015.

I am being very cruel: RWA to Donald and Erna Anderson, from London, Jan. 23, 1958.

CHAPTER ELEVEN: 1959–1965

excessively verbose: *NYT*, Dec. 4, 1949.

I might have written: Reed, *art.cit.*, March 26, 1967.

a great big junk heap: Mary Connelly, "Teresa Wright: Plain and Simple," *New York Post*, Oct. 4, 1969.

I once went to help: Mila Malden Doerner to DS, July 5, 2013.

In order to be: TW, quoted by RWA in a letter to Donald Anderson, Feb. 26, 1962.

She has no big: Ibid.

Teresa continues: RWA to Donald Anderson, July 9, 1962.

a lovely old farmhouse: RWA to Kathryn Hulme and Marie-Louise Habets, Jan. 3, 1966.

Many theatre friends lived there: Frank Rizzo, "Playwright Found Home At Long Wharf," *Hartford Courant*, Feb. 11, 2009.

It concerns: Ibid.

Miss Wright displays: *The Record*, June 26, 1963.

Teresa would rather: Rex Reed, *art.cit.*

CHAPTER TWELVE: 1966–1973

I had a fine day: TW to RWA (who was in London for the UK premiere of one of his plays), May 26, 1968.

I haven't had a hit: Rex Reed, *art.cit.*

We're never going: Mary Connelly, *art.cit.*

It was just a terribly painful: Jean Simmons to TW and DS, Dec. 1990.

with the naturalness: Clive Barnes, in *NYT*, Oct. 28, 1970.

Most of the time: Malcolm L. Johnson, *art.cit.*

Teresa loathed it: RWA to Eva Marie Saint, May 4, 1970.

Bob was very generous: Arvin Brown to DS, Sept. 24, 2014.

I never dreamed: William Glover, "Teresa Wright: She Found a New Stage," *Palm Beach Post*, Apr. 18, 1971.

At first I almost: Shafer, 201ff.

Wraithlike and lost: Clive Barnes, *NYT*, Mar. 21, 1971.

wonderfully low-key: Quoted in *Hartford Courant*, Nov. 6, 1977.

It's a marvelous work: Quoted in *Davenport (Iowa) Times-Democrat*, n.d. (1973).

CHAPTER THIRTEEN: 1974–1978

I told her/and insultingly/I think you want/as good as/both of us/I found it: RWA to Joseph Iseman, Sept. 13, 1975.

Linda is an exhausting role: Carragher, *art.cit.*

a woman of grave charm: Brendan Gill, in *The New Yorker*, July 7, 1975.

Face severely in repose: Walter Kerr, in *NYT*, June 29, 1975.

She is so poignant: Rex Reed, in *Daily News*, July 4, 1975.

We decided on a year's separation: Ibid.

luminous and totally unspoken: Talty, *art.cit.*

I tried for two years: RWA to Eva Marie Saint, Feb. 8, 1978; in the TW Papers at SG/AMPAS.

The *New York* magazine item about Bob and Hope Lange appeared in the issue of Nov. 13, 1978.

CHAPTER FOURTEEN: 1978–1984

I had been terribly spoiled: Rex Reed, "On Oscar night, who remembered Teresa Wright?" *New York Daily News*, Apr. 27, 1980.

I didn't audition Teresa: Vivian Matalon, at the memorial service for TW, New York, Mar. 2005; also, Matalon to DS, Oct. 23, 2014.

I told Osborn: Vivian Matalon to DS, Oct. 23, 2014.

doing the very best work: Walter Kerr, in *NYT*, Apr. 11, 1980.

These characters have: Harold Clurman, in *The Nation*, May 3, 1980, 540.

It's a joy: Garfield, *art.cit.*

Ponderous and irredeemable: Alvin Klein, in *NYT*, Apr. 17, 1983.

CHAPTER FIFTEEN: 1985–1990

Physicians don't need: Enid Nemy, "O'Neill Performed For Mayo Doctors," *NYT*, Apr. 15, 1985.

We took it: Shafer, 148; also, Nemy, *art.cit.*

For a person: Margaret Hunt, at TW's New York memorial, Mar. 19, 2005.

Teresa always had a wonderfully benign: Margaret Hunt to DS, Oct. 22, 2014.

There aren't many good roles: Jane Sumner, "Teresa Wright is Still Aglow," *Dallas Morning News*, Aug. 4, 1987.

He's a horse that can act: "A Closer Look: The Fig Tree," *Behind the Scenes*, Calvin Skaggs: booklet accompanying the DVD release by Public Media Video.

I do have a new play: Dan Sullivan, "Anderson Makes a Living—Between Killings," *Los Angeles Times*, Dec. 6, 1987.

I thought, well: Joe Brown, *art.cit.*

It's a great wonder: Ibid.

Diane was so kind: Vivian Matalon to DS, Oct. 23, 2014; similarly, Margaret Hunt to DS, Oct. 22, 2014.

a frail, bird-like: Fugard, 13.

I suppose I'm at an age: Eleanor Koblenz, "Teresa Wright Thrives Before Live Audience," *(Schenectady) Daily Gazette*, July 27, 1990.

I told many people/She makes fun of herself: RWA, typed notes for a journal, autumn 1990.

CHAPTER SIXTEEN: 1991–2005

I thought it was brave: Blake Green, "A Granny Who Really Gets Around," *New York Newsday*, Nov. 3, 1991.

Teresa's comments at the American Theatre Wing "Performance" seminar, Sept. 1991, were filmed by New York Public Television.

Have a good education: Garfield, *art.cit.*

It's a comedy: Blake Green, *art.cit.*

solid supporting: *NYT*, Oct. 10, 1991.

I saw Matt Damon: Steve Hochman, in *Los Angeles Times*, Dec. 28, 1997.

The flawless beauty: Bob Thomas, "Teresa Wright returns to movies in 'The Rainmaker,'" *Associated Press*, Dec. 26, 1997.

For an account of TW at Yankee Stadium, see Ray Robinson, "Becoming a Yankee Fan, By Way of Hollywood," *NYT*, July 4, 1999.

You see the skill: Tyler Kepner, "Baseball: Jeter Hopes to Stick Around for a While," *NYT*, Feb. 7, 2000.

✑

TERESA WRIGHT:
PROFESSIONAL CREDITS

TW performed in elementary school pageants and in high school plays (see the text). During the summers from 1937 through 1939, she was an apprentice with the nonprofit Wharf Theatre on Cape Cod and then with the Barnstormers, a traveling repertory group in New England. Her professional career began in 1939. (Contrary to many published sources, she did not appear in the original 1938 Broadway production of *Our Town*: she was understudy to Dorothy McGuire during the play's final weeks that autumn and then appeared in the road company of the play, first in the role of Rebecca and then as Emily.) Details, dates and performance histories are provided in the text.

IN 7 BROADWAY PLAYS:

Life With Father
The Dark at the Top of the Stairs
I Never Sang for My Father
Death of a Salesman
Ah, Wilderness!
Morning's at Seven
On Borrowed Time

IN 27 FEATURE FILMS:

The Little Foxes (Academy Award nomination for best supporting actress)
Mrs. Miniver (Academy Award for best supporting actress)
The Pride of the Yankees (Academy Award nomination for best actress)
Shadow of a Doubt
Casanova Brown
The Imperfect Lady
The Trouble With Women
The Best Years of Our Lives
Pursued

Enchantment
The Capture
The Men
Something to Live For
California Conquest
The Steel Trap
Count the Hours
The Actress
Track of the Cat
The Search for Bridey Murphy
The Restless Years
Escapade in Japan
Hail, Hero!
The Happy Ending
Roseland
Somewhere in Time
The Good Mother
The Rainmaker

IMPORTANT LEADING ROLES IN REPERTORY THEATRE AND OFF-BROADWAY, AND WITH TOURING COMPANIES AND PROVINCIAL THEATRES, FROM 1941:

The King's Maid
Salt of the Earth
The Country Girl
Bell, Book and Candle
The Heiress
The Rainmaker
Mary, Mary
Tchin-Tchin
Who's Happy Now?
The Effect of Gamma Rays on Main-in-the-Moon Marigolds
A Passage to E.M. Forster
Long Day's Journey into Night
The Soldier's Tale
The Knight of the Burning Pestle
Noël Coward in Two Keys
The Master Builder
All the Way Home
Threads
Wings
The Glass Menagerie
All's Well That Ends Well
You Can't Take It With You
The Road to Mecca

ON TELEVISION:

It is impossible to compile a complete list of TW's credits, as many early programs have been lost. Herewith a sampling of her major starring roles on TV from 1951. Some of these are frequently available on YouTube.com, and some may be viewed at the Paley Center for Media in New York and Beverly Hills:

"Manhattan Pastorale" (*Lux Video Theater*)
"The Sound of Waves Breaking" (*Lux Video Theater*)
"And Never Come Back" (*Robert Montgomery Presents*)
"Dress in the Window" (*Schlitz Playhouse of Stars*)
"Alicia" (*Hollywood Opening Night*)
"The Luckiest Day of My Life" (*Kate Smith Evening Hour*)
"And Suddenly You Knew" (*Ford Television Theater*)
"The Happiest Day" (*Ford Television Theater*)
"The End of Paul Dane" (*The United States Steel Hour*)
"The Long Goodbye" (*Climax!*)
"The White Carnation" (*Climax!*)
"Her Crowning Glory" (*Four Star Playhouse*)
"The Stars Don't Shine" (*Ford Television Theater*)
"The Good Sister" (*Four Star Playhouse*)
"Love Is Eternal" (*General Electric Theater*)
"Driftwood" (*The Elgin TV Hour*)
"The Red Gulch" (*The United States Steel Hour*)
"Intolerable Portrait 3" (*Your Play Time*)
"My Uncle O'Moore" (*The Loretta Young Show*)
"The Enchanted Cottage" (*Lux Video Theater*)
"The Lady in the Wind" (*Ford Television Theater*)
"Undertow" (*The Alcoa Hour*)
"The Devil's Disciple" (*Hallmark Hall of Fame*)
"Miracle on 34th Street" (*The 20th Century-Fox Hour*)
"Child of the Regiment" (*The 20th Century-Fox Hour*)
"Number Five Checked Out" (*Screen Directors Playhouse*)
"Once to Every Woman" (*Four Star Playhouse*)
"The Louella Parsons Story" (*Climax!*)
"The Secret Place"
"The Lonely Ones" (*Rheingold Theater*)
"The Faithful Heart" (*Studio One*)
"Witness to Condemn" (*Schlitz Playhouse of Stars*)
"The Miracle Worker" (*Playhouse 90*)
"Sister Louise Goes to Town" (*Schlitz Playhouse of Stars*)
"The Edge of Innocence" (*Playhouse 90*)
"Desperation" (*Ford Television Theater*)
"No Escape" (*Undercurrent*)
"Trap for a Stranger" (*United States Steel Hour*)
"The Hours Before Dawn" (*United States Steel Hour*)
"The Pit of Silence" (*Adventures in Paradise*)

"The Margaret Bourke-White Story" (*Sunday Showcase*)
"Shadow of a Soldier" (*Sunday Showcase*)
"Intermezzo" (*Theater '62*)
"The Big Laugh" (*United States Steel Hour*)
"Big Deal in Laredo" (*DuPont Show of the Week*)
"Three Wives Too Many" (*The Alfred Hitchcock Hour*)
"My Son, My Son" (*Bonanza*)
"The Pill Man" (*The Defenders*)
"Lonely Place" (*The Alfred Hitchcock Hour*)
"The Prosecutor" (*The Defenders*)
"Yesterday's Vengeance" (*Lancer*)
The Desperate Hours
"Appalachian Autumn" (*CBS Playhouse*)
Crawlspace
"The Camerons Are a Special Clan" (*Owen Marshall, Counselor at Law*)
"Murder on the 13th Floor" (*Hawkins*)
The Elevator
"Terror in the Night" (*Wide World of Mystery*)
Flood!
Grandpa Goes to Washington
The Golden Honeymoon (PBS)
"A Christmas Presence" (*The Love Boat*)
Bill: On His Own
Mothers by Daughters (PBS)
"The Firebird" (*Morningstar/Eveningstar*)
"A Rose for Alice" (*Morningstar/Eveningstar*)
The Guiding Light
The Fig Tree (WonderWorks/PBS)
"Mr. Penroy's Vacation" (*Murder, She Wrote*)
"The Elders" (*Dolphin Cove*)
"The Case of the Desperate Deception" (*Perry Mason*)
Lethal Innocence (PBS)
A Century of Women
"My Romance" (*Picket Fences*)

ON RADIO:

Abbreviated adaptations of feature films were often performed before live audiences in radio studios. A few, ranging from 1943 to 1979, have been preserved:

"Shadow of a Doubt" (*Lux Radio Theater*)
"The Little Foxes" (*Screen Guild Theatre*)
"The Men" (*Lux Radio Theater*)
"Dragonwyck" (*Screen Guild Theatre*)
"The Best Years of Our Lives" (*Screen Guild Theatre*)
"Enchantment" (*Screen Guild Theatre*)

"The Capture" (*Screen Guild Theatre*)
"Spindletop" (*Cavalcade of America*)
"I Never Sang for My Father" (NPR)

∽

BIBLIOGRAPHY

Adler, Thomas P. *Robert Anderson*. Boston: Twayne, 1978.

Anderson, Robert. *I Never Sang for My Father*. New York: Dramatists Play Service, 1996.

———. *Silent Night, Lonely Night*. New York: Samuel French, 1958 (published before the Broadway premiere).

———. *Solitaire/Double Solitaire*. New York: Dramatists Play Service, 1999.

———. *Tea and Sympathy*. New York and Hollywood: Samuel French, 1955.

———. *You Know I Can't Hear You When the Water's Running*. New York: Dramatists Play Service, 1995.

Berg, A. Scott, *Goldwyn: A Biography*. New York: Knopf, 1989.

Bergman, Ingrid, and Alan Burgess. *Ingrid Bergman—My Story*. New York: Delacorte, 1980.

Billetdoux, François (trans. Mark Rudkin). *Two Plays: Tchin-Tchin* and *Chez Torpe*. New York: Hill and Wang/Mermaid, 1963.

Busch, Niven (as Niven Busch Jr.) *21 Americans: Being Profiles of Some Famous People in Our Time*. New York: Doubleday Doran, 1930.

Busch, Niven. *The Actor*. New York: Simon & Schuster, 1955.

Callow, Simon. *Charles Laughton: A Difficult Actor*. London: Random House Vintage, 2012.

Cohen, Robert W. *The 50 Greatest Players in New York Yankees History*. Lanham, MD: Scarecrow Press/Rowman & Littlefield, 2012.

Coley, Thomas. *"Our Town" Remembered*. New York: Hudson Rudd, 1982 (privately printed limited edition).

Delmar, Viña. *About Mrs. Leslie*. New York: Pocket Books, 1951.

Egan, Leona Rust. *Provincetown as a Stage: Provincetown, The Provincetown Players, and the Discovery of Eugene O'Neill*. Orleans, MA: Parnassus Imprints, 1994.

Erickson, Glenn. *DVD Savant*. Rockville, MD: Wildside Press, 2004.

Fishgall, Gary. *Gregory Peck—A Biography*. New York: Scribners, 2002.

Fugard, Athol. *The Road to Mecca, A Drama in Two Acts*. New York and Hollywood: Samuel French, 1989.

Gehrig, Eleanor, and Joseph Durso. *My Luke and I*. New York: Crowell, 1976.

Haney, Lynn. *Gregory Peck—A Charmed Life*. New York: Carroll & Graf, 2003.

Herman, Jan. *A Talent for Trouble: The Life of Hollywood's Most Acclaimed Director, William Wyler*. New York: Putnam, 1995.

Inge, William. *The Dark at the Top of the Stairs*. New York: Dramatists Play Service, 1988.

Kashatus, William C. *Lou Gehrig: A Biography*. Westport, CT: Greenwood Press, 2004.

Kashner, Sam, and Jennifer MacNair. *The Bad and the Beautiful: Hollywood in the Fifties*. New York: Norton, 2003.

Kazan, Elia. *Elia Kazan: A Life*. New York: Knopf, 1988.

Kerr, Jean. *Mary, Mary*. New York: Dramatists Play Service, 1965.

Lindsay, Howard, and Russel Crouse. *Clarence Day's Life With Father*. New York: Dramatists Play Service, 1939, 1975.

McGilligan, Patrick. *Backstory 1: Interviews with Screenwriters of Hollywood's Golden Age*. Berkeley: University of California Press, 1988.

Newton, Michael. *The Ku Klux Klan in Mississippi: A History*. Jefferson, NC: McFarland, 2010.

Osborn, Paul. *Morning's at Seven*. New York and Hollywood: Samuel French, 1966.

———. *The Vinegar Tree*. New York: Samuel French, 1932.

Osborne, Robert. *70 Years of the Oscars: The Official History of the Academy Awards*. New York: Abbeville, 1999.

Robinson, Ray. *Iron Horse: Lou Gehrig in His Time*. New York: Norton, 2006.

Rollyson, Carl. *Hollywood Enigma: Dana Andrews*. Jackson: University Press of Mississippi, 2012.

Shafer, Yvonne. *Performing O'Neill: Conversations with Actors and Directors*. New York: St. Martin's, 2000.

Skinner, Edith. *Speak With Distinction* (rev. edition). New York: Applause Books, 2000.

Spoto, Donald. *The Art of Alfred Hitchcock* (rev. edition). New York: Doubleday Anchor, 1999.

———. *The Dark Side of Genius: The Life of Alfred Hitchcock*. Boston: Little, Brown, 1983.

———. *Enchantment: The Life of Audrey Hepburn*. New York: Crown/Random House, 2006.

———. *Notorious: The Life of Ingrid Bergman*. New York: HarperCollins, 1997.

———. *Spellbound by Beauty: Alfred Hitchcock and His Leading Ladies*. New York: Three Rivers/Random House, 2008.

———. *Stanley Kramer Film Maker*. New York: Putnam's, 1978; New York/Los Angeles: Samuel French, 1990.

Wilder, Thornton. *3 Plays: Our Town, The Skin of Our Teeth, The Matchmaker*. New York: Harper Perennial Classics, 1998.

∽

INDEX